Distributed Information Systems in Business

Springer
Berlin
Heidelberg
New York
Barcelona
Budapest
Hong Kong
London
Milan
Paris
Santa Clara
Singapore
Tokyo

W. König · K. Kurbel · P. Mertens
D. Pressmar (Eds.)

Distributed Information Systems in Business

With 99 Figures

Springer

Prof. Dr. Wolfgang König, University of Frankfurt,
Lehrstuhl für Betriebswirtschaftslehre, insbesondere
Wirtschaftsinformatik und Informationsmanagement,
Mertonstr. 17, D-60054 Frankfurt/Main

Prof. Dr. Karl Kurbel, Europa-Universität Viadrina Frankfurt/Oder,
Wirtschaftsinformatik II, Postfach 776, D-15207 Frankfurt/Oder

Prof. Dr. Peter Mertens, University of Erlangen-Nuremberg,
Betriebswirtschaftliches Institut, Bereich Wirtschaftsinformatik I,
Postfach 3931, D-90020 Nuremberg

Prof. Dr. Dieter Pressmar, University of Hamburg,
Fachbereich Wirtschaftswissenschaften,
Ordinariat für Betriebswirtschaftliche Datenverarbeitung,
Von-Melle-Park 5, D-22609 Hamburg

Die Deutsche Bibliothek - CIP-Einheitsaufnahme

Distributed information systems in business / W. König ... -
Berlin ; Heidelberg ; New York ; Barcelona ; Budapest ; Hong
Kong ; London ; Milan ; Paris ; Santa Clara ; Singapore ;
Tokyo : Springer, 1996
ISBN 3-540-61094-4
NE: König, Wolfgang [Hrsg.]

ISBN 3-540-61094-4 Springer-Verlag Berlin Heidelberg New York

SPIN 10536469 42/2202 - 5 4 3 2 1 0 – Printed on acid-free paper

Table of Contents

Managing Distributed Information Systems

Wolfgang Koenig, Karl Kurbel, Peter Mertens, Dieter Pressmar

Summary

This contribution sets up a general framework of how to manage distributed information systems. A 6-level model of network hierarchy is developed and common important tasks are identified. All 15 papers of this book are clustered accordingly, pinpointing research subjects and describing the influence on every-day decisions in information and workflow management.

1. Introduction

Current and future challenges in business and management include:

- increasing autonomy of business groups or individuals ("entrepreneurs"),
- globalization of business, including outsourcing of processes to low-cost countries,
- increasing parts of the gross national product are generated by service businesses, especially telecommunication-based value added network services (VANS).

One way to meet these challenges is to optimize the use of distributed information systems. What is a distributed information system? When coordinated work of different actors in socio-technical organizations (for example a company, or a public administration) takes place, we call this organization a distributed information system. Actors may be human or artificial actors, such as managers, operators, robots, knowledge-based software agents, and other hardware/software entities[1]. Actors receive information, transform it, and send it to 'colleagues' in the network. Actors cooperate in order to solve a common task or to achieve a common objective. The task of a distributed information system is to coordinate the interaction of the actors which are members of an organization-wide network. Extending this view, we may also talk of organizations which for example incorporate different enterprises or different individuals, e.g. estab-

[1] This definition extends the solely machine-oriented definition of Martin (1981). There, a distributed system is defined as a network of computers (nodes), each having parts of network-wide data and functions, which work cooperatively to solve a problem. The concept of actors is described in Shoham (1993).

lishing 'virtual enterprises' or 'interaction groups' which agree to communicate a particular issue by using a common standard.

Recently, two researchers of the University of California at Berkeley conducted two Delphi surveys in companies to elaborate how the information and communication technology function (IT function) will be developed within the next five years[2]. The first survey covered 30 executives of EDP / IT departments of large scale US companies (all major industries) as well as major consulting companies. So, the panel comprised people who in fact 'implement' the future. The second survey similarly covered 30 executives of 'application departments', like Marketing, Logistics, Accounting, etc. More than 50% of the executives of 'application departments' and almost 30% of the IT / EDP executives expect that EDP / IT departments will 'mutate into an infrastructure department' which is not only concentrating on communication networks and information processing nodes, but also integrates physical logistics functions (like for example streets, rail links, and pipes to perform inbound logistics, and waste disposal).

The primary tasks of such an infrastructural department in terms of EDP / IT are:

- Generate a layout of important physical infrastructural links between departments within an enterprise, and set the interfaces between the enterprise and other organizations (much like setting the layout of the interstate highway network by the federal transportation department), including the interfaces to local distribution networks. In the case of highways we talk about exits to state highways and municipal highways; and the interfaces to neighbor organizations, e.g. cross-national interstate interfaces between Canada and the US, or between Mexico and the US. In the case of major telecommunication links in an enterprise, we talk for example about FDDI or ATM networks. All departments of the enterprise are forced to use this network.
- Implement and run these important infrastructural links within the enterprise, as well as the interfaces to other organizations (to the outside world). In the case of highways, this means building and maintaining these highways and their exits and interfaces. In the case of major telecommunication links, this means to set-up switching nodes, deploy cables, or contract long-term rentals of existing infrastructure. Running the physical infrastructural links provides a set of basic services to customers. In the telecommunications business, a basic service is the transportation of a particular set of bits between two 'exits'. Note, that it is not necessary that these networks are run by an in-house EDP / IT department.

---

[2] Heinzl & Srikanth (1993), Heinzl & Srikanth (1994)

- Create a layout of the enterprise-wide value added network services (VANS) which the EDP / IT department provides on top of the basic services, or which are offered by external vendors via an enterprise-wide contract for which the EDP / IT department is responsible. We talk, for example, about a particular amount of transactions of an application system (like SAP), library interrogations, and accesses to external databases. Again, these VANS are compulsory to users within the enterprise. In fact, we not only identify VANS which are *provided by* the EDP / IT department but also services which will *not* be provided by the EDP / IT department so that "application departments" have both rights and duties to set up these services by their own. However, in the latter case, the "application departments" have to obey the standards set by the EDP / IT department for basic services.

- Implement and run enterprise-wide VANS. This may be done by an in-house EDP / IT department or bought from an outside vendor.

The secondary tasks of such an infrastructural department, like training, cost accounting of services, or coordination with controlling and organizational development departments will not be particularly addressed further on.

2. 6-level model of network hierarchy

In fact, we talk about a hierarchy of institutions, each executing power to subordinate institutions by setting standards within which subordinate institutions may solve their problems. Standards restrict the action alternatives in both the basic services as well as the VANS. The implementation of basic services sets standards to the enterprise-wide VANS; the basic services and the enterprise-wide VANS set standards for department-wide VANS; and all of these set standards for work group-wide VANS.

Fig. 1 shows a multi-level hierarchy of institutions and accordingly a multi-level hierarchy of networks, linking for example

- different enterprises into a multi-enterprise value chain,
- different departments or projects to an enterprise,
- different work groups to a project or department, and
- different individuals to projects, work groups, or departments.

All in all, we may distinguish 6 network levels:

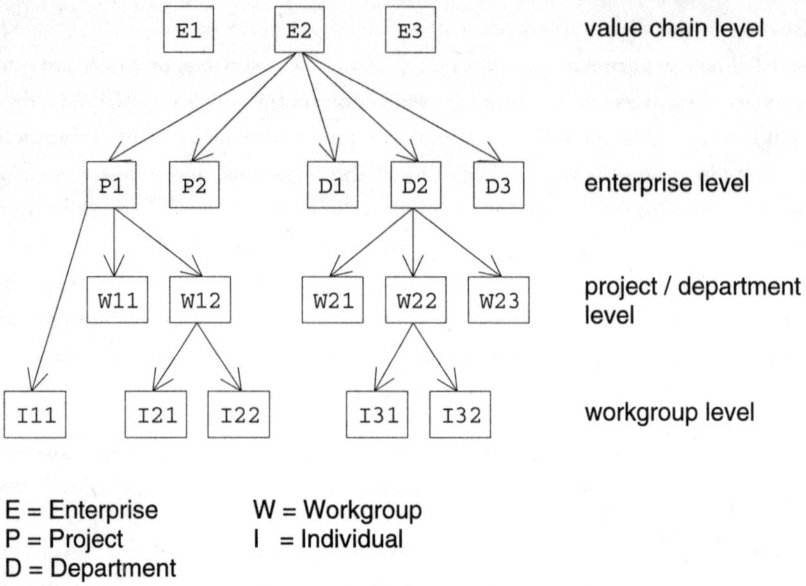

Fig. 1: Multi-level Hierarchy of Institutions and Networks

(1) individual: personal information management / personal workflow management (reflecting both roles of an individual: the business professional providing information services as well as the customer)

(2) small amount of people in a work group: group information management / group workflow management (also: family information management / workflow management)

(3) many people in a project or in a department: project or department information management / workflow management

(4) a lot of people in an enterprise: enterprise information management / workflow management

(5) a lot of people in a set of enterprises linked by value chains: information management / workflow management of a set of enterprises

(6) all people in a society: information management / workflow management of an information society.

Starting on the lowest level, the individual level, we encounter distributed information systems. For example, human actors have to coordinate multiple processing and storage sites (e.g. PCs at home, at the workplace in the company, and using a laptop on a business trip). On all superior levels, using distributed information systems is a must.

Domain-independent techniques and tools to manage and apply distributed information systems may be used on all levels of our network hierarchy. For example, database schema integration techniques and group scheduling methods and tools may be used in enterprise-wide systems as well as in personal information systems. On top of these common techniques and tools, additional specific knowledge may be about the respective institution of a particular network level (see for example group decision techniques), or particular application areas (for example budget planning, optimal logistics). These structures partly will be picked up again in chapter 4.

On each network level, the respective institution has to implement the decisions on all four issues put up in chapter 1: design and run important physical infrastructural links; and design and run Value Added Network Services. Each subordinate network level encounters restrictions set by the standardization decisions of superior network levels.

3. Goals of applying distributed information systems

The common goal is to set-up and maintain a 'modern' distributed information systems infrastructure of all institutions (network levels). More precisely, the long-term research and application goal is to develop a normative coordination scheme for interacting actors in this distributed information system, ideally covering all network levels. In Williamson (1975), two ideal ways of coordination are discussed: coordination through hierarchy and coordination through market.

In case of a market coordination mechanism, the task of the respective institution is to set up and maintain a full-fledged market, e.g. define independent VANS products, allow external vendors to easily "feed" internal systems, collect and compare prices, count service units, and perform quality control.

In case of a coordination through organizational hierarchy, we look for example for a work schedule which minimizes the duration of the production processes or which minimizes the production costs. Here, literature offers two main theoretical foundations to design distributed information systems: Theory of organization[3] is directed towards the creation of hierarchies of delegation and control and the distribution of business processes on actors in organizational units (like departments). In contrast, communication network theory of computer sciences[4] focuses on optimizing network topologies, channel capacities, and transmission fluxes, resembling a machine-oriented distribution of tasks. To what extent are these two fundamental approaches compatible with each other, mutually exclusive, or complementary? How do we have to properly set up communication infrastructures? How do we have to design business processes?

To answer some of these questions, the German National Science Foundation which is co-sponsored by industry has set up a research program to study these issues. In chapter 4, an overview of the best 15 project reports which are presented in this book is given[5]. Data presented here were collected in a semi-structured interview in spring 1995.

4. The contributions of this book to manage and apply distributed information systems

We have clustered the project reports into two sections, the Theoretical Section and the Application Section.

4.1. Theoretical section

The first section contains 8 projects that primarily focus on theoretical foundations of distributed information systems. In this context, 5 important questions arise:

1. How do we have to design distributed information systems themselves?

   Oberweis, Stucky and Zimmermann give an answer to this question in their paper "INCOME/STAR: Facing the Challenges for Cooperative Information System Development Environments". They use Petri nets to design distributed information systems. The design is supported by a powerful tool to create and simulate Petri nets.

---

[3] cf. Mintzberg (1979)

[4] cf. Tanenbaum (1988) and Purser (1987)

[5] The editors thank the program's referees for their efforts to rate the contributions and to propose improvements of the original texts.

2. How do we have to design databases of distributed information systems?

   In a distributed environment, databases are also distributed physically and/or logically. This means that the corresponding database schemata are developed locally and may therefore exhibit inconsistencies when being integrated. Should integration take place and if so, how is it done properly?

   Stickel, Hunstock, Ortmann and Ortmann address this problem in their contribution "A Business Process Oriented Approach to Data Integration".

3. How should distribution itself be performed?

   Three projects set out to solve this problem but taking different paths they found different, but equally valid solutions:

   Wendt, Rittgen and Koenig took a *problem-oriented* approach in "Solving Decision Problems by Distributed Decomposition and Delegation - Foundations of a Theory and its Application within a Normative Group Decision Support System framework". A complex problem is decomposed into smaller parts and these parts are delegated along the organizational hierarchy.

   Zwicker and Rottenbacher distribute *budget-oriented* in "Distributed cooperative budget-planning and -control". A global budget is disaggregated to decentralized budgets in order to control the coordination of cooperating agents.

   Mertens, Falk, Spieck and Weigelt approached the problem *agent-oriented* in "Decentralized Problem Solving in Logistics with Partly Intelligent Agents and Comparison with Alternative Approaches". An initial distribution of tasks to a set of partly intelligent agents (software agents) is improved by employing coordination agents. The pros and cons of centralized versus decentralized systems are determined by simulation.

4. How should we design the infrastructure of a distributed information system?

   Unland, Kirn, Wanka, O'Hare and Abbas suggest an answer to this question in their paper "Organizational Multi-Agent Systems: A Process Driven Approach". They build multi-agent systems that make use of "organizational intelligence".

5. How can distributed information systems profit by massive parallelization?

Two projects are dedicated to this problem. They investigate the advantages of transputers and workstation networks in distributed environments: Under which circumstances does parallelization gain outweigh the necessary overhead for synchronizing the participating transputers/workstations?

Holthaus, Rosenberg and Ziegler answer this question in the context of job-shop scheduling problems. The title of their contribution is 'Development and Simulation of Methods for Scheduling and Coordinating Decentralized Job Shops Using Multi-Computer Systems'. They use a demand-oriented look-ahead mechanism to improve scheduling results for decentralized job shops.

Kopfer, Utecht and Bierwirth inquire into the conditions and system architectures to achieve a speedup in 'Distributed Environments for Evolutionary Algorithms by means of Multi-Agent Applications'. They focus on production scheduling using evolution-based agent systems (e. g. genetic algorithms) to solve large-scale calculation problems.

Table 1 summarizes the projects in the theoretical section. The order in the table reflects the order given under 1 - 5 as well as the order of the papers.

authors	***key word / title of the project***	***most important research goals***	***type of empirical evaluation***[6]	***most important further research tasks***
Oberweis, Stucky, Zimmermann	INCOME / STAR: Cooperative CASE environment to develop and maintain distributed information systems	Evaluation of new Petri net-based concepts for CASE tools supporting the creation of distributed information systems	RUN, PTLAB	Enhanced support for collaborative work by using workflow, Multi-user version of the CASE tool
Stickel, Hunstock, Ortmann, A., Ortmann, J.	DSI: Database schema integration	Development of a method to perform automatic schema integration	RUN, 2-PTRC	Extend method of schema integration to construct federated systems
Wendt, Rittgen, Koenig	DRSS: Distributed reasoning support system	A model for the support of distributed problem decomposition and decision-making	PASLAB, RUN	Flexible Organization of distributed agents
Zwicker, Rottenbacher	DCBPC: Distributed cooperative budget planning and control	Equation-based system for decentralized budgeting and control	PASLAB	Disaggregation of the budgeting model into monthly periods
Mertens, Falk, Spieck, Weigelt	PIA: Deepening the theory of partly intelligent agents and its application in logistics	Determining a pro and con profile of applying distributed information systems compared to traditional centralized solutions	2-PASRC, PASLAB	Integrating more pro and con arguments for centralization and decentralization
Unland, Kirn, Wanka, O'Hare, Abbas	OI-CSS: Organizational intelligence and cooperative software systems	Information systems infrastructure for business processes in virtual organizations	RUN	Adapt Distributed Artificial Intelligence techniques to business processes and improve synchronization in DAI systems
Holthaus, Rosenberg, Ziegler	SCD: Scheduling and coordinating decentralized job-shops using multi-computer systems	Development of coordination rules for decentralized job-shops	PASLAB	Extending the method to coordinate subsystems with different organizational structures
Kopfer, Utecht, Bierwirth	PARNET: Distributed and parallel applications in local networks	Solving large-scale calculation problems by a team of distributed agents	PASLAB	Negotiation system based on distributed agents for multi-depot vehicle routing

Table 1: Projects in the Theoretical Section

[6] abbreviations:

PASLAB	Prototype of new application system tested in laboratory
PTLAB	Prototype of new tool tested in laboratory
n-PTRC	Prototype of new tool has been tested in n real-world cases
n-PASRC	Prototype of new application system tested in n real-world cases
RUN	Prototype of new tool or new module of basic technology runs

4.2. Application section

The second section comprises 7 projects that concentrate on the application dimension of distributed information systems. We can identify 4 major questions that occur when developing a distributed application on a practical level.

1. How do we have to develop a distributed information system?

   Ferstl and Sinz introduce an object-oriented CASE tool for this task in their paper "Multi-Layered Development of Business Process Models and Distributed Business Application Systems - An Object-Oriented Approach". The underlying method is called SOM (semantic object model).

2. How should we design the infrastructure of a distributed system of human agents?

   Two projects aim to solve this problem by groupware systems (computer supported cooperative work). Business process design is then based on the described infrastructure:

   Elgass, Krcmar, Ludwig and Schoenwaelder use *conversation structuring* to control the flow of information in distributed information systems. Their contribution "Computer Support for Distributed Information Management Tasks (CUVIMA)" also presents concepts for IS planning based on portfolio theory.

   Nastansky and Hilpert focus on modeling the *workflow* in groups in "The GroupFlow Framework: Enterprise Model and Architecture of the Workflow System".

3. How do we have to perform distributed problem solving?

   Two papers address this question in the context of financial consulting, another one does so in the context of group scheduling:

   Einsfeld, Roemer, Rossbach, Sandbiller and Will developed a comprehensive model of the consulting process following a novel approach for providing financial services based on discounted cash flows. Their paper is titled "ALLFIWIB: Customer Consulting in Financial Services with Distributed Knowledge Based Systems".

   Heissel, Krallmann, Meyer, Mueller-Wuensch, Schopf and Woltering built a tool to create systems that support cooperative problem solving. Their results are described in "A Generic Approach for Computer-Assistance of Complex Decision Processes".

Suhl, Reinecke and Pape developed a system for group scheduling that is especially suited for airline scheduling. Details can be found in "Group Scheduling - Methods and Tools for Distributed Scheduling Processes in a Corporate Environment".

4. How should we integrate legacy systems into new distributed architectures?

   A particular problem arises from the fact that enterprises regularly run voluminous legacy systems. These traditional systems often cannot be easily changed on a short-term basis due to, for example, limited staff or limited financial resources[7]. Thus, there is an additional objective to develop a 'migration architecture', capable to integrate both traditional as well as distributed information systems. One up-coming question is: how can we extract structural knowledge from traditional systems and properly re-use it in distributed information systems?

   Kurbel, Jung and Pietsch give the answer in "Modeling Knowledge about Long-term IS Integration and Integration-oriented Reengineering with KADS".

Table 2 summarizes the projects in the application section. Again, the order in the table reflects both the order given under 1 - 4 and that of the papers.

---

[7] cf. Arnold (1993)

authors	*key word / title of the project*	*most important goals*	*type of empirical evaluation*[8]	*most important further research tasks*
Ferstl, Sinz	ODDIS: Object-oriented development of distributed information systems	Development of a comprehensive method to model distributed information systems	RUN, 4-PTRC	Simulation of distributed information systems
Elgass, Krcmar, Ludwig, Schoenwaelder	CUVIMA: Computer Support for distributed information management tasks	Design of groupware systems for business process design and for information systems planning	PTLAB, 3-PTRC	Integration of IS planning tool into IS controlling, of process planner into workflow approaches and of conversation structuring into groupware
Nastansky, Hilpert	GFF: Group flow framework - a groupware-based approach to workflow management	Design of groupware systems to support the (re-) design of business processes	RUN, 5-PTRC	Extending the software kernel to wide area cooperations, Application in virtual firms
Einsfeld, Roemer, Rossbach, Sandbiller, Will	CCFS-DKS: Customer consulting in financial services with distributed knowledge-based systems	Comprehensive model of the consulting process; Prototype of a distributed application system	PASLAB	Analysis and modeling of the cooperation and coordination of human and artificial actors
Heissel, Krallmann, Meyer, Mueller-Wuensch, Schopf, Woltering	DPS: Distributed problem solving in the field of financial consulting and environmental management	Building a tool to create systems that support co-operative problem solving	PTLAB, PASLAB	Improving the methods for designing distributed application systems
Suhl, Reinecke, Pape	DCSP: Methods and tools for distributed corporate scheduling processes	Optimally distributed processes to generate schedules	RUN, PTLAB	Perform field tests of coordination mechanisms
Kurbel, Jung, Pietsch	EILS: Economic integration of legacy systems through gradual re-engineering	Methods for integrating legacy systems into modern distributed environments and assessment of economic impacts	PTLAB	Expert system prototype supporting decisions whether to develop a new software module or to re-engineer legacy systems

Table 2: Projects in the Application Section

5. References

Arnold, R.S. (Ed.): Software Reengineering, Los Alamitos CA, 1993.

---

[8] abbreviations:

PASLAB	Prototype of new application system tested in laboratory
PTLAB	Prototype of new tool tested in laboratory
n-PTRC	Prototype of new tool has been tested in n real-world cases
n-PASRC	Prototype of new application system tested in n real-world cases
RUN	Prototype of new tool or new module of basic technology runs

Heinzl; Srikanth: The Future of the Information Systems / Technology Function - 2000 and beyond - IS People Perspective, Research Report 12/93, Haas School of Business' Information Systems Research Group, Univ. of California at Berkeley, 1993.

Heinzl; Srikanth: The Future of the Information Systems / Technology Function - 2000 and beyond - Key Users Perspective, Research Report 3/94, Haas School of Business' Information Systems Research Group, Univ. of California at Berkeley, 1994.

Martin, J.: Design and Strategy for Distributed Data Processing, Englewood Cliffs NJ, 1981.

Mintzberg, H.: The Structuring of Organizations. A Synthesis of the Research, Englewood Cliffs NJ, 1979.

Purser, M.: Computers and Telecommunications Networks, Blackwell Scientific Publications, 1987.

Shoham, Y.: Agent-Oriented Programming, Artificial Intelligence, 60, pp 51-92, 1993.

Tanenbaum, A.S.: Computer Networks, 2nd edition, Englewood Cliffs NJ, 1988.

Williamson, O.E.: Markets and Hierarchies, Analysis and Antitrust Implications, New York, 1975.

Theoretical Section

INCOME/STAR: Facing the Challenges for Cooperative Information System Development Environments

Andreas Oberweis, Wolffried Stucky, Gabriele Zimmermann

Abstract

This paper surveys some innovative features of INCOME/STAR, an experimental environment for cooperative development of information systems.

First an extension of high-level Petri nets is described: *NR/T-nets* allow modeling of concurrent processes and related complex structured objects in distributed business applications. Further new concepts have been developed for *entity* and *relationship clustering* to support a stepwise top-down approach for entity/relationship based object modeling. Distributed *multi-user simulation and prototyping* are proposed for the evaluation and analysis of NR/T-nets and the involved object schemata.

Then, *ProMISE* - an evolutionary *process model* for information system development - is surveyed. A role-based *groupware component* is part of the INCOME/STAR architecture to support communication, organization and social interaction in development projects.

Keywords: cooperative system design, Petri nets, information systems, Petri net simulation, software development environments, software process support

1. Introduction

A major part of today's software systems are large, database supported information systems. Providing environments which support an efficient production of high-quality information systems has been - and still is - a major objective of information systems engineering. But an industrialization of software engineering in general and information systems engineering in particular is far from being achieved. More than a decade after the invention of CASE technology, there are still exciting challenges in this area, mainly because information systems have advanced in many aspects:

Complexity: Information systems are not only supposed to be specially suited for a certain application domain but also to support a wide range of functionality within this domain. On the one hand they must be capable, e.g., to handle production control data, on the other hand they must manage business and administration data of an enterprise.

Distribution: Systems may be geographically distributed and are quite frequently integrated in networks.

Interoperability: Systems are supposed to communicate and exchange data with other systems.

Flexibility: Requirements change frequently due to market factors, new technologies or strategical decisions. Moreover, systems are embedded in a heterogeneous software or hardware configuration which is subject to change.

One objective of the INCOME/STAR project[9] is to detect deficiencies of existing development support systems and to implement a prototype of an integrated environment supporting cooperative development of large, distributed information systems in the above sense. The INCOME/STAR prototype is based on INCOME[10], an existing tool for conceptual modeling and prototyping of information systems. INCOME was originally developed at our institute between 1985 and 1990. Basic concepts are: integration of structural and behavioral system aspects, prototyping facilities and design dictionary support *(Lausen et al. 1989).* Based on the academic version of INCOME, a commercially available methods and tools package was developed *(INCOME 1994).*

While INCOME is primarily suited for the development of new information systems, INCOME/STAR supports both the development of completely new systems and the integration of new components into existing hardware and software environments. Special emphasis is put on distributed, heterogeneous target systems (like modern information system networks).

These target systems require new or adapted methods and advanced simulation and prototyping concepts. Software process support and cooperative design techniques were identified as additional important research fields in the context of system development.

This paper summarizes the new concepts of INCOME/STAR which can be grouped into four research directions: methodological extensions (Section 2), software process support (Section 3), advanced simulation and prototyping concepts (Section 4) and cooperative system design (Section 5). The final section documents first practical experiences and gives a short outlook on future research work.

---

[9] The INCOME/STAR project is partially supported by the Deutsche Forschungsgemeinschaft DFG under grant Stu 98/9 in the program "Distributed Information Systems in Business".

[10] **I**nteractive **N**et-based **Co**nceptual **M**odeling **E**nvironment

2. Methodological Extensions

Modeling highly flexible information systems requires object structures that are not as restricted as postulated by the relational data model. Methodological extensions of INCOME/STAR aim at providing concepts for a behavior and structure model which is adequate for complex structured objects. An important step towards this goal is the conception of NR/T-nets - a new variant of high-level Petri nets closely related to NF^2 (Non First Normal Form) relational databases *(Schek, Scholl 1986)* - for behavior modeling (Section 2.1).

Another useful approach to cope with complex data and process structures is the use of hierarchically structured models which allow an incremental approach to conceptual modeling. Refinement and coarsening of Petri nets has already proven a successful technique in INCOME. INCOME/STAR provides an equivalent concept on the data side which extends existing Entity-Relationship model clustering techniques (Section 2.2).

2.1. Nested Relation/Transition Nets

Petri nets[11] are a graphical language for the formal specification of distributed system behavior. INCOME/STAR uses a new type of high-level Petri nets, called *nested relation/transition nets* (*NR/T-nets) (Oberweis, Sander, Stucky 1993)*.

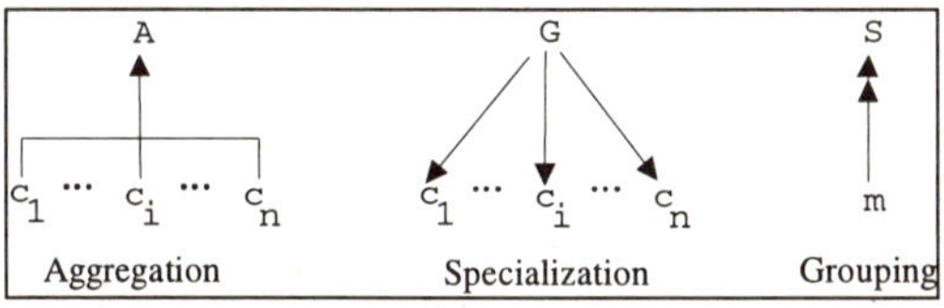

Fig. 1: Structuring concepts in SHM

To each place in an NR/T-net, a complex structured object type is assigned, specified in a semantic data model similar to SHM (Semantic Hierarchy Model*) (Brodie, Ridjanovic 1984)*. Basic constructs for data structuring are *classification*, *aggregation*, *specialization* and *grouping*. Figure 1 shows the graphical representation of these concepts. The marking of a place in an NR/T-net is a nested relation of the respective type, i.e. a set of so-called complex objects, where attribute values may again be nested relations.

A transition in an NR/T-net represents a class of operations on relations in the transition's input- and output-places. An occurrence of a transition denotes one single occurrence of the

---

[11] We suppose that the reader is familiar with the basic Petri net notation (cf. e.g. Reisig 1985).

respective operation. Operations may not only operate on whole tuples of a given relation but also on 'subtuples' of existing tuples.

NR/T-nets are an upwards compatible extension of *predicate/transition nets (Pr/T-nets)* (*Genrich, Lautenbach 1981)*: the marking of a place in a Pr/T-net is given as a normalized relation where attribute values of a tuple are atomic, i.e. unstructured. This is obviously not appropriate for modeling operations on complex structured objects, since it does not allow, e.g., concurrent accesses to different set-valued attributes of the same complex object. An example is a situation where different project team members access different parts of the same document.

Example

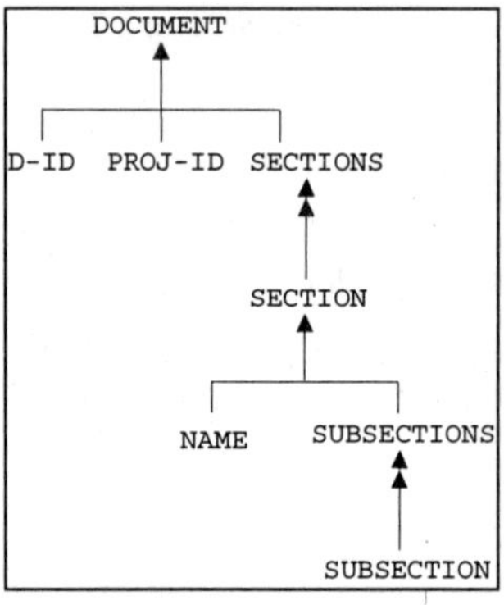

Fig. 2: Type DOCUMENT

Figure 2 shows the structure of a (simplified) object type DOCUMENT: An object of type DOCUMENT is composed of a document identifier (D-ID), a project identifier (PROJ-ID), and a set of sections (SECTIONS). Each section (SECTION) is composed of a section name (NAME) and a set of subsections (SUBSECTIONS). D-ID, PROJ-ID, NAME and SUBSECTION are atomic attributes.

Figure 3 shows the tabular representation of three example documents, doc1 and doc2 of project p1 and doc3 of project p2.

DOCUMENT			
D-ID	PROJ-ID	SECTIONS	
		NAME	SUBSECTIONS
			SUBSECTION
doc1	p1	{<sec1,	{sn1,sn2,sn3}>,
		<sec2,	{sn1,sn2,sn3}>
		<sec3,	{sn1,sn2}> }
doc2	p1	{<sec1,	{sn1,sn2,sn3}>,
		<sec2,	{sn1}>}
doc3	p2	{<sec1,	{sn1,sn2}>,
		<sec2,	{sn1,sn2,sn3}>,
		<sec3,	{sn1,sn2,sn3,sn4}>,
		<sec4,	{sn1,sn2,sn3}> }

Fig. 3: Tabular representation of three example objects of type DOCUMENT

Figure 4 shows an NR/T-net with three different transitions, each of them describing a different type of access to objects of the type DOCUMENT. A possible initial marking of the place DOCUMENT is given in Figure 3.

Arcs in an NR/T-net are inscribed with so-called *filter tables* which select data to be inserted into the adjacent output-place or to be removed from the adjacent input-place. Filter tables may be hierarchically structured to reflect the hierarchic structure of complex objects. This allows access to values which are located on lower levels of the attribute hierarchy.

A transition is enabled for an instantiation of the variables in the filter tables assigned to the incoming and outgoing arcs iff:

- the respective (instantiated) tuples in the filter tables at the ingoing arcs are contained in the adjacent input places, and

- the respective tuples in the filter tables at the outgoing arcs are *not* contained in the adjacent output places, and
- the logical rule which is optionally inscribed to the transition is *true* for the given instantiation.

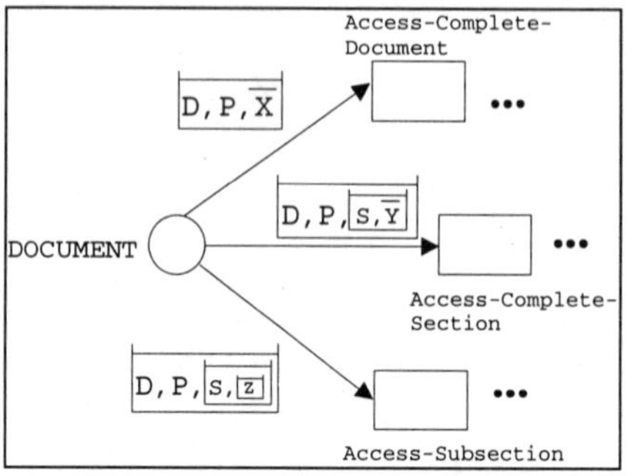

Fig. 4: Example NR/T-net (A)

For the set valued attributes we distinguish between two cases:

So-called *closed* variables which are overlined, e.g. $\overline{X}$ in Figure 4, always access complete attribute values. In Figure 4, $\overline{X}$ must be instantiated by complete sets of sections of a document. If, e.g., `D` is instantiated to `doc1` and `P` to `p1`, then $\overline{X}$ must be instantiated to

```
{<sec1, {sn1,sn2,sn3}>,
 <sec2, {sn1,sn2,sn3}>,
 <sec3, {sn1,sn2}>      }.
```

So-called *open* variables, e.g. X in Figure 5, may be instantiated by an arbitrary subset of a set attribute value. If `D` is instantiated to `doc1` and `P` to `p1`, then `X` may be instantiated, e.g., to

```
{<sec1, {sn1,sn2,sn3}>,
 <sec2, {sn1,sn2,sn3}> }.
```

In Figure 4 the following different access types are modeled:

- When transition `Access-Complete-Document` occurs, it removes a complete document tuple from the input place `DOCUMENT`, e.g.

```
<doc1,p1,{      <sec1, {sn1,sn2,sn3}>,
                <sec2, {sn1,sn2,sn3}>,
                <sec3, {sn1,sn2}>        }>.
```

- When transition `Access-Complete-Section` occurs, it removes a single section of a given document tuple from the input place DOCUMENT. The transition may occur concurrently to itself or to other transitions with respect to different sections - possibly of the same document. This corresponds to a situation where different persons/tools access different sections of the same document at the same time.

- When transition `Access-Subsection` occurs, it removes a single subsection of a given section of a given design document from the input place DOCUMENT. The transition may occur concurrently to itself or to other transitions with respect to different subsections - possibly of the same section of the same document. This corresponds to a situation where different persons/tools access different subsections of the same document at the same time.

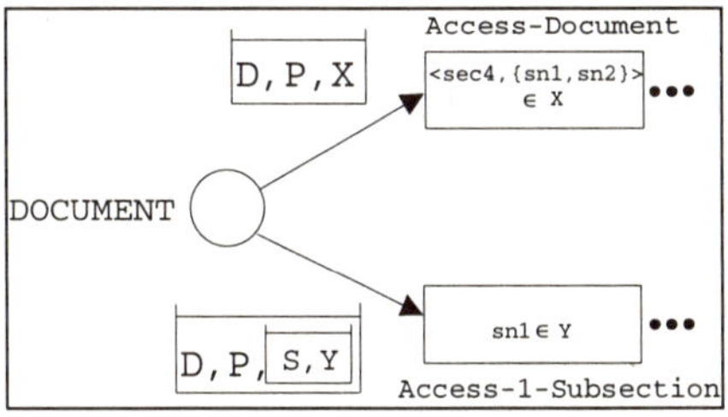

Fig. 5: Example NR/T-net (B)

The meaning of the transitions in the NR/T-net in Figure 5 is as follows:

- `Access-Document` removes a subset `X` of sections of a document in place DOCUMENT, such that `X` contains the section `<sec4, {sn1,sn2}>`.

- `Access-1-Subsection` removes a subset `Y` of subsections of a document in place DOCUMENT, such that `Y` contains the subsection `sn1`.

For a detailed description and further examples, the interested reader is referred to *(Oberweis, Sander, Stucky 1993).*

2.2. ER Model Clustering

The Entity-Relationship approach is a widely accepted method for conceptual database design. However, problems arise when ER modeling is applied to the design of really large databases concerning whole enterprises. There is, e.g., no way to obtain a general view or to perceive the global context of a detailed enterprise schema with hundreds of entity and relationship types.

Several approaches use ER model clustering to overcome these problems *(Feldman, Miller 1986; Teorey et al. 1989; Rauh, Stickel 1992).* Whole sections of the detailed diagram are mapped into so-called entity clusters, which are presented as (complex) entity types in a higher level ER diagram. All approaches are based on an already existing detailed ER diagram. Based on this, the abstraction layers are built *bottom-up.*

INCOME/STAR extends the approaches described above. It distinguishes between three kinds of clustering *(Jaeschke, Oberweis, Stucky 1993):*

① *Entity clustering* was first proposed by *(Feldman, Miller 1986).* An overview diagram leaving out several details is created from a detailed ER diagram. Sections of the detailed diagram are collected into so-called entity clusters, which are represented as (complex) entity types in a higher level ER diagram. The detailed relationship types between entity types existing in one cluster are not visible in the higher level ER diagram. The others - so-called outside-relationship types - are transformed to relationship types between the clusters containing the originally detailed entity types. The higher level diagram is iteratively abstracted by this method.

② *Simple relationship clustering* is newly introduced to refine relationship types by several semantically similar ones. *Simple relationship clustering* is used to formulate integrity constraints more precisely. In Figure 6, the relationship type 'works at' is refined by simple relationship clustering in the context of the refinement of 'Employee'. It is expressed that only members of the ground staff work at airports and that each member of the ground staff works at *exactly one* airport. *Simple relationship clustering* can as well be applied to represent integrity constraints in an ER diagram and to cluster semantically similar relationship types into one.

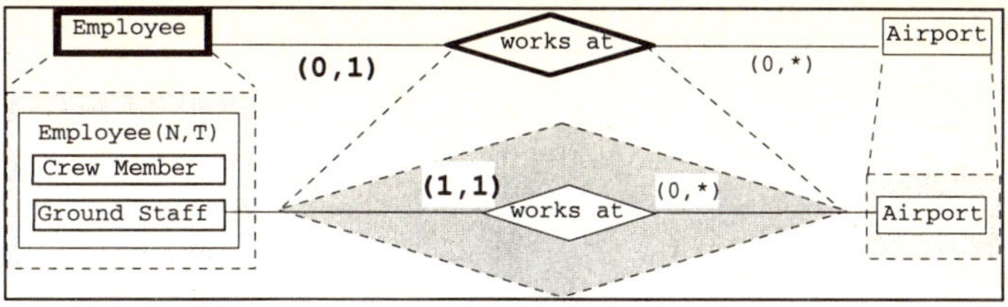

Fig. 6: Refinement of 'Employee' based on entity clustering; refinement of 'works at' based on simple relationship clustering

③ *Complex relationship clustering* is proposed to refine relationship types by whole ER diagrams. In contrast to simple relationship clustering not only the relationship type is divided into several similar relationship types, additional entity and relationship types are introduced as well. Either a single element is refined (non-contextsensitive refinement) or a single element together with its environment is refined (contextsensitive refinement).

For a detailed description and further examples, the interested reader is referred to *(Jaeschke, Oberweis, Stucky 1993).*

3. Software Process Support

Software process support in the INCOME/STAR project has two major concerns. First is to provide developers with a guideline of how to perform information system development with INCOME/STAR. A framework called ProMISE (**Pro**cess **M**odel for **I**nformation **S**ystem **E**volution) describes the methodology supported by INCOME/STAR and enables people involved in the development process to reflect, communicate and discuss the process. Its basic structure is lined out in Section 3.1.

Section 3.2 deals with the second concern of software process support which is *process model enactment*. Active assistance is offered for monitoring of development activities, document and workflow management (*Oberweis 1994)*, control of project responsibilities, capacity planning etc.

3.1. Basic Structure of ProMISE

System development with ProMISE takes an evolutionary approach, i.e. development and maintenance of a system are done as a sequence of sub-projects. ProMISE combines the advantages of a well-structured, stagewise approach to software development with other useful techniques, such as incremental refinement of documents, software reuse, prototyping, and cooperation support.

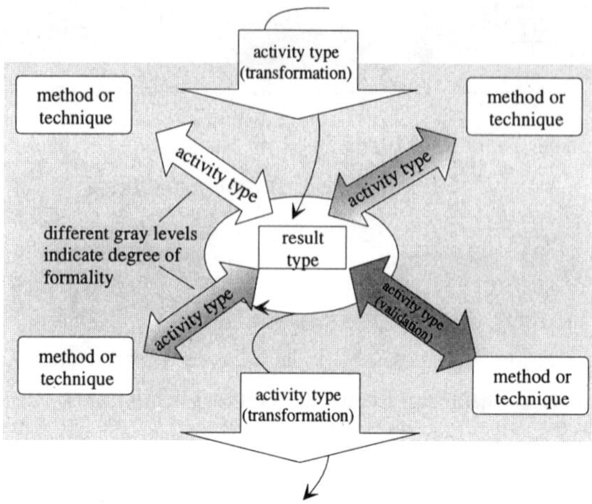

Fig. 7: Graphical representation of a generic development stage in ProMISE

Figure 7 shows the graphical representation of a generic development stage in ProMISE. A specific design document ('result type') has a certain status as, e.g., requirements schema, implementation module, etc. and is modified with stage specific activities (e.g. semantic data model editing, compilation, etc.). In the graphical representation activity types have a specific gray level indicating the activity's degree of formality. Usually, document creation starts with a - more or less formal - transformation step, converting documents of the preceding stage into (initial) documents of the current phase. Next, documents are iteratively adjusted by an activity sequence (refinement, structuring, information collection steps etc.). Software reuse is one potential alternative - either as an integration of standard components or as project specific adjustment of generic models.

The last activity type in an iteration is a validation step which checks the results of the preceding transformation and modification steps. Whenever it makes sense, end users will be involved in this process. When a document's quality is acceptable, it may be transformed into an initial document of the succeeding stage. Otherwise a new iteration of information collection, modification and quality checking steps starts. Sometimes a situation may require a go-back to an earlier stage, e.g. if requirements are added or changed.

A specific description for strategic planning, project specific planning, requirements collection and analysis, conceptual modeling, database design and implementation, program design and implementation is available in (Scherrer, Oberweis, Stucky 1994).

As an example, Figure 8 shows requirements collection and analysis in the introduced notation:

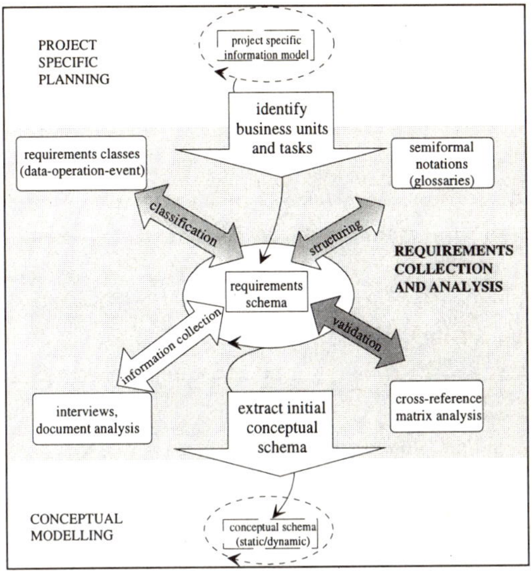

Fig. 8: Requirements collection and analysis stage

In the *initial transformation step*, a requirements collection plan is worked out by extracting business units and tasks from the *project specific information model*, which is the deliverable of the preceding stage. This initial document is refined to a complete *requirements schema* by iterating the following activity sequence: For each task/business unit combination in the requirements collection plan, *information is collected and completed* through interviews and an analysis of existing documents. Next, information items are *classified* as data, operation or event and then *recorded in structured glossaries.* Cross-reference matrix analysis is used for *validation.* If any inconsistency or incompleteness is detected, a new iteration is performed.

3.2. Process Model Enactment

To obtain an enactable version of ProMISE, it is specified as a hierarchy of Petri nets. A similar notation as in Figure 8 may be used on the top level. This top level representation provides a gross overview about the process model and may be used for communication between different groups of people involved in a software project. Manual and unstructured activities (like unstructured communication) are expressed by informal types of Petri nets inscribed with natural language expressions and enriched with icons that are easy to understand.

Stepwise refinement leads to a precise NR/T-net description of the process. The resulting nets are instantiated with a project-specific marking. Instantiation includes, e.g., association of activities and roles, roles and team members, deliverables and deadlines etc.

The instantiated nets can be enacted by a *process engine* (a Petri net interpreter) which is coupled to the central repository and can control access to tools and data and manage the flow of information between people and tools involved in the software development process.

4. Advanced Simulation and Prototyping Concepts

In INCOME/STAR, simulation is an integrated part of the development process: simulators are interfaced with the central design dictionary where the formal behavior specification is stored as a set of high-level Petri nets. Due to the formal semantics of the underlying net model, this specification is directly executable. Some innovative issues of the INCOME/STAR simulation and prototyping capabilities are now described in detail.

- **Simulation support for evolutionary development**

The simulation concepts in INCOME/STAR (*Mochel, Oberweis, Sänger 1993)* support the evolutionary development approach prescribed by the chosen software development process model ProMISE: a preliminary system behavior specification - given as a set of high-level Petri nets - is simulated and analyzed by a graphical query language (see next paragraph). As a result of this validation step the Petri net model is improved. The same procedure is executed for the resulting net, probably in several cycles, until the system behavior is modeled adequately.

- **Graphical query language for large simulation runs**

Practical experience showed that for large Petri net models, simulation runs which are generated by automatic simulation may consist of thousands of markings. Hence it is not obvious how to check a given simulation run for certain behavior patterns which are of interest to a system designer.

Our novel graphical query language GTL (**G**raphical **T**emporal **L**anguage) for simulation databases combines capabilities of temporal and graphical database languages. In the simulation database each net marking is interpreted as a single database state. GTL-queries are employed to check a simulation database for certain behaviour patterns. These patterns may be related to single states (e.g. *Is there a simulation state where condition c1 holds?*) or to sequences of database states (e.g. *Is there a simulation state sequence where first c1 holds, then c2, and finally c3?*). In GTL simulation states are graphically represented by circles and temporal relationships between simulation states can be expressed along an implicit time axis. So-called checkpoints (graphically represented as boxes) specify complex conditions to select a state (sequence) in the simulation database. For a detailed description of GTL see *(Oberweis, Sänger 1994)*.

- **Multiuser environment and application specific visualization of Petri net simulation**

An open simulation environment is provided which supports multiuser enactment and a coupling to external visualization devices. When dealing with large systems, several developers are involved in the design process of the corresponding Petri net model. Therefore, the applied tools should include appropriate multiuser support:

- Access control for Petri net models to avoid inconsistencies when multiple developers try to apply changes to the net at the same time.
- A possibility to visualize the simulation run on an arbitrary number of workstations.
- Developers should be enabled to influence the simulation run decentralized from their own workstation.

Another useful property of a simulation environment is *application specific visualization.* A common drawback of most today's graphical Petri net simulation tools is that they provide an animated view of the transition occurrences only in the graphical representations of the Petri net itself, i.e. they visualize the flow of information along the arcs of a net. For large systems, a visualization on this level is not particularly useful because with increasing net complexity it becomes more and more difficult to imagine how a certain system state translates to 'reality'. So what is needed is an open simulation environment integrating arbitrary visualization modules which can provide a problem oriented display of the current system state.

A prototype called GAPS (**G**raphical **A**nimated **P**etri net **S**imulator) *(Oberweis, Sänger, Weitz 1994)* implements these ideas: A person who initializes a simulation run becomes the 'master' of this process and can permit others to join in, either passively by letting them watch the simulation process or actively by granting them the right to influence the process. Beyond this external visualization, clients can register for certain events:

- The simulation starts.
- A given transition fires.
- The content of a given place changes.
- The simulation ends.

During simulation, the client is notified of the events it is registered for and reacts to such messages by updating its displays accordingly.

5. Cooperative System Design

Teamwork is an effective way to cope with the increasing complexity of software systems and high quality demands. Support for *cooperative development* work in a software engineering project includes different coordination aspects.

Process models like ProMISE imply different workflows as they support parallel processing of development deliverables. During the whole project, communication support and an efficient management of the flow of work items between different people or groups of people is required. While process and workflow management primarily deal with technical aspects of software development, communication support concentrates on the *social action perspective.*

A framework of a role-based groupware system called RoCoMan (**Ro**le **Co**llaboration **Man**ager) supporting communication, organization, and social interaction was worked out. The following teamwork support components are currently coupled to the INCOME/STAR repository *(Oberweis, Wendel, Stucky 1994)*:

- **Extended eMail system**

The eMail system maintains a semi-structured message exchange which supports message filtering methods to avoid information overload, a typical problem of existing communication systems. Therefore, the eMail system was extended by a component which interprets rule expressions like 'if mail arrives from team member Smith then put mail into dictionary smithMail'.

There are four different types of eMail are supported: common, formatted, extended and conversational eMail. Common eMail corresponds to conventional eMail. Formatted eMail supports structuring of the mail content. Extended eMail allows the declaration of specific message types, for instance a request or a question. Conversational eMail is embedded in a so-called conversation which declares valid sequences of messages which can be modeled by a conversation editor. Main components of the extended eMail system are a mail desktop and a mail editor. The desktop supports filtering methods for analyzing incoming mails. The editor maintains the creation of mail with respect to the selected eMail type.

- **Day planner**

The day planner maintains three kinds of electronic calendar: personal, group and common project calendar. A personal electronic calendar consists of private and shared spaces. Shared spaces - in contrast to private spaces - are periods of time which can be read and manipulated by other authorized team members. Shared spaces of team members are used to arrange group appointments which get registered in a *group calendar*. Deadlines and project dates are registered in a *project day plan* which is accessible by all group members.

- **Conversation manager**

The conversation manager allows planning and modeling of conversations and monitors progress information about current conversation processes. Conversations are represented by *conversation diagrams*, a semi-formal graphical language which allows to specify communication processes in an easy and intuitive way *(Oberweis, Wendel, Stucky 1994*). Each conversation consists of a *conversation act* representing a team member conversation activity, and a *processing relation* which links the conversation act to other conversation acts. A processing relation represents so-called conditions of completion to execute a conversation act: the importance (*conversational relevance*) of the conversation act, the *personal competence* and the *organizational role* of the team members performing the conversation act.

6. Practical Experience and Outlook

INCOME/STAR is implemented in a workstation environment, using *Smalltalk* for the user interface (including the graphical editors) and *Prolog* for the simulation kernel. A relational database system is used as basis for the repository.

Since some of the methods and tools are still under development, a practical evaluation of the complete system is not possible so far. Still, some valuable experiences were gained by evaluating parts of the system in some smaller case studies:

An information system for the administration of examination data was entirely developed with methods and tools available in the INCOME/STAR development environment *(Jaeschke, Stucky 1994*).

Several other case studies were carried out in cooperation with external partners to determine practical requirements and gain experiences with some specific methods. Two questions were of particular interest:

① Which semantic data model is most applicable in practice and should therefore be supported by the INCOME/STAR methodology? What is more important in practice: rich semantics or simplicity? Three alternatives were taken into consideration:

- a simple binary Entity-Relationship model
- an extended Entity-Relationship model

- the semantic hierarchy object model

One (surprising) result was that it can make sense to use different variants of the ER model in the same project. In spite of its restricted expressiveness, the simple, binary variant seems to be an adequate basis for discussion with end users, while versions with enriched semantics are preferred by software experts. But even developers sometimes switch to the binary variant at later stages, mainly because it can easily be converted into a relational database schema.

The semantic hierarchy object model seems to fit best with the NR/T-net concept and NF^2 databases. Consequently, instead of restricting INCOME/ STAR to one data model, we are thinking about a component which supports a conversion between models.

② Is there a reasonable degree of acceptance for Petri nets in practice? How should methodological support for Petri nets look like?

Experiences in this area were quite contradictory: Acceptance for Petri nets seem to be much better in manufacturing than in administration. One possible explanation could be that behavioral aspects of technical processes are more obvious and can therefore be modeled more easily. There is a lack of methodological support for the development of Petri net models, especially for applications in administration, where behavioral aspects can normally not be recognized as intuitively as in technical applications. Most advantageous for practical acceptance seem to be user-friendly visualization techniques and an automated generation of nets and markings.

Future research work includes the following issues:

While our graphical editors support both Pr/T- and NR/T-nets, our simulators currently work with strict Pr/T-nets. For the future, both net types will be supported. Furthermore, we are planning methodological support for a conversion from one net type into the other.

Our support for process modeling currently concentrates on qualitative aspects of software process management. Now we are planning to consider quantitative aspects as well by adding a component for software productivity and quality measurement.

As far as teamwork coordination is concerned, an important aspect of future research is the support of other system environments, e.g. available commercial groupware applications.

References

Brodie, M.L.; Ridjanovic, D.: On the design and specification of database transactions; in: Brodie, M.L.; Mylopoulos, J.; Schmidt, J.W. (Eds.): On Conceptual Modelling, Springer 1984, pp. 278-306.

Feldman, P.; Miller, D.: Entity model clustering: Structuring a data model by abstraction; The Computer Journal, 29(4), 1986, pp. 348-360.

Genrich, H.J.; Lautenbach, K.: System modelling with high-level Petri nets; Theoretical Computer Science, 13, 1981, pp. 109-136.

INCOME User Manuals: INCOME/Designer, INCOME/Dictionary, INCOME/Generator, INCOME/Simulator; PROMATIS Informatik, Karlsbad 1994.

Jaeschke, P.; Oberweis, A.; Stucky, W.: Extending ER model clustering by relationship clustering; in: Elmasri, R.; Kouramajian, V. (Eds.): Proc. 12th Int. Conf. on the Entity-Relationship Approach, Arlington 1993, pp. 447-459.

Jaeschke, P.; Stucky, W.: An integrated tool for information system development: practical experience; Universität Karlsruhe, Institut für Angewandte Informatik und Formale Beschreibungsverfahren, Forschungsbericht 297, Karlsruhe 1994.

Lausen, G.; Németh, T.; Oberweis, A.; Schönthaler, F.; Stucky, W.: The INCOME approach for conceptual modelling and prototyping of information systems; Proc. 1st Nordic Conf. on Advanced Systems Engineering, Stockholm 1989.

Mochel, T.; Oberweis, A.; Sänger, V.: INCOME/STAR: The Petri net simulation concepts; Systems Analysis - Modelling - Simulation, Journal of Modelling and Simulation in Systems Analysis, 13, 1993, pp. 21-36.

Oberweis, A.: Workflow management in software engineering projects; in: Medhat, S. (Ed.): Proc. 2nd Int. Conf. on Concurrent Engineering and Electronic Design Automation, Bournemouth 1994, pp. 55-60.

Oberweis, A.; Sänger, V.: Graphical query language for simulation runs; Journal of Microcomputer Applications, Vol. 17, Issue 4, 1994.

Oberweis, A.; Sänger, V.; Weitz, W.: GAPS - A multiuser tool for graphical simulation of Petri Nets; in: Halin, J.; Karplus, W.; Rimane, R. (Eds.): Proc. 1st Joint Conf. of Int. Simulation Societies, Zurich 1994, pp. 377-381.

Oberweis, A.; Sander, P.; Stucky, W.: Petri net based modelling of procedures in complex object database applications; in: Cooke, D. (Ed.): Proc. IEEE 17th Annual Int. Computer Software and Applications Conf., Phoenix 1993, pp. 138-144.

Oberweis, A.; Wendel, T.; Stucky, W.: Teamwork coordination in a distributed software development environment; in: Wolfinger, B. (Ed.): Innovationen bei Rechen- und Kommunikationssystemen, Springer 1994, pp. 423-429.

Rauh, O.; Stickel, E.: Entity tree clustering - a method for simplifying ER design; in: Pernul, G.; Tjoa, A.M. (Eds.): Proc. 11th Int. Conf. on the Entity-Relationship Approach, Springer 1992, pp. 62-78.

Reisig, W.: Petri Nets; EATCS Monographs on Theoretical Computer Science, Springer 1985.

Schek, H.-J.; Scholl, M.: The relational model with relation-valued attributes; Information Systems, 11(2), 1986, pp. 137-147.

Scherrer, G.; Oberweis, A.; Stucky, W.: ProMISE - a process model for information system evolution; Proc. 3rd Maghrebian Conf. on Software Engineering and Artificial Intelligence, Rabat 1994, pp. 27-36.

Teorey, T.J.; Wei, G.; Bolton, D.L.; Koenig, J.A.: ER model clustering as an aid for user communication and documentation in database design; Communications of the ACM 32(8), 1989, pp. 975-987.

A Business Process Oriented Approach to Data Integration

Eberhard Stickel, Jens Hunstock, Anke Ortmann, Jan Ortmann

Abstract

In most of today's companies we find heterogeneous database systems containing redundant and inconsistent data. This threatens the ability to make coordinated, organization-wide responses to business problems. Although benefits of data integration need not dominate the costs, we argue that some kind of common understanding of data structures is an absolute must. Thus, data integration is necessary at least to some degree. In literature, only technical aspects of schema integration are treated. Also, the complexity issue (large schemata are hard to understand) is usually not treated explicitly. We present a business process oriented strategy for data integration. This method allows the determination of the order and the degree of integration. Complexity is reduced by schema clustering during the pre-integration phase.

Keywords: Data integration, interoperability, data modeling.

1. Introduction

In most of today's companies redundant and inconsistent data are contained in various isolated databases. These data have grown in an uncoordinated manner over time and there have hardly been any coordination efforts. This threatens the ability of companies to make coordinated, organization-wide responses to today's business problems[12]. As a result of this situation, managers often complain that their information needs are not properly satisfied. Aggregated information has to be produced at high costs and with a certain time lag[13].

It seems reasonable to expect that companies are eager to integrate their data and to provide 'a common formal language for communicating about business events'[14]. We would expect companies to try to create enterprise-wide views of relevant data structures. Empirical investigations, however, show that this is not the case[15]. Reasons for this observation may be as follows:

---

12 cf. Goodhue et al., 1992b.

13 see e.g. the case study presented in Goodhue et al., 1992b, p. 301.

14 cf. Goodhue et al., 1992b, p. 293.

15 cf. Sprague, McNurlin,1993, pp. 208-212.

1. The complexity of the integration task is simply not manageable. The top down creation of an enterprise-wide information model is a costly and extremely time consuming project[16]. Analysts and designers are exposed to the full complexity of the enterprise at once. Moreover, data models created during earlier projects may not be used in this process since the structures defined there are not compatible with high level enterprise-wide views.

2. Bottom up approaches that try to integrate existing project data models lead to problems since structural and semantic heterogeneity have to be addressed. In literature, various approaches for schema integration have been presented[17]. However, the various approaches still remain isolated and do not address the issue of real world complexity. *Coulson* pointed out that this approach (he calls it a data dictionary approach to resemble the more technical nature of this approach) did not solve data management problems[18]. Recent case studies in the financial services industry also stress this point[19].

3. Data integration projects may lack top management support[20]. Numerous objections to the need for information systems planning stress the argument that things change so quickly that any plans will soon be obsolete[21]. On the other hand, management has realized the importance of data as a valuable company asset[22].

4. Data integration efforts may fail since they do not provide sufficient benefits. In literature, it was always assumed that benefits outweigh costs[23]. *Goodhue et al.* challenge this argument by presenting a framework for judging the merits of data integration[24]. Based on different case studies it is pointed out that data integration need not be beneficial for every organization.

We argue that even in heavily decentralized organizations there is a need for data sharing. As pointed out by *Sheth*: 'With high interconnectivity and access to many information sources, the primary issue in the future will not be how to efficiently process the data that is known to be relevant, but which data is relevant and where it is located'[25]. Companies will have to deal with heterogeneous database systems and will have to use information 'distributed' over various such systems.

---

16 for a discussion of this technique refer to Martin, 1989 or Goodhue et al., 1992a.
17 see e.g. Batini et al., 1986 or Sheth, Larson, 1990.
18 cf. Coulson, 1982.
19 cf. Seitz, Stickel, 1992 and Kühlmann, Stickel, 1990.
20 cf. Lederer, Sethi, 1990.
21 cf. Sprague, McNurlin, 1993, p. 106.
22 cf. O'Brien, 1990, p. 22.
23 cf. Huber, 1990.
24 cf. Goodhue et al., 1992b.
25 cf. Sheth, 1991.

We agree on the argument that top down development of enterprise-wide views is a rather complex and expensive task and that other strategies should be developed and investigated. For this purpose, we present a business process oriented strategy for data integration in section 4. Business processes that are critical to the company need to be adequately supported by information systems. Hence, studying business processes should give some insight as to which data are needed for its support. We will present a method based on an affinity measure that links databases to business processes and that allows the determination of the order and the degree to which schemata should be integrated. Finally, we turn to the actual integration task. Schema complexity is reduced through clustering steps in the pre-integration phase. The integration process is described in general in section 3. Some details of our approach are presented in sections 3 and 5.

2. Costs and Benefits of Data Integration

The main purpose of information is to reduce uncertainty. Uncertainty is the driving force for information processing requirements[26]. *Tushman* and *Nadler* basically distinguish two types of uncertainty[27]. The first type is uncertainty in the sense that needed information is absent. The second type is called equivocality. Equivocality means that there may be a couple of possibly conflicting interpretations of a situation. In the case of uncertainty, more information is beneficial in any case since it reduces the degree of uncertainty. In the case of equivocality, this is not necessarily true. The main focus now lies on the appropriateness of information provided.

A study by *Todd* and *Benbasat* adds the problem of the decision maker's trade-off between improving decision quality and minimizing or maintaining personal effort[28]. Empirical studies have not proved that managers having access to more information that was preselected by a decision aid used this option[29]. Quantitative analysis of a binary decision problem shows that more information might lead to lower expected misclassification costs, but to a higher variance and therefore to results that are worse, at least in the near future[30]. If the costs of getting appropriate information are considered, results may be worse in the long run. Again these findings support the argument that more information is not always beneficial.

26 cf. Galbraith, 1973.
27 cf. Tushman, Nadler, 1978.
28 cf. Todd, Benbasat, 1992.
29 cf. Benbasat, Nault, 1990 and Sharda et al., 1988.
30 cf. Stickel, 1994.

Tushman and *Nadler* use the following classification for sources of uncertainty and/or equivocality[31]:

1. complex and/or non-routine tasks;

2. unstable task environment;

3. interdependence between organizational subunits.

Complex and non-routine tasks usually are associated with equivocality. The same basically holds for unstable task environments. A high degree of interdependence between organizational subunits leads to the necessity of information sharing. Here we have to deal with the first type of uncertainty due to lack of information. *Goodhue et al.* look at data integration in the light of this classification and present a number of 'propositions' based on these scenarios and on suitable case studies[32]:

1. All other things being equal, as the interdependence between subunits increases, the benefits of data integration will increase, and the amount of data integration in rational organizations should also increase.

2. All other things being equal, as the differentiation between subunits increases, data integration will impose more and more compromise costs on local units; therefore, the amount of data integration in rational firms should decrease.

3. All other things being equal, firms with increased data integration will experience greater bureaucratic delay in getting approval for changes affecting the data models used by individual subunits.

4. All other things being equal, as the number and heterogeneity of subunit information needs increase, the difficulty of arriving at acceptable design compromises increases, and the costs of the resulting design will increase more than linearly. Thus, rational firms will integrate less extensively when there are many heterogeneous subunits involved.

5. As organizations face greater instability in their environments and their information requirements, the importance of the fourth point will increase. In turbulent environments, firms with many heterogeneous subunits will be even less likely to integrate extensively, and firms with homogeneous subunits will be more likely to integrate extensively.

---

[31] cf. Tushman, Nadler, 1978.

[32] cf. Goodhue et al., 1992b, pp. 301-306.

These arguments suggest that the benefits and costs of data integration heavily depend on the organizational structure and on the business environment of the particular firm. We may expect that these topics are reflected in the business processes that are critical to the company. We may hope that studying those business processes on a sufficiently detailed level will give hints on the level of data integration that should be performed. An actual computation of costs and benefits of data integration seems to be a very difficult task. The number of relevant parameters is large. At the same time, their interaction is sometimes not clear. Finally, a corresponding optimization problem needs to be formulated and solved in an enterprise-wide context, such that we have to deal with a large degree of complexity. Note that technological issues (e.g. economies of scale as discussed by King[33]) are not considered as being relevant in the first place. Current information technology allows the treatment of physical distribution and logical distribution of data separately (at least to a large degree).

We finally present one more argument for (partial) data integration. There is growing interest in highly decentralized organizational structures. Information technology supports decentralization by reducing communication costs (note that at the same time decentralization generally leads to higher coordination costs and the net result of these effects is not automatically evident). The decentralized units are based on profit centers, projects, products and customers (e.g. self managed work groups)[34]. It is well-known, however, that optimizing subproblems does not lead to a global optimum. Agency theory addresses this problem in detail[35]. Agency costs (e.g. monitoring costs) incur as a result of discrepancies between the objectives of the principal (top managers that are judged on the overall performance of the firm) and those of the agents (e.g. managers of profit centers). *Gurbaxani* and *Whang* present an illustrative example[36]: Manufacturing is rewarded for operational efficiency while marketing is rewarded for increasing sales. These two measures are not necessarily maximized by a consistent set of actions. Close monitoring of respective departmental performance is suggested. Close monitoring, however, means collecting data about the performance of the agents. Again this calls for data sharing and hence for at least partial data integration.

Also note that political or cultural aspects of an organization might lead to other decisions than those suggested by the rational perspective of an organization[37].

---

[33] cf. King, 1983.
[34] refer to Sprague, McNurlin, 1993, pp. 152-156 for more details.
[35] cf. Alchian, Demsetz, 1972 and Ross, 1973.
[36] cf. Gurbaxani, Whang, 1991.
[37] see Goodhue et al., 1992b, pp. 306-307 for some examples and Cohen et al., 1993 for more of these issues.

3. Data Integration

3.1. View Integration and Database Integration

Data integration means creating a common formal language for reasoning about a firm's data resources. Conceptual database modeling is usually done with the help of the well-known entity-relationship method[38]. An entity-relationship model may be transformed 'automatically' into a relational database design[39]. In the context of schema integration we assume that we have an entity-relationship model for every database under investigation. In general, we will find several variations of the entity-relationship method even in the same company.

The goal of view integration is to extract a common view on at least two conceptual database schemata. Database integration is concerned with physically integrating two databases. Thus, view integration may be seen as a first step towards database integration.

Note that data integration in our context means view integration. The goal is to create a common language for reasoning about data. We do not assume that integration will be performed physically. This observation corresponds to the two basic strategies presented below.

1. Federated database approach: The generation of a global conceptual schema allows global queries while at the same time existing databases remain active. Hence, heterogeneity of the database systems is assumed. The global schema acts as some kind of mediator. The global query is transformed into local queries.

2. Distributed database approach: Existing heterogeneous database systems are migrated to a new so called distributed database system. The global schema serves as a basis for redistributing physical data (fragmentation and allocation)[40]. Note that we use the term distributed database system in a wide sense.

Whatever strategy is chosen, however, view integration is necessary. Various strategies for view integration are proposed in the literature[41]. We use a binary approach. Hence, in each step two schemata are integrated.

---

[38] see Chen, 1976.
[39] transformation rules may be found in Elmasri, Navathe, 1994.
[40] see Özsu, Valduriez, 1991 for details.
[41] a summary may be found in Batini et al., 1986.

3.2. Problems of View and Database Integration

Problems of view integration result from structural and semantic heterogeneity of schemata that are to be integrated. An excellent summary of those problems, as well as possible solutions are provided by *Batini et al.*[42]. For completeness, we list the most important issues:

- *Use of different modeling concepts.* The ER-method as originally published has three modeling concepts, namely entity sets, relationship sets and attributes[43]. Extensions of this model, e.g. the EER-method[44], allow the modeling of subclasses and superclasses. The same real world concept may be modeled differently depending on the variant of the ER-method used. Also it is quite often up to the designer to choose whether a real world object is modeled as a separate entity set or as an attribute.

- *Naming conflicts.* Here we have the problem of homonyms and synonyms in various schemata.

- *Contradictory design specifications.* Consider the example of cardinality constraints. In one of the local schemata an entity set may depend existentially on another entity set while in the other schema this is not the case.

- *Detection of interschema dependencies.* These dependencies are not included in the local schemata but they should be visible in the global schema, since a larger domain is now described.

- *Detection of redundant modeling constructs* (e.g. derivable attributes or relationship sets). Attributes may be non-derivable in the local schemata but derivable in the global schema. Also we may have redundant relationship sets that may be eliminated in the global schema. The latter problem is treated in detail by *Rauh* and *Stickel*[45].

In the case of database integration, another major problem is that of entity identification on the instance level. The same real world object may be modeled by different instances in the local database systems. The problem is to identify the various pieces and to put them together correctly[46].

Batini et al. identify various stages of the integration process[47]:

---

42 cf. Batini et al., 1986.
43 cf. Chen, 1976.
44 cf. Elmasri, Navathe, 1994.
45 cf. Rauh, Stickel, 1993.
46 see e.g. Lim, Prabhakar, 1993.
47 cf. Batini et al., 1986.

1. *Pre-integration.* If we have to integrate more than two schemata, a choice of the strategy and/or the order of integration has to be made. In literature, it is proposed that the relative importance of schemata be determined[48]. More details are not presented.

2. *Comparison of schemata.* Within this integration step we analyze and compare the two schemata to be merged. We may detect interschema relationships and naming conflicts (e.g. homonyms and synonyms), as well as structural conflicts and the use of different constructs.

3. *Conforming the schemata.* If conflicts have been identified, they need to be resolved in this step.

4. *Merging and possible restructuring of the schemata.* In this step, the two schemata are superimposed and merged. We then have to check the quality of the global schema[49].

Note that in most of those integration steps domain specific knowledge has to be used to address the problem of semantic heterogeneity. If the integration task is to be automated, this knowledge has to be collected in an encyclopaedia. For this purpose, data dictionary approaches have been presented in the literature[50]. We use a dictionary approach in combination with concept hierarchies[51].

4. Order and Degree of Schema Integration

4.1. Basic Concepts

We now turn to the problem of the order in which conceptual database schemata should be integrated. Greater competitive pressure forces companies to look for new forms of organization. Today, highly decentralized organizational units are favoured in a lot of companies. The organization of critical business processes is a key success issue. Information systems need to support the key business processes identified. Thus, looking at critical business processes will indicate the kind of data that is necessary for their support. Our method uses these observations and collects information about existing local databases and business processes in a database/process matrix. Fig. 1 shows such an incidence matrix. A '1' in the *i*-th row and *j*-th column indicates that database *i* is used by business process *j*. A '0' indicates that the database is not used by this business process. The left side of Fig. 1 contains data of a sample matrix which we will use to illustrate our approach.

---

48 cf. Batini et al., 1986, p. 343.
49 cf. Rauh, Stickel, 1993.
50 cf. Metais et al., 1993 for a discussion of different approaches and their efficiency.

$$A := \begin{bmatrix} 0 & 1 & 1 & 0 \\ 1 & 1 & 0 & 1 \\ 0 & 0 & 0 & 1 \\ 1 & 0 & 0 & 0 \\ 1 & 1 & 0 & 0 \\ 0 & 0 & 1 & 1 \\ 0 & 1 & 1 & 0 \\ 0 & 1 & 0 & 1 \end{bmatrix} \quad B := A \cdot A^T \quad C_{i,j} := \frac{B_{i,j}}{\sqrt{B_{i,i} \cdot B_{j,j}}} \quad C = \begin{bmatrix} 1.00 & 0.41 & 0.00 & 0.00 & 0.50 & 0.50 & 1.00 & 0.50 \\ 0.41 & 1.00 & 0.58 & 0.58 & 0.82 & 0.41 & 0.41 & 0.82 \\ 0.00 & 0.58 & 1.00 & 0.00 & 0.00 & 0.71 & 0.00 & 0.71 \\ 0.00 & 0.58 & 0.00 & 1.00 & 0.71 & 0.00 & 0.00 & 0.00 \\ 0.50 & 0.82 & 0.00 & 0.71 & 1.00 & 0.00 & 0.50 & 0.50 \\ 0.50 & 0.41 & 0.71 & 0.00 & 0.00 & 1.00 & 0.50 & 0.50 \\ 1.00 & 0.41 & 0.00 & 0.00 & 0.50 & 0.50 & 1.00 & 0.50 \\ 0.50 & 0.82 & 0.71 & 0.00 & 0.50 & 0.50 & 0.50 & 1.00 \end{bmatrix}$$

Fig. 1: Sample Database/Process Matrix and resulting Affinity Matrix

If we multiply this database/process-matrix A from the right by its transpose A^T, we get the matrix $B=AA^T$ that shows how often various databases support the same business process. The number b_{ij} in the i-th row and j-th column indicates how many business processes require information from both database i and database j. We use this matrix to determine the affinity between local databases or local schemata respectively. From the matrix B we derive an affinity matrix C[52]. The entry c_{ij} is defined by

$$c_{ij} = \frac{bij}{\sqrt{biibjj}}$$

The right side of Fig. 1 contains the entries of the matrix C for our sample database/process-matrix. Note that C is a symmetric matrix.

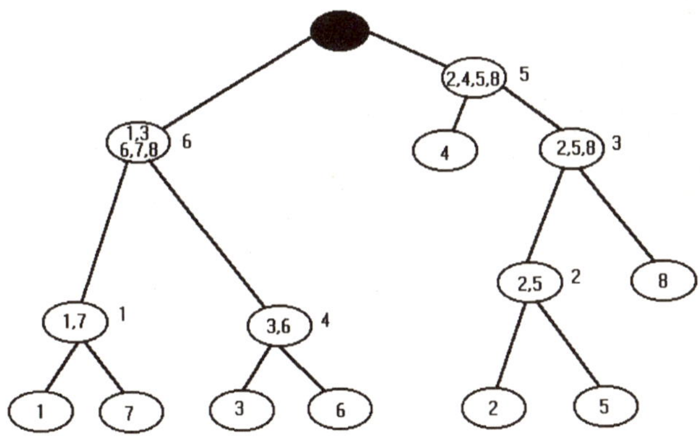

Fig. 2: Order of the Integration Process

[51] cf. Johannesson, 1993.

[52] for a treatment of affinity analysis in the context of information engineering see Martin, 1990.

We now choose the maximal non-diagonal entry of the matrix C. In our example, this is the entry c_{71}. Note that this entry need not be unique. In that case, we choose one of the maximal entries. Note that in this respect our algorithm is not deterministic. We now integrate the databases labelled 1 and 7. Next we add row 7 of matrix A to row 1 of matrix A and finally delete row 7 from this matrix. Since A is an incidence matrix any values greater than 1 are adjusted to 1. We then again postmultiply A by its transpose, compute the resulting affinity matrix C and choose a maximal non-diagonal element. This process continues until the matrix A is reduced to only one row. In our small example, we get the integration sequence documented in Fig. 2. The algorithm presented is very easy to implement. Fig. 3 shows the user interface that has been developed for this purpose. We finally note again that the algorithm is not deterministic. Depending on the choice of the maximum (if the maximum is not unique), we may get different possibilities for the order of integration. We do not think, however, that this is a drawback of our method. The intention is to influence the order of integration such that schemata with a high affinity are merged at an earlier stage while others are not merged at all or only partially. Also note that Fig. 2 suggests checking if total integration is worthwhile. It may be sufficient to leave the left and right subtree isolated.

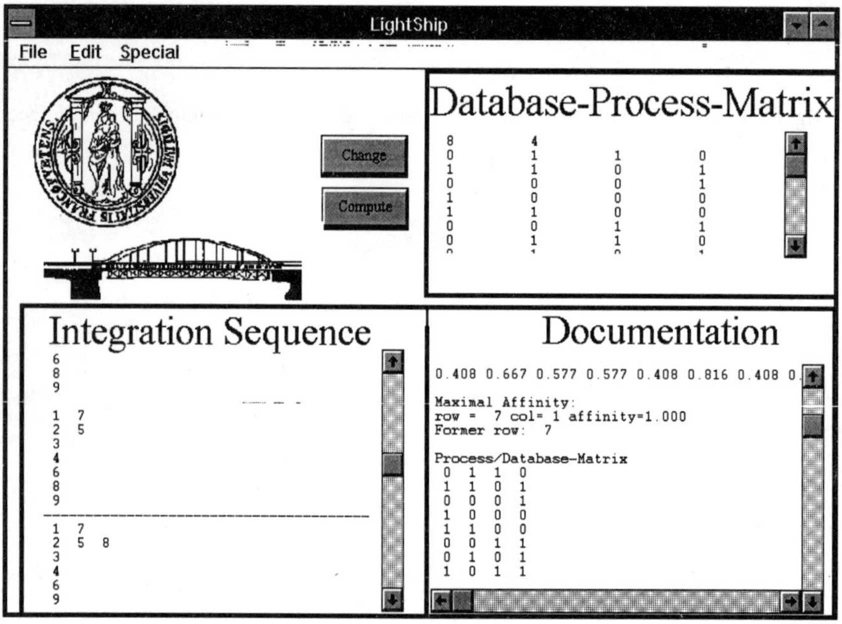

Fig. 3: User Interface

4.2. Extensions

Note that the approach presented here is still rather imprecise since we use only the information that a certain database system includes data that are used by a critical business process. We may expect more detailed results by using incidence matrices on the entity level. Of course, it does not make sense to check for every entity set of a local database schema whether it is used in one of the critical business processes. Otherwise, the problem of homonym and synonym detection, as well as semantic heterogeneity issues have to be addressed before the actual integration phase takes place. Instead, we use the results of our clustering algorithm as presented in section 5. After a couple of clustering steps, only the most important entity sets remain. We then check how these entity sets are related to business processes. The details are as follows.

- The entity sets that remain after terminating the clustering process are attributed to the critical business processes. The result is an entity/process matrix *EP*.
- A database/entity matrix *DE* showing in which database the above-mentioned entity sets are contained is created. Multiplication of *DE* with *EP* yields a new database/process matrix *DP*. The entry *(i,j)* of this matrix is the number of (kernel) entity sets of database *i* that are used in business process *j*.
- We now again postmultiply the matrix *DP* by its transpose and again compute a corresponding affinity matrix (the formula previously introduced is used). Having determined a maximum of the affinity matrix we now reduce the database/entity-matrix *DE*.

We have implemented this approach in a similar way as the basic approach presented earlier. Fig. 4 contains an example for illustrative purposes. The matrices *EP*, *DE*, *DP=DE*EP* and the affinity matrix *C* are shown. Note that in *EP* entity sets are shown in rows, processes in columns while in *DE* entity sets are shown in columns and database systems in rows.

$$EP = \begin{bmatrix} 1&0&1&1&0&0 \\ 0&1&1&0&0&1 \\ 0&1&1&0&0&1 \\ 1&1&0&0&0&0 \\ 1&1&0&0&1&1 \\ 1&0&0&0&1&1 \\ 0&1&0&0&1&1 \\ 0&0&0&1&1&1 \\ 0&0&1&0&1&1 \\ 1&0&1&0&1&0 \end{bmatrix} \quad DE = \begin{bmatrix} 1&0&1&1&0&1&0&1&0&1 \\ 0&1&1&1&0&0&0&1&0&1 \\ 0&0&0&1&0&0&1&0&0&0 \\ 1&0&1&0&1&0&0&0&1&1 \\ 0&0&0&0&1&1&1&1&0&1 \end{bmatrix} \quad DP = \begin{bmatrix} 4&2&3&2&3&3 \\ 2&3&3&1&2&3 \\ 1&2&0&0&1&1 \\ 3&2&4&1&3&3 \\ 3&2&1&1&5&4 \end{bmatrix} \quad C = \begin{bmatrix} 1.00&0.93&0.74&0.97&0.90 \\ 0.93&1.00&0.82&0.96&0.85 \\ 0.74&0.82&1.00&0.71&0.81 \\ 0.97&0.96&0.71&1.00&0.87 \\ 0.90&0.85&0.81&0.87&1.00 \end{bmatrix}$$

Fig. 4: Computational Steps for Extended Method - An Example

In Fig. 4 we would integrate the schemata 1 and 4 at the beginning. We may also use this method to determine whether partial integration is more appropriate. If the affinity of two databases is small, this means that those databases have only a small number of (kernel) entity sets in common that are needed by critical business processes.

We would expect this extension to yield more accurate results. Empirical tests conducted so far did not justify this assumption. The results basically were of the same quality as if the basic approach were used. We used an affinity analysis technique for determining the integration sequence for 17 conceptual schemata of a large financial institution in Germany. The method yielded an extremely plausible integration sequence. At the same time it was indicated that 'total integration' would be of no great use. Instead, three clusters of schemata should be formed. We are currently trying to estimate the benefits of the application of our method for this particular case.

5. Complexity Reduction through Schema Clustering

Large schemata are complex and hard to understand. In particular, it seems to be impossible to integrate two complex schemata. This is one of the reasons why we try to simplify existing schemata by means of clustering. Clustering was introduced by *Teorey et al.* as an aid for documentation[53]. We stress the importance of automatic clustering and our approach is different from the method presented by *Teorey et al.*.

In each clustering step, entity sets are absorbed by so called parent entity sets. Finally, only the most important entity sets remain. Thus, the design process is in a certain sense reversed. With regard to schema integration we use clustering to simplify both schemata during the pre-

---

[53] cf. Teorey et al., 1989.

integration phase. Let n_1 and n_2 be the number of clustering steps performed for schema 1 and schema 2, respectively. We start by resolving conflicts and then merge the two schemata on the particular clustering level (n_1,n_2). Finally, we reverse the last clustering step for both schemata and then try to refine the integrated schema by integrating the clustered schemata of level n_1-1 and n_2-1, respectively. Note that the overall structure of the integrated schema is already defined. Hence, the integration step is some kind of refinement.

We now present only the most important characteristics of our clustering algorithm[54]. We first introduce a partial ordering on the set of cardinality constraints given by $C = \{(0{:}1), (1{:}1), (0{:}n), (1{:}n)\}$. This partial ordering is defined as follows:

$$(1{:}1) \succ (0{:}1) \succ (0{:}n);\quad (1{:}1) \succ (1{:}n) \succ (0{:}n);\ (0{:}1) \succ (1{:}n).$$

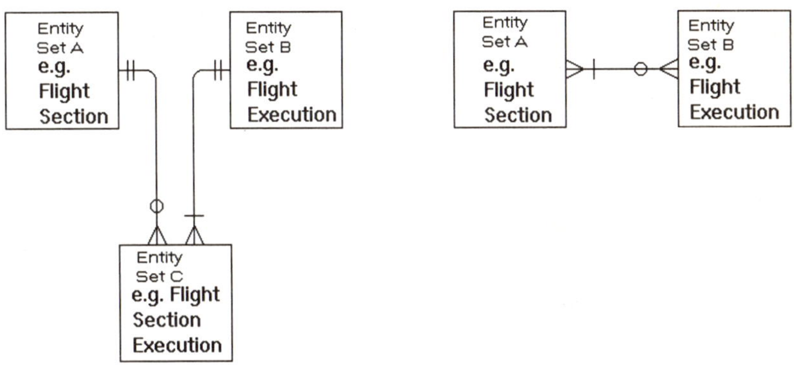

Fig. 5: Clustering Step

We assume that many-to-many relationship sets, as well as relationship sets of degree greater than two have been resolved by introducing associative entity sets. We also assume that bijective one-to-one relationship sets between two entity sets (cardinality (1:1) on both sides) have been resolved by merging the two entity sets. Finally, relationship sets of cardinality (0:1) on both sides are not clustered at all or are resolved by merging the two entity sets. Our tool automatically enforces these restrictions and allows the choice between different options if applicable. Refer to Fig. 5. The entity sets used in the example correspond to Table 2. Entity sets *A* and *B* are called parents of entity set *C*. Thus, due to the dominance of cardinality constraints defined by our partial ordering ($(1{:}1) \succ (0{:}n)$ and $(1{:}1) \succ (1{:}n)$), entity set *C* is then absorbed by its parent entity sets and becomes an entity-valued attribute of them. This induces a relationship set between entity sets *A* and *B*. We call this a complex relationship set. The cardi-

[54] refer to Rauh, Stickel, 1992 for further details.

nalities of the complex relationship set follow from Table 1. Entity set A (as well as B) is called an existential parent since C depends existentially on A (as well as on B).

X/Y	(0:1)	(1:1)	(0:n)	(1:n)
(0:1)	(0:1)	(0:1)	(0:n)	(0:n)
(1:1)	(0:1)	(1:1)	(0:n)	(1:n)
(0:n)	(0:n)	(0:n)	(0:n)	(0:n)
(1:n)	(0:n)	(1:n)	(0:n)	(1:n)

Table 1: Cardinality Transformation

No information concerning instances of entity sets and their relationships should be lost. For that purpose, cardinality transformations have been introduced in Table 1. Also, the following rules that handle clustering if more than two existential or non-existential parents are present need to be observed for that reason. We include those rules for the sake of completeness.

- Suppose that E is to be absorbed and that more than one existential parent exists. Then, complex relationship sets have to be established in such a way that all absorbing existential parents are connected. This means that there has to be a path from an arbitrary absorbing entity set to another one, but no cycles are allowed.

- Suppose that E has at least one existential parent, say P, and that E is to be absorbed by E' where E' is not an existential parent of E. Then, E' has to be connected with P (or with any other existential parent). Again we have non-determinism if more than one existential parent exists. The same applies if a complex relationship between E and an entity set E'' exists.

- Suppose that E has no existential parent. Then, all entity sets absorbing E have to be connected with each other. The same applies again if a complex relationship between E and an entity set E'' exists.

- If E is engaged in a recursive relationship set, recursive relationship sets for the absorbing parents of E need to be generated.

We now present an example and show how our tool clusters schemata. The entity sets and relationship sets with their cardinalities are given in Table 2. The example refers to an airport information system that models flights (scheduled and executed), as well as staffing of employees and airplanes.

The cardinalities given in Table 2 need to be interpreted as the following example suggests. An instance of entity set 'Airplane' is used in 0 or many (cardinality (0:*n*)) flight section executions. A particular instance of the entity set 'Flight Section Execution' requires exactly one airplane. Fig. 6 shows an ER-diagram of the example.

Entity-Sets			
Ground Staff	Employee	Airport	Section
Flight Section	Flight	Flight Execution	Flight Section Execution
Member Action	Crew Member	Rating	Airplane Type
Airplane			

Relationship Sets			
Ground Staff	Airport	0:n	1:1
Airport	Section	1:1	0:n
Section	Flight Section	1:1	0:n
Flight Section	Flight	0:n	1:1
Flight Section Execution	Flight Section	0:n	1:1
Flight Section Execution	Flight Execution	1:n	1:1
Flight Section Execution	Member Action	1:1	0:n
Member Action	Crew Member	0:n	1:1
Crew Member	Rating	1:1	0:n
Crew Member	Employee	0:1	1:1
Employee	Ground Staff	1:1	0:1
Rating	Airplane Type	0:n	1:1
Airplane Type	Airplane	1:1	0:n
Flight Section Execution	Airplane	0:n	0:1

Table 2: Entity and Relationship Sets - An Example

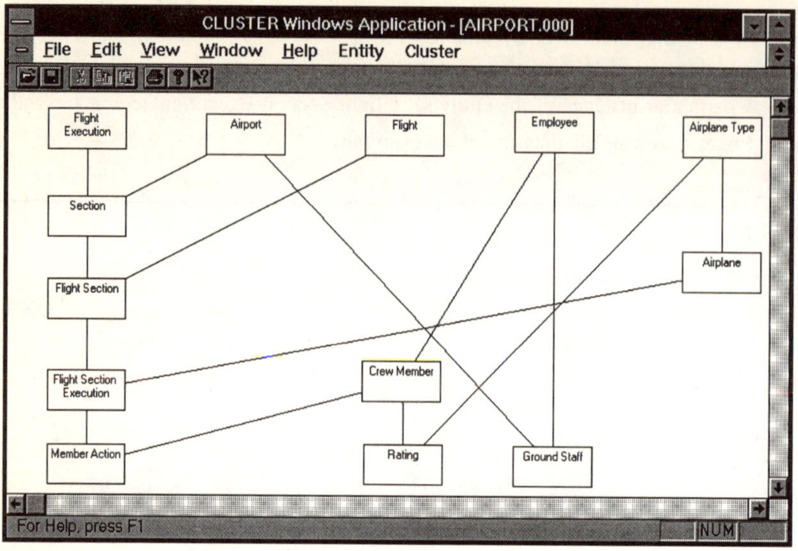

Fig. 6: Clustering - Before First Clustering Step

The presented example shows that clustered schemata get simpler after a few steps (see Fig. 7). Also note that after a total of four clustering steps only the most important entity sets (Employee, Airport, Airplane Type, Flight, Flight Execution) remain.

We may use these kernel entity sets for the algorithm presented in section 4.2. We would then get a database/process-matrix consisting of kernel entity sets and critical business processes. Our clustering tool documents all clustering steps in a data dictionary. Various reports and clustering options (e.g. restricting the partial ordering such that only existential relationship sets are clustered, manual clustering) are available. The clustering algorithm is not deterministic (there is a choice in the clustering steps if more than two existential or non-existential parents exist). Therefore, we have defined the notion of equivalent clustered schema. It is possible to characterize equivalent schemata up to a certain degree and hence to switch from one to another[55].

[55] a detailed description of the implementation may be found in Ortmann et al., 1994.

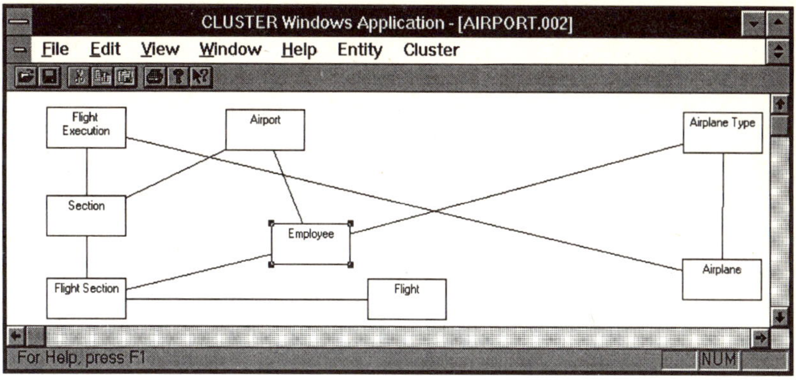

Fig. 7: Clustering - After Second Clustering Step

6. Conclusion

We have presented arguments that schema integration is - at least partially - necessary in today's business environment, although this is questioned in the literature especially for highly decentralized (heterogeneous) organizational units. One reason is agency costs. Based on the argument that data integration is necessary to some degree, we have presented a method to determine the order in which database schemata should be merged and the degree of their integration (totally or only partially). This method links data structures to critical business processes and thus considers actual business needs as a prerequisite for schema and/or database integration.

During the pre-integration phase, we use a clustering step to simplify existing database schemata. This reduces the complexity of view integration. Clustering is done automatically and the information from later clustering steps may be used to determine the order and degree of integration on the level of entity sets. Clustered schemata are merged after conflicts have been resolved. We use well-known classical methods for this task whenever possible. In some sort of 'forward-engineering' step the effect of clustering is reversed. This allows the incremental clustering of two schemata by subsequently adding more detail to the integrated schema. Various difficulties with respect to the use of this clustering method have been pointed out (e.g. non-determinism of the algorithm) and possible solutions have been presented. The development of our tool that is supposed to automate the integration process as far as possible is still continuing.

Acknowledgement

The authors wish to thank Mrs. Edna Bloxham for checking English style and grammar.

References

Alchian, A. A.; Demsetz, H.: Production, Information Costs and Economic Organization. American Economic Review Vol. 62, 5, Dec. 1972, pp. 777-795.

Batini, C.; Lenzerini, M.; Navathe, S. B.: A Comparative Analysis of Methodologies for Database Schema Integration. ACM Computing Surveys, Vol. 18, 4, 1986, pp. 323-364.

Benbasat, I.; Nault, B.: An Evaluation of Empirical Research in Managerial Support Systems. Decision Support Systems Vol. 6, 2, July 1990, pp. 439-449.

Chen, P.: The Entity-Relationship Model - Toward a Unified View of Data. TODS Vol. 1, 1, March 1976, pp. 9-36.

Cohen, D.; Larson, G.; Berke, L.: Role of Interoperability in Business Application Development. Proc. of the 1993 ACM SIGMOD International Conference on Management of Data. SIGMOD Record Vol. 22, 2, June 1993, pp. 487-490.

Coulson, C. J.: People Just Aren't Using Data Dictionaries. Computerworld, August 16, 1982, pp. 15-22.

Elmasri, R.; Navathe, S.: Fundamentals of Database Systems. 2nd Ed., Redwood City, CA (1994).

Galbraith, J.: Designing Complex Organizations. Reading, MA. (1973).

Goodhue, D. L.; Kirsch, L. J.; Quillard, J. A.; Wybo, M. D.: Strategic Data Planning: Lessons From the Field. MIS Quaterly Vol. 16, 1, March 1992a, pp. 11-34.

Goodhue, D. L.; Wybo, M. D.; Kirsch, L. J.: The Impact of Data Integration on the Costs and Benefits of Information Systems. MIS Quaterly Vol. 16, 3, September 1992b, pp. 293-311.

Gurbaxani, V.; Whang, S.: The Impact of Information Systems on Organizations and Markets. Communications of the ACM Vol. 34, 1, Jan. 1991, pp. 59-73.

Huber, G.: A Theory of the Effects of Advanced Information Technology on Organizational Design, Intelligence, and Decision Making. Academy of Management Review Vol. 15, 1, 1990, pp. 47-71.

Johannesson, P.: Using Conceptual Graph Theory to Support Schema Integration. In: Elmasri, R., Kouramajian, V. (Eds.): Proc. of the 12th Interantional Conference on the Entity-Relationship Approach, Dallas, TX. 1993, pp. 277-288.

King, J. L.: Centralized versus Decentralized Computing: Organizational Considerations and Management Options. ACM Computing Surveys Vol. 15, 4, Dec. 1983, pp. 319-349.

Kühlmann, K.; Stickel, E.: Datenmodellierung als strategisches Instrument für Anbieter von Versicherungen und ergänzenden Finanzdienstleistungen; Zeitschrift für Versicherungswesen, 24, 1990, pp. 618-620.

Lederer, A. L.; Sethi, V.: Critical Dimensions of Strategic Information Systems Planning. Decision Sciences Vol. 22, 1, Winter 1991, pp. 104-119.

Lim, E. P.; Prabhakar, S.: Entity Identification in Database Integration. In: Proc. 9th Conference on Data Engineering, Vienna 1993, pp. 294-301.

Martin, J.: Information Engineering. Book I: Introduction. Englewood Cliffs, NJ. (1989).

Martin, J.: Information Engineering. Book II: Planning and Analysis. Englewood Cliffs, NJ. (1990).

Metais, E.; Meunier, J.-N.; Levreau, G.: Database Schema Design: A Perspective from natural Language Techniques to Validation and View Integration. In: Elmasri, R., Kouramajian, V. (Eds.): Proc. of the 12th Interantional Conference on the Entity-Relationship Approach, Dallas, TX. 1993, pp. 187-198.

O'Brien, J. A.: Management Information Systems: A Managerial End User Perspective. Homewood, Ill. (1990).

Ortmann, A.; Ortmann, J.; Stickel, E.: Implementierung von ETC. Fakultät für Wirtschaftswissenschaften der Europa-Universität Frankfurt (Oder), Arbeitsbericht 6, 1994.

Özsu, M. T.; Valduriez, P.: Principles of Distributed Database Systems. Englewood Cliffs, NJ (1991)

Rauh, O.; Stickel, E.: Entity Tree Clustering - A Method for Simplifying ER-Designs. In: Pernul, G., Tjoa, A. M. (Eds): Entity-Relationship Approach - ER '92. Proc. 11th International Conference on the Entity Relationship Approach, Karlsruhe 1992, LNCS 645, pp. 62-78, Berlin (1992).

Rauh, O., Stickel, E.: Searching for Compositions in ER Schemata. In: Elmasri, R., Kouramajian, V. (Eds.): Proceedings of the 12th International Conference on the Entity-Relationship Approach, Arlington, TX 1993, pp. 75-86.

Ross, S.: The Economic Theory of Agency: The Principal's Problem. American Economic Review Vol. 63, 2, May 1973, pp. 134-139.

Seitz, J.; Stickel, E.: Data Structures for Product Design in Financial Institutions. In: SWIFT (Eds.): Proceedings of the BANKAI Workshop on Intelligent Information Access; Brüssel 1991, pp. 47-59, Amsterdam (1992).

Sharda, R.; Barr, S. H.; McDonnell, J. C.: Decision Support Systems Effectiveness. A Review and Empirical Test. Management Science Vol. 43, 2, February 1988, pp. 139-159.

Sheth, A.; Larson, J.: Federated Database Systems for Managing Distributed, Heterogeneous, and Autonomous Databases. ACM Computing Surveys Vol. 22, 3, Sept. 1990, pp. 183-236.

Sheth, A.: Semantic Issues in Multidatabase Systems. SIGMOD Record, Dec. 1991, pp. 5-9.

Sprague, R. H.; McNurlin, B.: Information Systems Management in Practice. Third Edition. Englewood Cliffs, NJ. (1993).

Stickel, E.: Information und Risiko. Fakultät für Wirtschaftswissenschaften der Europa-Universität Frankfurt (Oder), Arbeitsbericht 5, 1994.

Teorey, T. J.; Wei, G.; Bolton, D. L.; Koenig, J. A.: ER Model Clustering as an Aid for User Communication in Database Design and Documentation. Communications of the ACM Vol. 38, 8, 1989 pp. 975-987.

Todd, P.; Benbasat, I.: The Use of Information in Decision Making: An Experimental Investigation of the Impact of Computer Based Decision Aids. MIS Quaterly Vol. 16, 1, March 1992, pp. 11-34.

Tushman, M.; Nadler, D.: Information Processing as an Integrating Concept in Organizational Design. Academy of Management Review Vol. 3, 3, July 1978, pp. 613-624.

Solving Decision Problems by Distributed Decomposition and Delegation
---
Foundations of a Theory and its Application within a Normative Group Decision Support System Framework

Oliver Wendt, Peter Rittgen, Wolfgang Koenig

Abstract

This paper is based on the paradigm that the solution of a yet unstructured decision problem with discrete action alternatives requires planning of the problem solution process (the invention of a new solution) prior to the execution of this plan. First, we concentrate on the design of a distributed planning process using several agents (first phase of a decision process). Following a "modeling cost approach", the foundations of a general theory of problem decomposition and delegation of sub-problems will be developed.

Based on this description of the decompositions and delegations using the domain independent and extendible language ANDORI, we derive rules to identify the particular region of a decomposition tree promising the best compromise between modeling cost and solution quality. That means that we provide means to select the optimal node to be decomposed next. Furthermore, models of task distribution to agents are evaluated. Finally, we describe a preliminary prototype of a group decision support system based on this theory as well as the organizational environment necessary for its application.

1. Introduction

Imagine being the manager of a project that aims to *reorganize and optimize the distribution logistics* of your company. Your project team consists of several members, each member being an expert on a different domain. Imagine furthermore, your team members would be geographically dispersed. We assume that the team members are linked by phone, fax, or electronic mail. Moreover, all team members use a tool like Lotus Notes to structure and access their documents. Still, you and your team members require the use of a *normative group decision support system* that

- ❒ provides imperatives on how to logically structure the decision problem and the solution process, and

- provides optimization tools.

As we are talking about so-called *unstructured decision problems*, we cannot set up an imperative to optimize the decision object (e.g. "You have to buy this particular part of the logistics services from an outside vendor!"). We do not even know which way of partitioning the problem is most suitable. Instead, we can only try to *optimize the planning and decision process within a group of collaborators* (which then, when being executed, may lead to optimal solutions of the decision problem).

We set up on the paradigm that the solution of an unstructured decision problem is created by *repeatedly decomposing the original decision problem and its components* into less complex / unstructured components until we reach a sub-problem which in fact is structured (i.e. there is an imperative available on how to solve this particular sub-problem). So, integrating the solutions bottom up along the decomposition graph yields the solution of the originally unstructured problem.

However, the decomposition structure of an unstructured problem is not trivial. We introduce the so-called ANDORI language which enables users to describe *both AND and OR decomposition of an original problem as well as the description of so-called information edges* between ANDed components of an original problem (e.g. precedence structures, see chapter 2).

The process of structuring and solving unstructured decision problems occurs facing a *trade-off* between

- trying to find an optimal solution for the decision problem (in our case for example reducing the logistics costs by buying appropriate services from outside vendors), and

- trying to minimize the search costs to obtain this solution (in our case for example hiring a consultant to buy special expertise in logistics).

In particular, modeling all possible decompositions of a problem seems to be far too expensive. Instead, we need a technique that enables us to selectively build up a problem decomposition graph, top down, directed towards an optimal decomposition path. Thus, we develop a so-called modeling cost theory (chapter 3) that integrates both the benefits of a particular problem decomposition on the level of the decision object and the modeling costs that are necessary to realize this solution. Using particular *estimators for both classes of costs*, our normative group decision support system identifies the node in the decomposition graph which has to be expanded next (see chapter 4).

Moreover, this decomposition graph also acts as a basis to *optimize the delegation of the decomposition of sub-problems*. There are two contrary approaches to coordinate delegates during the distributed process of decomposition: Either there is no coordination (i.e. all possible nodes for further decomposition are modeled in parallel, without for example learning particular structures of the global problem or its solution from other decomposers). Or we perform a centralized coordination (causing high communication costs and requiring a large central throughput). By evaluating the trade-off between the expected number of nodes to be expanded in the course of problem decomposition (in fact the modeling costs of all of these nodes) an the coordination costs, we may determine an optimal distribution degree of the problem decomposition (see chapter 5).

All these tasks of structuring yet unstructured decision problems belong to phase 1 of the decision process which terminates when a decomposition graph representing a valid solution to the problem is found. In phase 2 the normative group decision support system supports the integration of the sub-solutions from the different collaborators and, in case of conflicts, suggests a revision of the original problem decomposition. After completion, in phase 3 the normative group decision support system controls the distributed execution of the decentralized problem solution process. However, in this present article we concentrate only on phase 1 of the decision process, the distributed decomposition and delegation and its support by a normative group decision support system which is called "Distributed Reasoning Support System (DRSS)".

Syntax and semantics of ANDORI graphs

We further specify our logistics case: Due to the fact that you (the project manager) received several offers of third-party forwarders that sound reasonable to you, you consider your logistics problem being a MAKE-OR-BUY problem (refer to fig. 1).

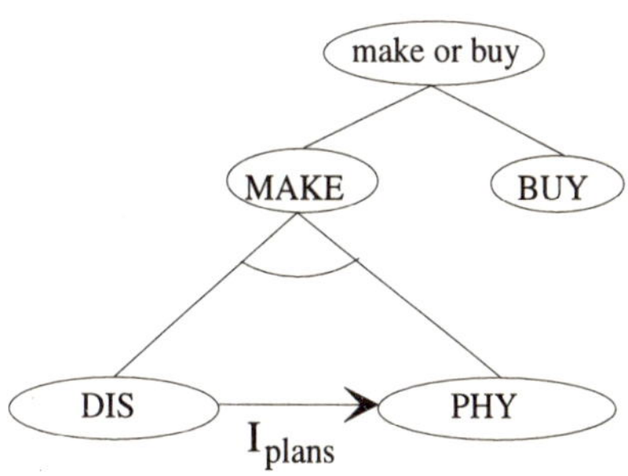

Figure 1: Simple ANDORI graph

You could either go on providing the distribution logistics all by yourself or buy a packaged service from one of those external forwarders[56].

The relation between the MAKE-OR-BUY problem and its two sub-problems is called an OR relation, due to the fact that the alternatives are mutually exclusive, which means that you will never implement both of the two partial plans, MAKE and BUY, to the real world, although you have to solve both of the two planning problems in order to find out which alternative is the one with the lowest cost.

In case you decided to reason about the MAKE alternative first, you may want to think of distribution logistics as some sort of compound of *physical logistics* activities, in the sense of driving from customer A to customer B or loading the cargo into a truck, and *dispositive logistics,* which consist of planning the allocation of a given set of cargo to the available trucks and planning the routing for each of them. The relation between the MAKE problem and its two sub-problems is quite different to the one discussed on top level: It is not enough to just implement the solution of either one of the two sub-problems, you rather have to solve them both in order to find an appropriate plan for the MAKE problem. For this reason, the relation is called an AND relation and is denoted by an arc connecting the two vertical edges.

The sub-problems of an AND decomposition may have functional dependencies denoted by information edges. Figure 1 shows a *precedence relation* between two nodes: in order to execute the physical logistics, the dispositve logistics department has to provide the plans for routing your trucks[57]. The plan itself is passed from the DIS node to the PHY node (I_{plan}). Other types of functional dependencies are discussed in Wendt and Rittgen (1993). So, the domain independent problem statement language ANDORI extends the well-known AND/OR graphs[58] by the so-called information edges (I edges), hence its name.

Due to time restrictions or a lack of competence you decide to consult (internal or external) experts and delegate the partial tasks to them. The three partial tasks are:

DIS: Find the best organization for planning our distribution logistics; evaluate the cost of implementing this organization and using it for the next five years.

PHY: Find the best organization for physically distributing goods to our customers, evaluate the cost of implementing this organization and using it for the next five years.

---

[56] This is a simplification, since it might be possible to find "mixtures" of making some services and buying the others.

[57] It has to be noted here that the information edge I states a precedence relation constraining the execution of the partial plans and not the planning process itself. Planning may still be performed in parallel, although when designing the organization of the physical logistics we have to design a "business process" which is capable to execute any possible plan which might be provided by the DIS process in the excecution phase.

[58] Cf. Pearl (1984).

BUY: Find the best external forwarder by evaluating the quality and cost of their service for the next five years.

None of these problems is trivial in the sense that a solution might be given without further investigations. Unfortunately, the cost of further investigations into the BUY branch of the search tree will be sunk when it finally turns out that the MAKE branch leads to a superior solution (and vice versa). To constrain the search and modeling cost, we need an estimation telling us which parts of the global decomposition graph lead to an optimal solution and which cost this modeling brings about. This means identifying the correct sub-graph in the decomposition hierarchy which rewards modeling (refer to chapter 4.5).

Formally, an ANDORI graph is a tuple (V, E_A, E_O, E_I, I, F) consisting of a set of vertices V, also called nodes, a set of AND edges E_A, a set of OR edges E_O, a set of information flow edges E_I, a set of information flows I associated with the corresponding edges in E_I, and a set of goal functions F associated with each vertex. The tuple elements are defined as follows:

V: is a set of vertices (or nodes) representing problems (or solutions in case that all sub-problems have been solved).

2^V: is the set of all sub-sets of V (collections of problems).

$E_A \subset V \times 2^V$: is a set of AND edges, the first element of each pair being the parent vertex (super-problem), and the second being a set of child vertices (sub-problems).

$E_O \subset V \times 2^V$: is a set of OR edges with tuple elements as in E_A.

$E_I \subset V \times V$: is a set of directed I edges (information edges); the first element of each pair is the source vertex, the second one the destination of the information flow.

$I = \{I_i | i \in E_I\}$: is a set of information flows (one for each I edge).

$I_i \in \{(d,b) | d \subset D, b{:}d \rightarrow \{true, false\}\}$:

The first element of the pair is a set of variables (data flow), the second is a boolean function on this set (control flow).

D: is the set of all variables (data).

$F = \{f_i | i \in V\}$: is a goal function f_i (for each vertex i) which has to be minimized[59].

Restrictions:

$\forall(p,C) \in E_A \cup E_O : p \notin C \wedge |C| \geq 2$: No parent is its own child, and at least two children are required (no renaming).

$\forall(s,d) \in E_I : \exists(p,C) \in E_A : \{s,d\} \subseteq C$: Information can only flow between the ANDed children of a node[60].

$\forall(p,C) \in E_A \cup E_O : f_p = \Theta(\{f_c | c \in C\})$: aggregation of goal functions along the hierarchy[61]

For the example of figure 1 we have:

$$V = \{make\_or\_buy, MAKE, BUY, DIS, PHY\}$$

$$E_A = \{(MAKE, \{DIS, PHY\})\}, \quad E_O = \{(make\_or\_buy, \{make, buy\})\}$$

$$E_I = \{(DIS, PHY)\}, \quad I = \{I_{(DIS,PHY)}\}, \quad I_{(DIS,PHY)} = I_{plans}$$

$$F = \{f_{make\_or\_buy}, f_{MAKE}, f_{BUY}, f_{DIS}, f_{PHY}\}$$

$$f_{make\_or\_buy} = \min(f_{MAKE}, f_{BUY}), \qquad f_{MAKE} = f_{DIS} + f_{PHY}$$

Semantically, the ANDORI framework adopts the state space view of problems and problem solving, i.e. a problem P may be defined by a tuple (X, S_0, H, f, O) consisting of the set of all states X (the state space), a set of initial states S_0, a set of hard constraints H, a goal function f defined on all states complying with all hard constraints in H and a set of operators O transforming states (going from one state to another). Imagine the *state space* $X = X_1 \times X_2 \times \ldots \times X_n$ to be the set of all possible combinations of action variables $X_1 .. X_n$ the decision maker can control[62]. Initially the "world" is in a state $x \in X$. You may change this state x into a state x' by applying an operator $o: X \to X$ to the initial state. By applying a se-

---

[59] We do not have to consider maximization problems explicitly, since maximization of a term f can be accomplished by minimizing -f.

[60] Since OR nodes represent a choice between mutually exclusive alternatives, information cannot flow between them.

[61] This restriction forces the goal function fp of the parent node p to be expressed by some arbitrary function Θ on the goal functions of its children. It ensures that the decomposition of a parent node is complete in the sense that the quality of the solution of p does not depend on anything else but the solution of its sub-problems.

[62] In this paper we assume certainty about the environmental variables, i.e. we do not cope with uncertainty here, which would change the focus from "minimizing the cost f of the solution" to "minimizing the expected cost".

quence of operators $o \in O$ to the state x and its transformations you try to reach some optimal goal state x^*, the solution of your problem P.

What are the properties of this goal state x^*? First of all, it must not violate any hard constraint $h_i \in H$. Each of these hard constraints can be represented by a boolean function $h: X \to \{true, false\}$. Let us define the *solution space* $S \subseteq X$ to be the subset of all states in X, which do not violate *any* of the hard constraints, i.e. $S = \{x \in X | h_1(x), \cdots, h_k(x)\}$. Our final goal is to find an $x^* \in S$ for which the value of our goal (cost) function $f: S \to \text{Real}$ is minimized.

We introduce a set S_0 of initial states here (instead of just one initial state) to enable the description and solution of a *problem class*. The sequence of operators that solves the instance of the problem class associated with a specific initial state $x \in S_0$ is a function of that state x. For example, our planning task PHY in the make-or-buy example is of this type, since we do not know the plans delivered by DIS in advance. Therefore, the solution to PHY is a "program" capable to process all possible results of DIS correctly.

In the light of these definitions, the *semantics of an OR decomposition* can be outlined as follows: The total solution space S for the given problem P is partitioned into p sets of alternatives that can be explored separately[63]. The solution to P is the one alternative with the minimal cost f. The following restrictions have to hold:

$S = S_1 \cup S_2 \cup \cdots \cup S_p$: The total solution space S of the parent node is covered by its children.

$x_S^* = x_{S_i}^* : f_S(x_{S_i}^*) = \min\left(f_{S_1}(x_{S_1}^*), \cdots, f_{S_p}(x_{S_p}^*)\right)$: The best alternative x_S^* of the parent problem is identical to the best solution $x_{S_i}^*$ over all subspaces S_i.

Regarding the *semantics of an AND decomposition*, we define the following: The action variables $X_1, X_2, \cdots, X_n$ are partitioned into q different groups in such a way that the following equations should[64] hold true:

$S = S_1 \times S_2 \times \cdots \times S_q$: All variables are accounted for exactly once.

---

[63] Note that in the case of unstructured problems (like our make-or-buy example) we do not know the solution space S in advance, i.e. we cannot enumerate the nodes of our search tree. Nevertheless, we are able to partition this unknown set S into smaller subsets S_1 and S_2, namely the set of all MAKE alternatives and the set of all BUY alternatives.

[64] In many cases it may be advantageous to violate those constraints in order to derive partial models that are easier to solve. This is "paid for" by higher costs for integrating the partial solutions.

$f_S\left(\left(x^*_{S_1}, x^*_{S_2}, \cdots, x^*_{S_q}\right)\right) = \min\left(\left\{f_S(x) \middle| x \in S\right\}\right)$: The combination of the partial maxima is also a global maximum for the parent problem.

The principal advantage of ANDORI graphs over AND/OR graphs is that the I edges enable the modeling of *information flow* between nodes, thus explicating the functional dependencies between partial sub-problems and their respective solutions. These dependencies are hidden in pure AND/OR graphs, and can therefore not be dealt with. Different types of dependencies exist:

Temporal precedence: Task A has to be performed before task B (see figure 1).

Conditional sequence: The execution of task B depends on the result of task A.

Conditional loop: A sequence of tasks is iterated depending on a loop condition.

Based on interpreting the information edge as the joint data and control flow we have developed an algorithm[65] for detecting *latent parallelism*, which is described in Wendt and Rittgen (1993). This algorithm supports the decision maker(s) when deciding which parts of the ANDORI graph may be delegated to independent problem solvers and where such a distributed problem solving leads to high coordination costs when integrating the (potentially incompatible) results.

We have now completed the description of the ANDORI language itself. The following chapter addresses the search for an optimal solution in ANDORI graphs.

2. Modeling cost theory as a guide to optimal search in problem decomposition hierarchies

Consider again the MAKE branch of our logistics problem. Different domains of the economic sciences have developed different methods of determining an optimal organization, for example Cost Accounting or Operations Research. You may either set up complex combinatorial optimization models for tour planning and simulate their results in order to get a cost figure or you may apply simple heuristic methods (for example take last years cost of your logis-

[65] This algorithm is based on a data flow analysis as used in compiler theory. Cf. Aho, Sethi, Ullman (1984).

tics department as a budget for this year's activities). Both methods solve the given task but differ in the solution process as well as in the solution quality.

The simple heuristic only requires modeling a small part of the global problem and aiming for an "acceptable" solution, which can be handled much easier. But the heuristic cannot guarantee that the optimal solution of the global problem is reached. On the contrary, optimization methods lead to the optimum, but usually require a higher amount of modeling and computation time. Generally speaking, the more you spend on modeling, the higher the quality of the solution and the lower the cost of the execution.

Between these two poles, various methods are known which provide a specific mixture of modeling simplicity, solution speed, quality of the solution and distance of the modeled problem to the original problem. The theory of complexity[66] may be used to compare the computational resources needed for two algorithms A and B, solving the same problem to optimality. But it does not help us in the case of an unstructured problem, where we try to achieve the "best compromise" between the quality of the solution (in our case e.g. the number of miles of a round-trip) and the cost invested for obtaining this solution. Using a modeling cost theoretic approach[67] we get:

Minimize: $C = C_f + C_m$,

C_f being the cost of executing the solution found in the decision process

C_m being the cost of modeling and solving the problem.

The cost of modeling includes for example:

- the cost of learning a domain terminology of a solution method,
- the cost of learning and applying this method,
- the associated hardware and software cost,
- the cost of convincing the members of the project team of the quality of this method, and,
- the cost of assuring the quality of the correct application of the method.

---

[66] Cf. Garey, Johnson (1979)

[67] Cf. Koenig, Wendt (1994).

While for example the cost of learning a new method is usually paid only once, the cost of applying this method to a problem as well as the opportunity cost incurred by applying a suboptimal method have to be viewed as a sum of discounted cash flows occurring over a long period of time.

How can we apply these criteria in order to develop guidelines for distributed problem solving in the ANDORI framework? To answer this question, let us focus on a search in *pure OR-trees* from now on[68].

3. Economic search: Optimally trading off solution quality and planning cost

When we constructed our ANDORI tree for the logistics example (Fig. 1), it was clear that the bottom nodes of this tree are not leaf nodes in the sense that they represent "trivial problems". Therefore, in order to solve our global problem, planning has to proceed by "expanding" one of the bottom nodes, i.e. transforming it into simpler sub-problems.

But, which of the nodes should we expand first? We are looking for a function $f(i \in V)$, telling us the cost of the optimal leaf node, that an expansion of node i will eventually reveal. Unfortunately, we may only *estimate* the true cost value $f(i \in V)$ by an estimator $f'(i \in V)$.

It can be shown[69] that performing a *best-first search* in an OR tree, which means to always expand the node i with the lowest cost estimator $f'(i \in V)$ leads to an optimal solution of the problem *if the estimator is optimistic*, i.e.

$$f'(i) \leq f(i) \quad \forall i \in V .$$

We have to continue our expansion process until the following condition is true: The node i with the lowest cost estimator is a leaf node. For leaf nodes $f'(i) = f(i)$ and due to the optimism of the estimator f' we therefore know that all other branches of our tree could only yield solutions with higher costs than $f(i)$. This in turn guarantees that i is one of the optimal solutions to our problem, i.e. it does not pay to continue the search process.

Unfortunately, the total number of nodes that we will have to expand depends on the quality of our cost estimator f'. If it is too optimistic (just imagine $f'(i) = 0 \quad \forall i \in V$), almost every node of the search tree will have to be expanded in order to guarantee the optimality of a so-

[68] The extension of this search to general AND/OR graphs or ANDORI graphs is much more involved but does not add new insight to the findings presented here. The reader interested in the details of those extensions is referred to Wendt and Rittgen (1993).

[69] Cf. Pearl (1984), p. 75.

lution. In contrast, we reduce the number of nodes to be expanded by minimizing the difference between $f'(i)$ and $f(i)$. On the other hand, when we observe complex decision processes in organizations, we find people rather looking for *realistic* than for *optimistic* cost estimates for a given subset of all possible actions. This phenomenon can easily be explained by the existence of modeling costs: The best-first search described above just focuses on how to obtain an *optimal* solution in a minimal number of search steps. In contrast, when we encounter substantial modeling costs, it may be advantageous to give up the requirement of finding an optimal plan in order to reduce the cost of planning.

Basically, we have to replace our old cost estimator $f'(i)$, which was just representing the estimated cost of executing the best plan obtainable by pursuing alternative i by a new one $f''(i) = f'(i) + m'(i)$ that also accounts for the estimated modeling cost $m'(i)$ that we will have to pay in order to *find* this solution.

A central finding of our modeling cost theory is, that (contrary to the results for $f'(i)$ in the case of no modeling costs) it is *not advisable* to use an *optimistic* estimator $f''(i)$. While in the case of no search cost you could easily "backtrack" to another, more promising branch of the search tree, once your initial cost estimation had turned out to be too optimistic, the exploration of a misleading branch of the search tree will now cause search costs that are sunk. That means that search errors cannot be undone anymore without losing invested modeling and search costs.

Since we cannot use an optimistic estimator alone in the presence of search costs, we assume that it is possible[70] to bind the costs from above, too, i.e. for every node i of our search tree we estimate the plan execution costs to be within the interval $\left[\underline{f}'(i); \overline{f}'(i)\right]$ and the cost of planning to be bound within $\left[\underline{m}'(i); \overline{m}'(i)\right]$. Graphically we may represent this available cost information on each node by a box as in figure 2.

[70] In practice, you will frequently hear people estimating costs to be "within the range of X and Y". We therefore believe this to be a valid assumption.

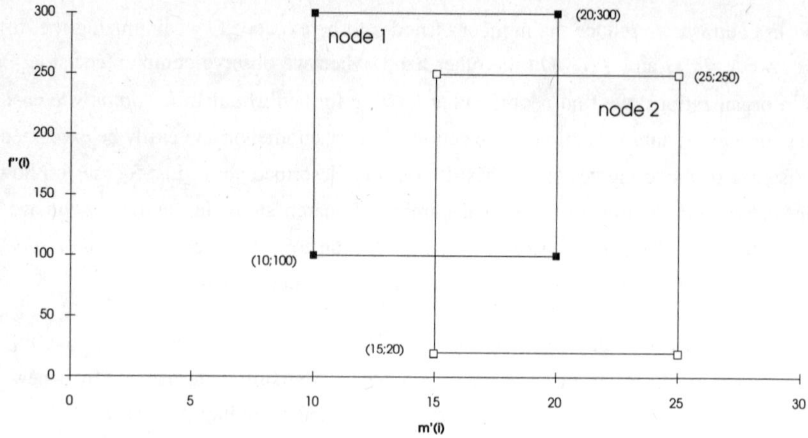

Figure 2: Characterization of two possible branches of the search tree

Which of the two nodes given in fig. 2 should we expand? For every point $(m'(i); f'(i))$ within the box i there is a probability density $p(m'(i); f'(i))$ indicating the chance that the search for a leaf node beneath node i will eventually yield a leaf of cost $f'(i)$ after investing $m'(i)$ for further planning activities. The expected total cost $f''(i)$ for continuing the search with node i may be calculated to be

$$f''(i) = \int_{\underline{m}'(i)}^{\overline{m}'(i)} \int_{\underline{f}'(i)}^{\overline{f}'(i)} p(m; f) \cdot (m + f) \cdot df \cdot dm \qquad \forall i \in V.$$

As long as we do not have any further information on the probability density within the boxes, we will assume a uniform distribution. In this case, we may simply determine the center of gravity for each box and calculate the total cost for this point. With this method we get a total expected cost of 215 for node 1 and a cost of 155 for node 2. We therefore decide to expand node 2. Let us assume that node 2 decomposes into two new nodes, namely node 21 and node 22. One of them (node 21) being a leaf node of cost 170 and the second one having the upper and lower cost bounds illustrated in figure 3. As we see, the expanded node 2 itself disappeared, but the alternative node 1 is still available. The leaf node 21 is just a point (0; 170) on the y-axis, since it provides a plan of sure cost 170 which does not require any further modeling.

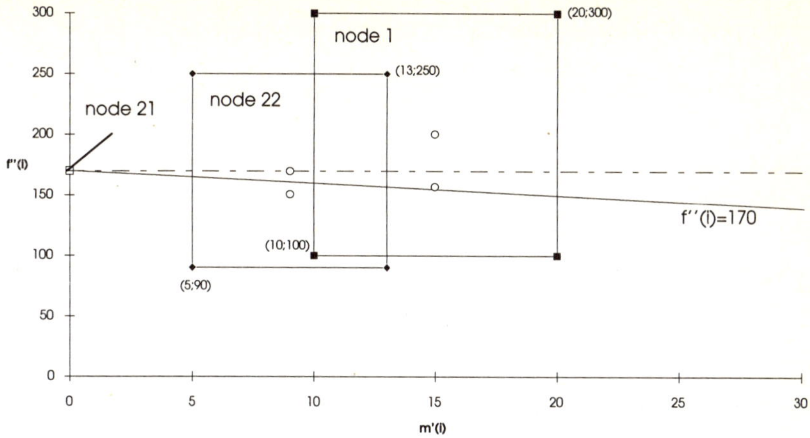

Figure 3: Should there be any further planning activities ?

How to proceed from this situation? Should we stop planning and execute the solution provided by node 21? When we calculate the centers of gravity for the two yet unexpanded nodes we obtain expected costs of 215 for node 1 (as before) and 179 for node 22. We see, that the centers of gravity for both boxes lie above the line through all points of total cost $f''(i)=170$.

Although these results recommend to stop the search, we should not do so. In fact, the old way of calculating the expected cost for the two unexpanded nodes is no longer appropriate as soon as we have an executable plan available! Since we can always use this plan with costs of 170 as a "backup solution" we do not have to fear obtaining a solution worse than 170 by continuing the search. Consider an expansion of node 22: Should we decide to expand this node and after a total investment of 10 units of search cost end up with a plan of execution cost 200, we will of course discard this plan and use plan 21 instead. Graphically this means, that once a solution of cost $\bar{b}$ is obtained, the probability density above the dashed line "shrinks down" onto this line for every unexpanded node. Formally, this means

$$f''(i) = \int_{\underline{m}'(i)}^{\overline{m}'(i)} \int_{\underline{f}'(i)}^{\overline{f}'(i)} p(m;f) \cdot \left(m + \min\left(f;\bar{b}\right)\right) \cdot df \cdot dm \qquad \forall i \in V.$$

Using this rationale to recalculate the expected costs for the two yet unexpanded nodes, we obtain expected total cost of 173 for node 1 and 159 for node 22. Thus it is indeed advisable to expand node 22 although there is a 50% chance of not finding any solution better than 170 by doing so. The expansion should be stopped when all unexpanded nodes yield estimates above the cost bound $\bar{b}$.

4. Distribution of decomposition tasks to cooperating agents

When discussing the motivation for our ANDORI graphs, we assumed that each node of the graph can be assigned to some *actor* who creates a plan to solve this partial problem. Apart from the information edges which indicate dependencies, the actors do not require any coordination before they return their (partial) results to the delegator. As we have seen in the last chapter, this totally parallel processing of the problem decomposition graph would lead to a rather inefficient search when the ANDORI graph contains many OR nodes. We therefore explored different mechanisms for coordinating such a parallel search.

Totally distributed processing with no coordination (NC)

Just imagine that you may dispose of n actors helping you with your task of searching an OR tree for the best solution to a given problem. Once you have expanded the top node of a pure OR tree, you may distribute the work of further exploring the m sub-problems to the n actors. Even if we assume that $m=n$ and every actor receives one "chunk" of the solution space S, it will eventually turn out that n-1 of the n agents did explore the "wrong regions" of the solution space instead of helping the one agent (who got the right region assigned) to explore his region faster.

Centralized coordination (CC)

The other extreme would be to require each of the n agents just to expand the one assigned node and *immediately* return all child nodes to the delegator. After the delegator has collected all child nodes from all agents he sorts them by their cost estimator $f''(i)$ and distributes the n best nodes of the list to the n actors in order to ask them again for just one expansion.

As you may imagine, this model will reduce the total number of node expansions significantly, compared to the NC model. On the other hand, there will be a huge communication load compared to the NC model. Especially, the central coordinator becomes a bottleneck, when the number of available actors increases, thereby restricting the possible speedup[71].

Distributed coordination (DC)

We therefore explored a distributed coordination model. After the initial distribution of $m \geq n$ nodes to the n agents there is no *global* coordination anymore until the point in time when all

71 Cf. Finkel, Manber (1987).

n agents have terminated their search. But in contrast to the NC model, each of the n processors "informs" the other agents of the intermediate results. To do this, we simply introduce a node distribution step after the node expansion step. This means that after all n actors have expanded the best node of their "private" list of yet unexpanded nodes, these lists get resorted by increasing values of the estimator $f''(i)$. Now each actor distributes the best nodes from its list of unexpanded nodes (up to a fraction d of the total number of nodes on this list) to other actors by deleting the nodes from its own list and "mailing" them to a different actor.

The receiving actor for the transferred work could either be chosen randomly among all "co-workers" or by a predefined "distribution topology"[72].

Our empirical tests with the different distribution models yielded the following results[73]:

- Whether parallel search "pays off" strongly depends on the quality of the estimator $f''(i)$. When its quality is poor (i.e. it is too optimistic) and modeling costs are low, many branches of the search tree eventually have to be explored. A lack of coordination does not matter in this case, almost every actor will always expand a so-called efficient node, i.e. a node that would have been expanded by a single actor system, too. In contrast, a very good estimator allows for a "straight forward" expansion from the root node to the optimal leaf node. By adding actors to the "task force" we may only expand inefficient nodes and therefore waste resources.

- For the three parallel models, the total number of node expansions in a DC model is bounded from below by the number of expansions in the CC model and from above by the number of expansions in the NC model.

- Nevertheless, not the CC but the DC model was the right choice in most of our tests: Especially when employing a higher number of actors, the "central agent" of the CC model became a serious bottleneck. Thus, the saved communication and waiting time largely offset the search time spent on the excess nodes for the DC model[74].

- For the DC model, only a relatively small fraction d of nodes[75] needs to be distributed in order to focus all actors on the most promising regions of the search tree.

---

72 This means that each actor may only send work to a specified subset of the total number n of available actors. In the extreme case this may only be one of them, thus defining a ring topology.

73 For a detailed description of the tested problems and the numerical results refer to Wendt and Rittgen (1994).

74 Especially for larger problems, the number of nodes expanded by DC did not even exceed the number expanded by the CC model significantly.

75 In the presence of high communication cost and likewise high central processing cost just the first node should be send to another actor.

- In the DC model, a random topology of the communication network[76] outperformed all fixed topologies[77]. Among the latter, the networks with a small diameter performed best.

5. Application of the ANDORI framework within a Group Decision Support System (GDSS): Requirements and current status

The use of a normative group decision support system based on ANDORI graphs and the decomposition and delegation theory outlined above requires the implementation of a decision-oriented information management. For yet unstructured decision problems, the decision-makers are required to describe their problem decomposition and delegation hierarchy (including the cost estimators described in chapter 4). For a well-structured problem or sub-problem the system should search a library for available solution methods that match the problem's structure and the decision maker should document the method he finally chooses for solving it.

A preliminary prototype of such a systems called DRSS (Distributed Reasoning Support System) is based on the decomposition and delegation theory presented so far and has been implemented on a UNIX network under KEE (Knowledge Engineering Environment). In particular, it allows the graphical specification of decompositions and information edges between the ANDed sub-nodes. The DRSS identifies the node to be decomposed next and exploits possible parallelization of sub-processes according to a data-flow analysis. This node is allocated to an appropriate agent either by the agent of the parent node or by an automatic job-shop scheduling algorithm (especially when the agents are machines). This agent receives the current ANDORI graph of the original problem so he can explore the relevant context of his own partial problem before he will extend the ANDORI graph at the current node. Again, to solve his partial problem, an agent may specify an acceptable solution method for his sub-problem, or he can likewise further decompose it. This method of repeated decomposition terminates, if for the solution of a sub-problem no further decomposition is necessary since the solution is obvious.

Generally, the GDSS allows the distributed administration of plan versions and their comparison. Furthermore it maintains a history of the revised decision structures, which serves as a basis for empirical analysis of the decomposition and delegation work.

Later, in phase two of the decision process, the GDSS shall support the integration of the sub-solutions, or, in the case of conflicts, suggest a revision of the problem decomposition. In phase three, the GDSS shall control the execution of the derived solutions, i.e. the distributed

---

[76] i.e. a random selection of the "receiving" agents in the distribution phase

[77] Actually, the speedup achieved with the DC model did not deviate much from the theoretical upper bounds recently derived by Karp and Zhang (1992).

execution of the decentralized problem solution process which has been planned in phases 1 and 2.

So far, the following important arguments against our approach have been identified:

- Managers are occasionally reluctant to clearly model their decision indicating the parameters mentioned in chapter 4. Especially in larger companies, there is a tendency that managers expect their subordinates to structure the manager's decision problems. Managers do not like to expose their personal models to a decentralized evaluation by subordinate employees, who might reveal inconsistencies.

- The integrated optimization of both, the execution cost and the modeling cost produces a high complexity that may arise in the mental handling of the process and in quantifying the corresponding parameters under the pressure of everyday business.

- A cultural and organizational resistance arises from the fact that in many companies the decisions of the employees and the information inputs necessary for these decisions do not yet play a central role of the information management department. In these cases there is no institution within a company that actually introduces a group decision support system; the departments do not feel responsible for interfaces between the departments.

7. Outlook

The most important work that remains to be done concerns the following topics:

- A support of the re-integration of the sub-processes and their solutions worked out by the different agents (phase 2 of the decision process) needs to be developed. In addition, an adequate classification of partially structured decision problems with the aim to aid the re-use of historical decompositions of decision problems and their components is not yet provided.

- An algorithmic support for allocating tasks to agents (solving an extended job-shop scheduling problem) should be developed and implemented.

- The modeling cost theory outlined in chapter 4 easily extends to AND/OR trees. Adapting it for searching ANDORI graphs still remains an open question.

- Although we empirically validated the superiority of the distributed coordination model, a normative theory which dynamically controls the optimal amount of communication is not yet available.

8. References

Aho, A.; Sethi R.; Ullman J.: Compilers: Principles, Techniques and Tools; Reading (Addison-Wesley) 1984.

Finkel, R.A.; Manber U.: DIB - A distributed implementation of backtracking; ACM Trans. Prog. Lang. Syst. 9 (1987); pp. 235-256.

Garey, M.R.; Johnson, D.S.: Computers and Intractability; San Francisco (Freeman) 1979.

Karp, R.M.; Zhang Y.: Randomized Parallel Algorithms for Backtrack Search and Branch-and-Bound Computation; Journal of the ACM 40 (1993); pp. 765-789.

Koenig, W.; Wendt O.: Optimale DV-Unterstützung der Logistik - dargestellt am Anwendungsbeispiel der Luftfrachtkommissionierung; submitted to WIRTSCHAFTSINFORMATIK.

Pearl, J.: Heuristics: Intelligent search strategies for computer problem solving; Reading (Addison-Wesley) 1984.

Wendt, O.; Rittgen P.: ANDORI Graphs - an Extension of AND/OR Graphs for Distributed Problem Solving and Reasoning; Research Paper (93-09); Institute of Applied Computer Sciences; Frankfurt University 1993.

Wendt, O.; Rittgen P.: Coordination of Distributed Planning and Problem Solving; Research Paper (94-13); Institute of Applied Computer Sciences; Frankfurt University 1994.

Distributed Cooperative Budget-Planning and -Control

Eckart Zwicker, Claus Rottenbacher

Abstract

This presentation summarizes our efforts to implement a budgeting computer system, named INZPLA, that allows managers to realize a cooperative budgeting and control system for decentralized organizations applying network- and database-technology in a distributed environment. The INZPLA system is based upon the theory of ITP. The theory determines INZPLA to be a highly specified application of commonly known technology of equation based systems. It enables a complete decentralized budget planning and control procedure to be performed. Up to now, equation based systems have not been employed for this economic purpose. We have found that the application of an equation based system has significant advantages.

INZPLA is a client server application based on a relational DBMS.

1. Introduction

Everywhere in business the trend towards decentralization of responsibility to managers down the line can be observed due to increasing complexity of markets as well as the internationalization of many companies. Many authors demand the 'entrepreneur within a company' to have autonomous profit responsibility and wide ranging freedom to act. They would like companies to shift towards profit-centre organizations.

Information technology systems must be developed to meet this trend. However, large-scale development of corporate software should be founded upon a thorough economic theory.[78]

In part two the theory of 'incremental target planning and control' (ITP) will be outlined. Part three describes the INZPLA computer system and the hard- and software applied for the development.

---

[78] Scheer (1990), p. 15.

2. Theory of 'incremental target planning and control' (ITP)

2.1. Introduction

ITP ('incremental target planning and control') has been developed by Eckart Zwicker at the Technische Universität Berlin.[79] It is a normative theory for budget planning and control. ITP is based on the leadership style 'Management By Objectives' (MBO). Management By Objectives is a leadership style 'specifying that superiors and those who report to them will jointly establish objectives over a specified time frame, meeting periodically to evaluate their progress in meeting these goals.'[80] However, it is extended and formalized into a consistent and general theory for budget planning and control.

Negotiations between executing and leading departments about the objectives for a planning period are an integral part of the ITP theory. At the outset of negotiations executing and leading departments tend to have different opinions about objectives. The ITP concept provides a special, structured method to define the two negotiation positions and to reach an agreement between the two groups of interest, using a three step planning procedure which will be described in chapter 2.5.

2.2. The ITP model

The ITP theory rests on the incremental target planning model (ITP model). Exhibit 1 shows its basic structure.

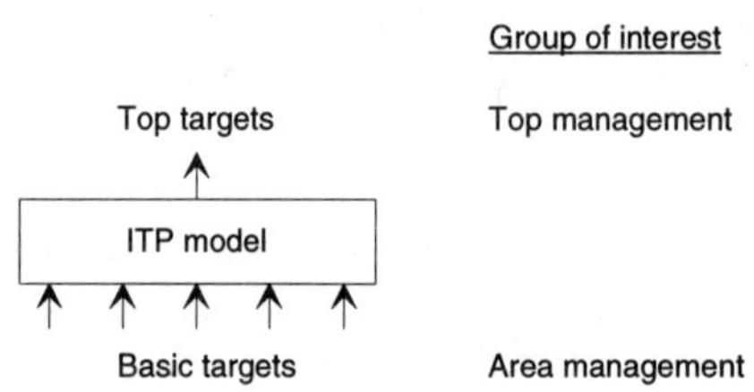

Exhibit 1: Basic structure of an ITP model

The ITP model consists of equations. The equations for an application in a firm must be determined by the user. These equations link the so called *top targets* with the so called *basic*

---

[79] See Zwicker (1988).

[80] Rosenberg (1978), p.281.

investment (ROI) or cash-flow. Basic targets are targets of the executing departments (area of responsibility, AOR) such as sales volume, demand rates (e.g. in tons per hour) or fixed costs. Basic targets are the objectives of the AOR's.

The ITP model is an equation system linking the targets of top management with the targets of executing departments (AOR's). Each AOR is defined as an independent profit-centre. It has its own equations and forms a small self-contained ITP model (AOR model) which is subsequently used for decentralized budgeting.

```
SEGMENT PC_1:
operational_profit_PC1.Y = earnings_PC1.Y - costs_PC1.Y
earnings_PC1.Y = price_PC1.Y * sales_volume_PC1.Y
costs_PC1.Y = variable_costs_PC1.Y + fixed_costs_PC1.Y
ENDSEGMENT

SEGMENT PC_2:
operational_profit_PC2.Y = earnings_PC2.Y - costs_PC2.Y
earnings_PC2.Y = price_PC2.Y * sales_volume_PC2.Y
costs_PC2.Y = variable_costs_PC2.Y + fixed_costs_PC2.Y
ENDSEGMENT
```

Exhibit 2: ITP model for profit-centre budgeting

All equations of one AOR are contained in one segment. The ITP model in exhibit 2 has two segments. Each segment has two basic targets (`sales_volume_PCx.Y`, `fixed_costs_PCx.Y`). In order to reduce the number of objectives that must be negotiated, the results of equations that are influenced by basic targets are recombined into a new equation, resulting in a single new objective, the area target. The area target in exhibit 2 is `operational_profit_PCx.Y`. As a matter of fact the area target of an AOR is always operational profit.

With the area target being the new objective of a profit-centre, there is no further obligation to meet the values of basic targets. Basic target values can now vary and must be adjusted to meet the value of the area target.

Once the area targets of all AOR's are established they can then again be combined into another single area target (see exhibit 3).

```
SEGMENT HEADQUARTER:
operational_profit_HQ.Y =    operational_profit_PC1.Y +
   operational_profit_PC2.Y -
   overheads.Y

ENDSEGMENT
```

Exhibit 3: Equation of a superior AOR

Taking overheads into consideration, `operational_profit_PC1.Y` is added to `operational_profit_PC2.Y` and results in the area target of the so called headquarter AOR. The area target of the headquarter AOR is the top target of an ITP model. The headquarter AOR is not only responsible for its own area target but also the area targets as well as the basic targets of all subordinated AOR's.

So far a rather rudimentary description of AOR models has been presented. It is important, however, to mention that is is possible to consider any number and sort of accounting and organizational issues (e.g. choice of transfer prices, determination of overhead costs share for AOR's) when AOR model equations are constructed.

2.3. The global ITP model

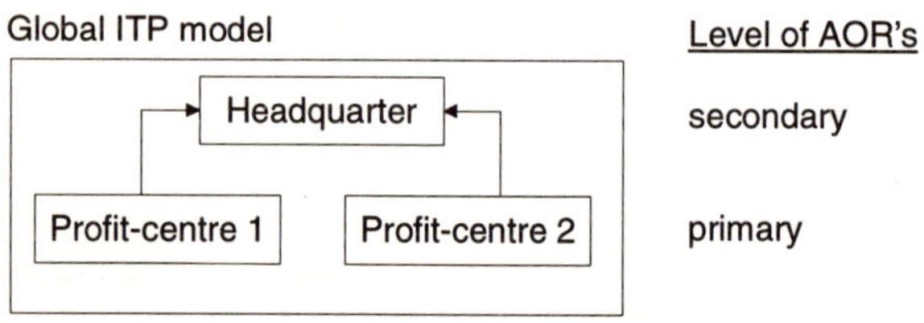

Exhibit 4: Global ITP model

The sum of all equations of all AOR's is called the global ITP model. In the global ITP model AOR's that aggregate area targets of subordinated AOR's into a single area target are called secondary AOR's. Secondary AOR's are leading departments. The highest secondary level always represents the corporate headquarter.

Executing departments are called primary AOR's. Exhibit 4 shows an example of a global ITP model with only one secondary level; however, there can be a hierarchy of secondary levels. A global ITP model for profit-centre budgeting is always organized hierarchically, because even if there is only one secondary level, several area-targets of AOR's on the same level will be combined into one area target of the headquarter AOR.

2.4. The four states of basic variables

Mathematically, both top and basic targets are variables within an equation system, the ITP model. To be more specific, basic targets are one state of basic variables. In total, there are four states of basic variables, see exhibit 5.

States of basic variables

- basic targets
- decision parameters
- uncontrollable basic variables
- objectionfree basic variables

Exhibit 5: States of basic variables

The differences between the states are as follows:

(1) The basic targets are the 'objectives' as described by MBO. The AOR's are responsible to meet their basic targets. The sets of basic targets of the AOR's are mutually exclusive. Thus each AOR is responsible for different basic targets. Values of basic targets are initially set by the area management. The values are voluntary target obligations and will change during the planning procedure. (see in 2.5). At the end of the planning procedure the values of basic targets become the objectives for the AOR's.

(2) Values of decision parameters are set by the top management and will remain unchanged throughout the planning. Examples are product sale prices or the desired inventory at the end of the planning period. The values of decision parameters are fixed. Decision parameters are always totally controllable.

(3) Values of uncontrollable basic variables are estimated for planning and usually remain unchanged during the planning procedure. An example is the currency exchange rate. When the values of uncontrollable basic variables do change, the variations then lie beyond a firm's sphere of influence. AOR's cannot be hold responsible for deviations between planned and

real values of uncontrollable basic parameters. Uncontrollable basic parameters are not objectives that have to be met.

(4) Objectionfree basic variables are rare in corporate accounting systems. An example is the loan change rate. The state of objectionfree basic variables is special. Variations of their values have no influence on the AOR's in meeting their objectives. Therefore, values of objectionfree basic variables are not determined exactly till the end of a planning procedure. They are changed and adjusted once or several times within a planning procedure in order to optimize top targets.

The distinction between the four types of basic variables has considerable implications:

(1) Once the equations of an ITP model are determined, all basic variables can and must be classified into one of the four states described above. The classification guarantees that only basic targets, which are controllable by AOR's and therefore need to be negotiated, will in fact be negotiated.

(2) Sometimes the state 'objectionfree' can be assigned to one or more of the basic variables in an ITP model. It is then possible to adjust those basic variables in order to optimize top targets, without affecting the commitment of any AOR to meet its objectives. In this case negotiation of objectives and optimization are not contradictory.

2.5. The three step planning procedure

The planning procedure includes (1) the bottom up step, (2) the top down step and (3) the bottom up top down step (confrontation), see exhibit 6. In the following these three steps will be discussed in detail.

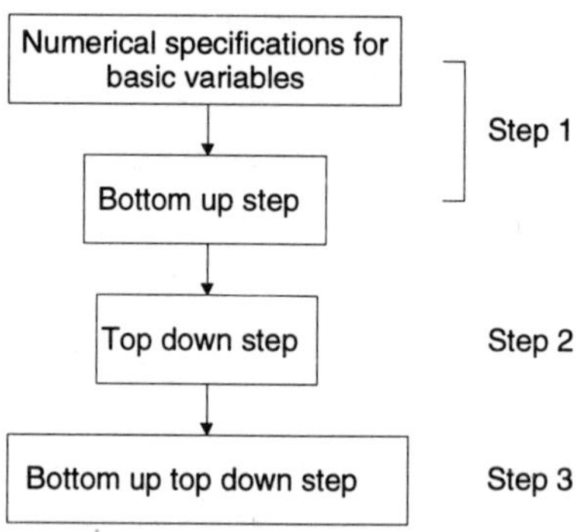

Exhibit 6: The three step planning procedure

Bottom up step

In the bottom up step the AOR's must provide numerical specifications (bottom up values) for all basic targets.[81] Once the values of all basic variables are given, the area targets can then be calculated. The area targets represent the negotiation position of AOR's.

Top down step

The top down step serves to present the negotiation position of the top management. The top management usually postulates a higher operational profit than the one resulting from the bottom up step.

Top targets are calculated from basic targets by means of equations. In order to determine the top down value of a basic target, the top management specifies a load margin for each basic target, that is the highest admissible change towards increased load.[82] For example, the sales volume of a certain product can only be increased by +10% due to the limit of maximum market demand. If the basic target is a cost target the additional load percentage would show a negative direction. Once the load margins are specified, basic target values are then adapted within their individual load margin in order to reach the top targets postulates of the top management. This is done by an optimization procedure.

At this point of the planning procedure the two initial positions for the negotiation process are established: (1) the position representing the interests of the area management which has been determined in the bottom up step and (2) the position representing the interests of the top management which has been determined in the top down step.

Bottom up top down step

In the bottom up top down step ('confrontation'), the final numerical values of the area targets are negotiated between top management and the management of all primary AOR's through another adaptation of the values of basic targets.

Each basic target influences the top targets differently. Some basic targets have a greater influence on the value of top targets than others. The degree of influence of one specific basic target is represented by a parameter. This parameter depicts the change of a top target value resulting from a 1% change of a basic target value. Consequently, it is possible to devote the main attention to the basic targets of greater influence.

---

[81] Specific persons are authorized to enter bottom-up-values of the other basic-variables.

[82] The idea of establishing load margins is based on the theory of 'Organizational Slack', see Cyert, March (1963).

The determination of the final numerical values of area targets preceeds on the determination of specific values for the basic targets. In the AOR's these values are called accepted basic targets because they represent one possible combination of figures that will definitely fulfill the agreed area target.

Due to the option of choosing different sets of basic target values, the actual value of the headquarter area target will probably differ from the planned value, even when the planned values of all area targets are met. The deviation of actual top target values from planned top target values can be represented graphically. The range of values within which top target values can vary is called the uncertainty area of top target values. An example of the uncertainty area of two top targets is shown in exhibit 7.

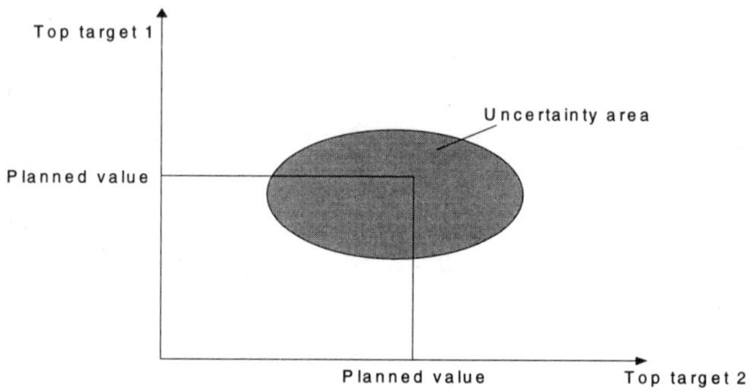

Exhibit 7: Uncertainty area of two top targets

The top management must define an admissible region for the choice of each basic target value in order to be able to influence the size of the uncertainty area. The more the top management limits the choice of basic target values, the smaller will be the uncertainty area of top target values and the less will be the deviation of actual from planned top target values. It is important to mention that the accepted basic target values must always lie in the admissible region of the basic targets. The admissible region is called 'area of variation'.

The possibility of showing and comparing different uncertainty areas enables the top management to make a calculated decision about the areas of variation with regard to their own ideas and targets. Beside strategic considerations there is also a fundamental economic need for the top management to define the areas of variation. A negative example: A profit-centre produces and sells two products P_1 and P_2 with the sales volume X_{P1} and X_{P2} being the accepted basic targets. In the bottom up top down step an operating profit (area target) of that profit-centre has been negotiated. If the profit-centre has complete freedom in choosing its sets of basic target values (which still meets the planned area target value), X_{P1} or X_{P2} could be assigned a value of zero. The negotiated operating profit would then be achieved by producing and selling only one of the two products.

Once an agreement on area target values is reached between top management and executing departments and once the areas of variation are established by top management, the planning procedure is finished and the area targets have to be realized.

2.6. Decentralized budgeting ('post confrontation')

While the negotiated objectives are being realized, each AOR has the possibility to assign any numerical values to its basic targets within the given areas of variation. In other words, even after the objectives are agreed upon, the planning is not finished but continues in decentralized budgeting. This marks a fundamental difference of the ITP method from other MBO planning systems.

For example, for an objective of 30 an AOR can choose a set of basic targets of 10+10+10 or 12+10+8, etc. The optimal set of basic targets is calculated by each AOR using its self-contained AOR model. The possibility to define the sets of basic targets to their best advantage has a motivating effect on AOR's.

However, AOR's are not isolated. They are embedded within the corporate cost centre structure and hierarchy. Each variation of numerical values of basic targets affects the amounts of mutual profit-centre transfers and leads to a higher request or release of capacities of interrelated AOR's. Therefore, the degree of variation of basic target values is restricted by the capacities of interrelated AOR's. Because each AOR works with a self-contained AOR model it does not know the occupations of interrelated AOR's. Occupations of all AOR's are part of the global ITP model. Therefore every change of basic target values within decentralized budgeting must be approved by the top management. This guarantees the observance of capacity restrictions of interrelated AOR's.

2.7. Target control

In order to perform the ex post control process, the actual values (as opposed to the negotiated values) of basic variables must be registered. Some actual values can be observed or calculated. Others, such as the total amount of monthly salaries, can be retrieved from other corporate computer systems. They are the parameters of a further model which is used to calculate the actual values of the area targets. In the target control the actual values of the objectives are compared with the negotiated values. The target control takes place on a monthly or quarterly basis. However, the above described planning procedure provides objectives on an annual basis only. The splitting up of the negotiated yearly values of basic targets is done by a procedure that will not be described in this essay.

Each AOR is only responsible for the deviations of planned and actual area target values which result from changes of its own basic target values. No AOR is responsible for deviations produced by value changes of decision parameters or uncontrollable basic variables.

3. The INZPLA system

3.1. Overview

The architecture of the INZPLA planning and control system is based on requirements established by the theory of ITP. A fundamental requirement is that the INZPLA system must be an equation-based system, since the ITP model consists of equations.

The application of an equation based system for budget planning and control has significant advantages. With former cost accounting systems the calculation of top targets and, when simultanious equations occur, the calculation of mutual transfer prices has been rather complicated. This is because former cost accounting systems are no equation based systems. Values of transfer prices, once calculated, have been accepted for monthly or annual periods, ignoring the fact that in the course of a month or a year the actual values of transfer prices usually differ from the calculated values. With the INZPLA system beeing an equation based system, it is much easier to determine top target values and transfer prices. Therefore a set of precise values is available at any time.

As mentioned above, there is the possibility to define objectionfree basic variables. When objectionfree variables occur, negotiation of objectives and optimization are no longer contradictory.

As opposed to other equation based systems, INZPLA is not a further attachment to existing corporate planning systems. It distinguishes itself as a special corporate budgeting and control procedure, based on the ITP theory.

There is another important difference: equation based systems usually work on a highly aggregated level and are therefore used to evaluate aggregated business planning problems (such as the DuPont-system or other management ratio systems). [83] Unlike these systems, INZPLA employs highly disaggregated models to achieve the requirements of a MBO planning process. In that respect the global ITP model presented in exhibit 4 is not representative for INZPLA (it

83 Reichmann (1990), p. 15 ff.

is considerably simplified). For example, ITP models representing individual firm-accounting systems that have been developed within this research project consist of some ten thousand equations. In the recent time we have been working on reconstructing the model described by Kilger.[84] The Kilger ITP model consists of 38 cost centres, 149 cost units and 11 products. It contains 19864 variables, 3353 of which are basic variables. A printout of the Kilger ITP model would amount up to ca. 1150 pages. The size of a database of another ITP test model, containing some 58000 variables, has turned out to be approximately 500 MB.

3.2. Applied hard- and software

The INZPLA system uses client server architecture of relational database management systems. To develop the INZPLA system the following platform is being employed:

Hardware and operating system: 486 PC network using Windows for Workgroups 3.11 and NOVELL 3.11.

Language interface system: An editor to feed model equations into the system plus a compiler to generate executable libraries (DLL). The compiler processes a non procedural order of equations and encodes simultanities (e.g. the mutual cost centre charge transfers) by using the Gauss Seidel algorithm.

Database (RDBMS): Gupta's SQLBase, Version 5.12.

User interface system: Gupta's SQLWindows 4.01 (object oriented 4GL) to develop all client applications and Borland's PASCAL 7.1 with SQL interface for object oriented methods. MS-EXCEL and Gupta's ReportWindows as report systems.

3.3. The distributed system

INZPLA as a distributed budgeting and control system is spread throughout the organization of a firm. The AOR's use client frontends to work with their self-contained AOR model and independent RDBMS. Each AOR database is a copy of a part of the central RDBMS (storing the global ITP model) and contains all information concerning itself. Mutual updates are performed periodically on an asynchronous basis.

The INZPLA system has the following subsystems:

(1) Control station for the following tasks

---

[84] See Kilger (1988).

- administration of users of the INZPLA system, this includes: entering and deleting of users; relating users to primary and secondary AOR's; granting and revoking user authorizations concerning back- and frontend
- defining the sequence of tasks and a planning calender
- distributing tasks to users
- supervising the execution of tasks.

(2) Specific modules for the following tasks

- creating the ITP model equations
- data entry for values of basic variables
- scenario calculations
- planning procedure
- determination of the uncertainty area
- post confrontation
- reporting.

(3) Various tools to analyze the structure of the ITP model

- tool for graphical analysis of interrelations between AOR's
- tool for generating reduced equations based on the ITP equation model
- tool for graphical analysis of the the syntax-tree of ITP models

Exhibit 8 shows the structure of a disaggregated global ITP model for a decentralized profit-centre budgeting process. This ITP model of a fictitious firm consists of seven AOR's, four primary and three secondary ones.

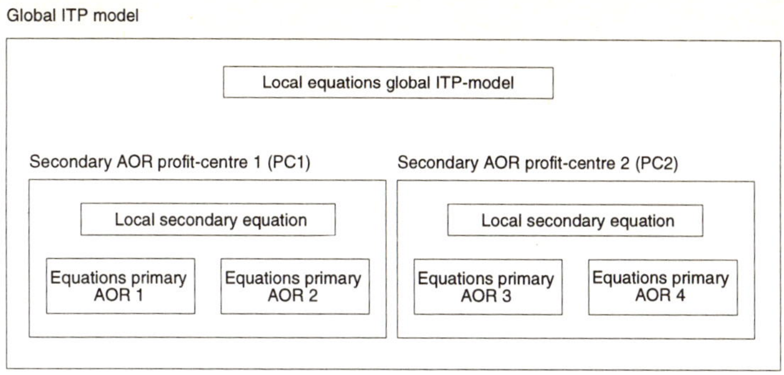

Exhibit 8: Disaggregated global ITP model for decentralized profit-centre budgeting

All seven AOR's form a hierarchy within which the secondary AOR consists of all subordinated AOR's plus a local model equation which aggregates subordinated area targets. Exhibit 9 illustrates a possible configuration of the global ITP model shown in exhibit 8.

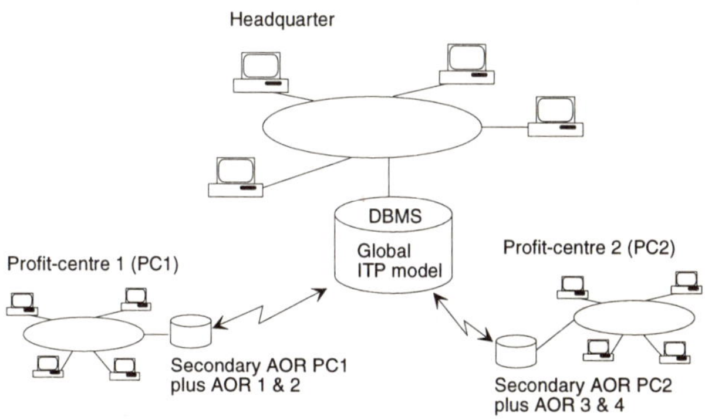

Exhibit 9: Possible configuration of the global ITP model shown in exhibit 8

References

Cyert, R.M.; March, J.G.: A behavioral theory of the firm; Englewood Cliffs 1963.

Kilger, W.: Flexible Plankostenrechnung und Deckungsbeitragsrechnung; Wiesbaden 1988.

Reichmann, T.: Controlling mit Kennzahlen. Grundlagen einer systemgestützten Controlling-Konzeption; München 1990.

Rosenberg, J.: Dictionary of business and management; New York 1978.

Scheer, A.-W.: EDV-orientierte Betriebswirtschaftslehre, Grundlagen für ein effizientes Informationsmanagement; Berlin 1990.

Zwicker, E.: INZPLA - Ein Konzept der computergestützten Unternehmensgesamtplanung, in: W. Lücke (ed.): Betriebswirtschaftliche Steuerungs- und Kontrollprobleme; Wiesbaden 1988, p. 341 ff.

Decentralized Problem Solving in Logistics with Partly Intelligent Agents and Comparison with Alternative Approaches

Peter Mertens, Jürgen Falk, Stefan Spieck, Mark Weigelt

Abstract

The research work described in this paper pursues two goals. Firstly, it deals with how Distributed Artificial Intelligence (DAI) techniques are used to solve "real-world" logistical problems. Secondly, it compares decentralized solutions (agent systems) with alternative centralized approaches. The results of most of the cases indicate that concerning the main objectives the agent systems can outperform alternative approaches. A general statement in favour of the DAI-approaches is not possible, though.

Keywords: Distributed Artificial Intelligence, Agent Systems, Partly Intelligent Agents, Logistical Problems

1. Introduction

This paper focuses on the applicability of Distributed Artificial Intelligence (DAI) techniques to solving "real-world" logistical problems. The Partly Intelligent Agents (PIAs) we use are equipped with simple algorithms supplemented by knowledge-based components. By comparison with centralized methods we can judge the benefits of our new DAI approaches. It is a central objective of our work to present in detail how to make "practicable" agent systems and thereby reduce the gap between theory and practice.

The second chapter starts with a description of the freight allotment problem in demand-driven truckload carrying. Afterwards, decentralized approaches realized as the agent systems TRAMPAS-1 and -2 (Tramping Truck Dispatching Agent System) as well as a centralized approach realized as the system TRAMP-Z are discussed.

The third chapter deals with another logistical issue. We introduce the problem of shipping scarce goods and present centralized and decentralized approaches as well as the corresponding systems RATAS-1 and -2 (Rationing Agent System) and RAT-Z.

Our results of comparisons are discussed at the end of chapter 2 and 3. In order to complete the impressions concerning DAI-benefits, we can furthermore exploit results of an adjacent project conducting research in the field of production control. Concluding the text, we evaluate and try to combine the outcomes of all three problem areas.

2. Freight Allotment in Demand-Driven Truckload Carrying

2.1. Problem Setting

In demand-driven truckload carrying, regional shipping agencies attempt to assign incoming freight orders during the day to the "best-qualified" truck. The dispatchers of the agencies must be informed about the current locations of "their" trucks. Quite often, they have to decide quickly which truck might be assigned to a new order, so that it can be accepted or refused. The German carrier we focus on is a specialist in transporting pieces of art (70 per cent), computer (15 per cent), and furniture (15 per cent). The regional agencies are located in Cologne (head office), Hamburg, Berlin, Frankfurt and Munich. The vehicle fleet of Cologne encompasses 24 trucks, the fleets of the other depots up to ten (total 64).

The different "hard" and "soft" constraints for each freight allotment that may not be violated include precedence relationships (*first* pickup and *then* delivery of the goods), time windows, load capacities, commodity compatibility, traffic congestion, and crew and vehicle maintenance requirements. Additionally, it is typical for this kind of truckload carrier that every freight order needs special attention due to its unique service quality- and handling-constraints. For example, special safety boxes must be produced in the internal joiner's workshop before the pieces of art can be loaded. Therefore, it has to be scheduled separately.

Conventional vehicle routing programs do not allow consideration of all these non-quantifiable order-dependent constraints. Furthermore, for that partly *Dynamic Vehicle Routing*-problem, information (a new freight order) is also made known to the decision-maker concurrently with the determination of the route[85]. There is no definite closing time for incoming orders[86]. Obviously, round-trip scheduling performed by conventional programs is unsuitable.

The dispatchers assign their trucks locally and attempt to coordinate freight orders having pickup and delivery locations in different regions via telephone and fax (see figure 1). The objective is to attain cost-reducing load consolidation. Coordination is a thorny process in daily practice and takes a lot of time. The dispatchers of the carrier we investigated deplore that they sometimes negotiate via phone the whole day without achieving sufficient consolidation results.

---

[85] see Psaraftis (1992).

[86] see Bodin et al. (1983).

In this problem field, knowledge-based agents could offer new opportunities[87] since they are "smart": They take all the constraints into account and are able to communicate. We call them Partly Intelligent Agents (PIA) since in addition to a knowledge-based component reflecting the qualitative constraints they are provided with scheduling algorithms (e. g., calculating cheapest load insertions).

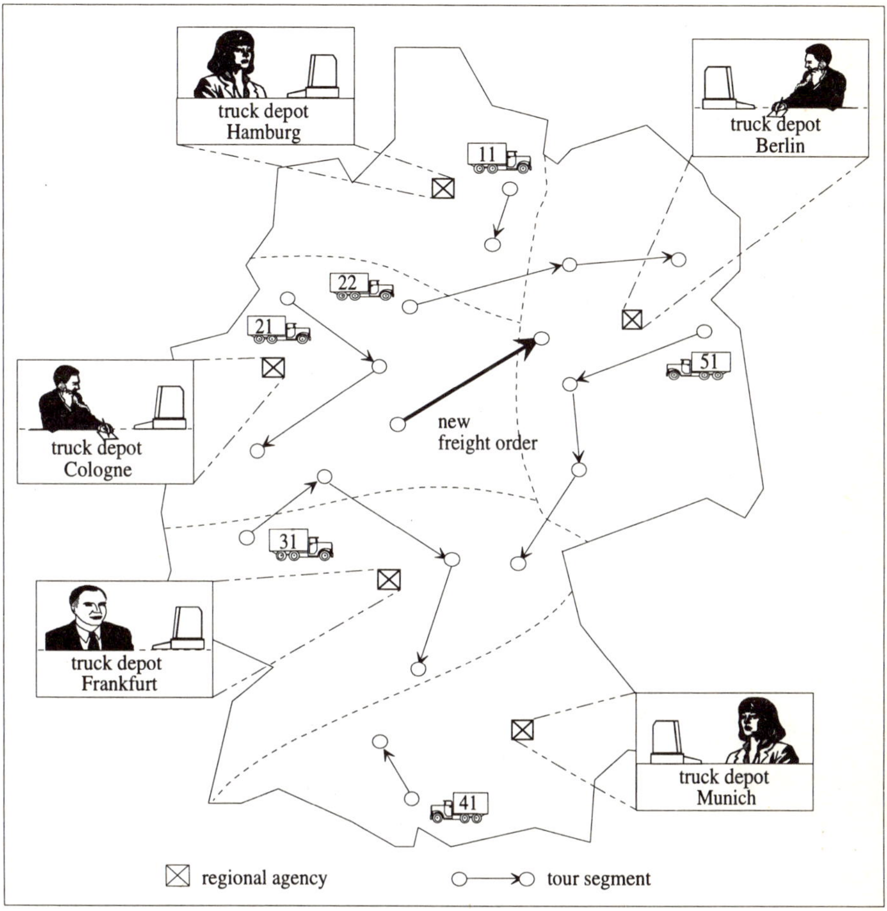

Fig. 1: Distributed freight allotment of a demand-driven carrier in Germany

[87] see Shaw et al. (1993).

2.2. Decentralized Approach

2.2.1. Architecture

In our strongly decentralized I.T.-approach, freight orders are assigned and consolidated by the PIAs mentioned above. The PIA-system is based on a region-centered cooperative architecture which means that one agent has the disposal of several trucks[88]. An object-centered approach mentioned in literature considers single trucks as negotiation units in a contract carrier scenario[89]. However, the dispatchers have to be able to duplicate what the agents do. We think that will be more difficult for them when introducing truck-agents which support the (non-realistic) negotiation process of single vehicles.

In the regional agencies, the depot-agents schedule the local vehicle fleet. They have to coordinate the assignments with agents representing other depots especially if incoming freight orders have delivery locations outside their own regions. When a load is called in, the agent closest to the pickup-location of the new freight order is designated for coordinating the planning process (Coordinating PIA = C-PIA). Agents controlling trucks close to the new load (neighboring trucks) have to take part in the assignment process as Participating PIAs (= P-PIAs). Obviously, the composition of a planning course varies from order to order.

2.2.2. Operators

The PIAs are equipped with an extensible set of operators[90] for scheduling and combining freight orders. The operators utilize scheduling algorithms[91] and a knowledge-based component to check the constraints.

1. *Insertion-Operator*: A new freight order can be easily added to a current tour without changing the pickup and delivery times of the orders already scheduled.

2. *Shifting-Operator*: To achieve a wider time gap which enables the insertion of a new load, pickup and delivery times of existing orders are moved within the corresponding time windows (if defined).

3. *Reloading-Operator:* Following a successful insertion, it might be possible to "save" a car by reloading several trucks passing a regional agency. This means collecting loads in short-haul traffic and consolidating them at specified points of exchange (e. g. the truck depots) to optimize load ratios for long-distance traffic.

---

[88] see Steeb et al. (1981).
[89] see Fischer et al. (1993).
[90] see Falk et al. (1993).
[91] see Jaw (1986).

4. *Chaining-Operator*: This operator is intended to examine possible combinations of tour segments of different trucks to reduce distances travelled without load.

5. *Exchanging-Operator*: Quite often temporal and spatial gaps in the schedule can be filled by interchanging orders between tours and trucks. Exchanging loads is also very important to diverting trucks and thereby avoiding congestion in case of traffic jams.

The P-PIAs rate each allotment or consolidation alternative by calculating a value of success (SUCC). SUCC is defined as the difference between freight revenues and transportation costs.

2.2.3. Coordination Process

To coordinate the freight order assignment and consolidation processes we utilize two different kinds of a Contract-Net (CN)[92] which make the difference between the both versions of the PIA-system TRAMPAS: an "original" CN is realized in TRAMPAS-1 (chapter 2.3) and a more flexible variant in TRAMPAS-2 (chapter 2.4).

2.3. TRAMPAS-1

In TRAMPAS-1, the C-PIA decomposes each allotment or consolidation task in a predefined order of operators to be applied by the participating agents (see figure 2a). The operators are sequenced by some "central" criteria which characterize the specific dispatching situations. To those criteria, we count the amount of available planning time and the desired SUCC. A possible sequence could be the following:

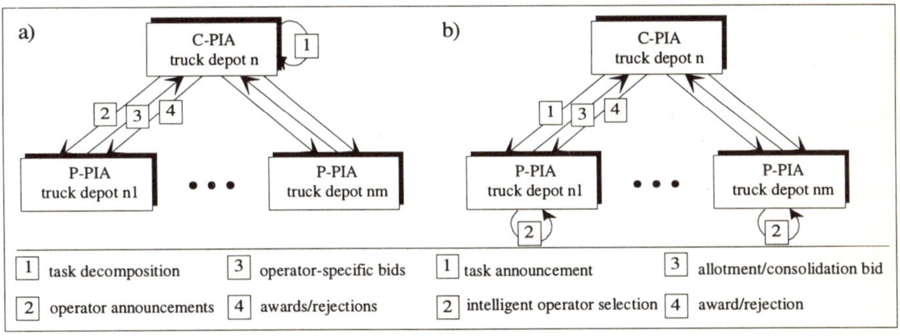

Fig. 2: a) CN in TRAMPAS-1, b) CN in TRAMPAS-2

[92] see Smith et al. (1980).

After the arrival of a new order, the C-PIA invokes its partners to plan *cheapest insertions* for their neighboring tours first. The C-PIA collects and ranks the insertion proposals and selects the agent with the highest SUCC, but only if SUCC exceeds a certain threshold value which might be determined individually for each order.

Next, the coordinator requests the P-PIAs to consolidate truckloads (operator 2) and/or to chain tour segments. Using the *reloading-operator*, the P-PIAs examine the pick-up and delivery locations of their tours to find out whether they are marked as points of exchange or not. Only at such locations freights can be moved from one truck to another. In case of deploying the chaining-operator, the corresponding P-PIAs try to find out combinations of tour segments. As an assumption, an agent must have calculated at least one insertion proposal for a tour as to where the new freight order will be added to the end. For the new end location of this alternative, the P-PIA determines neighboring tours. If any exist, it requests chaining-bids from the corresponding agents containing the information whether and how segments can be connected. In this way, the coordination process has branched twice (second stage of CN).

If SUCC remains under the threshold, in the last step the PIAs have to interchange freight orders between tours and trucks taking advantage of varying time and capacity gaps by inserting additional orders and releasing already scheduled orders (*exchanging-operator*). If in this way a new order promising a high SUCC could be inserted successfully, the P-PIAs start a new planning cycle for the released orders. If the removed orders cannot be inserted any more, the dispatcher has to decide what to do.

2.4. TRAMPAS-2

In TRAMPAS-2, we achieved a higher degree of decentralization by having implemented a further knowledge-base enabling the P-PIAs to select the appropriate operator(s) by themselves. The agent structure is outlined in figure 3.

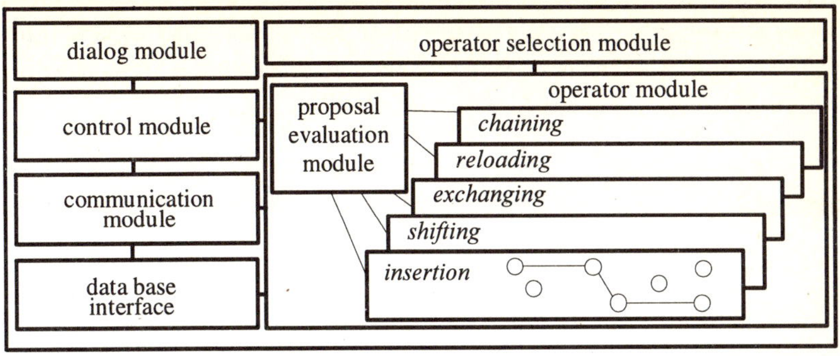

Fig. 3: Module structure of an agent in TRAMPAS-2

The C-PIA announces the allotment task as a whole. The P-PIAs investigate the local dispatching situation considering local objectives, handling-constraints and experiences and select the appropriate operator(s) (see figure 2b). The following questions are a subset of those influencing the local operator selection decision of an agent:

- What kind of service quality- and handling-constraints has to be considered?
- Which objective should be preferred: full-loaded truck or minimized distance?
- Which customers have highest priority?

Whereas in TRAMPAS-1 the P-PIAs only *react* to predetermined operators, they *reflect* their future actions in TRAMPAS-2. With this additional knowledge it is more likely that the agents act as flexible as human dispatchers do.

2.5. TRAMP-Z

TRAMP-Z is a **centralized** decision support system. One single "agent" controls the whole vehicle fleet of the company and dispatches all incoming freight orders by itself[93]. The system is equipped with the operators developed for TRAMPAS to calculate all the freight allotment and consolidation possibilities for neighboring tours and trucks. The operators are sequenced in the same way as it is done by the C-PIA in TRAMPAS-1. To achieve tolerable response times we had to simplify the scheduling component (leading to the fact that scheduling with TRAMP-Z is more inaccurate).

---

[93] see Bagchi et al. (1991).

Introducing this kind of system into practice means that the tasks of the regional dispatchers will be reduced to "collecting data" for the central dispatching office. Local knowledge for assessing the current tour constellation cannot be taken into account.

2.6. Results

As the hardware backbone, a PC network (Intel 80486) under NOVELL with an integrated data base server of GUPTA is used. We have implemented the scheduling component, the knowledge-base, and the communication component in the programming language C/C++. We measured the speed of solution of TRAMPAS-2. The scheduling of 99 generated freight orders was performed in about 1 hour and 30 minutes.

We have reproduced the organizational structure of the regarded German carrier by configuring depot agents for all agencies. To compare the solution quality of the decentralized and centralized approaches, we at first simulated an input of 99 orders (one week time window) and afterwards evaluated the corresponding schedules using the following performance index numbers: number of orders assigned (Noa, to be maximized), number of vehicles allocated (Nva, to be minimized), ratio of order distances to distances travelled (Roddt, to be maximized) and load balance (Lb, degree of loading space utilization, to be maximized).

Table 1 depicts detailed results achieved by the depot agent "Cologne" of the TRAMPAS-systems. In table 2 results accomplished by the decentralized *and* centralized approaches valid for the whole company are contrasted.

Agent "Cologne"	Noa	Nva	Roddt	Lb
TRAMPAS-1	36	6	68,83 %	41,14 %
TRAMPAS-2	37	6	76,21 %	51,89 %

Table 1: Results of comparisons valid for truck depot Cologne

	Noa	Nva	Roddt	Lb
TRAMPAS-1	93	14	69,10 %	42,76 %
TRAMPAS-2	99	14	75,02 %	51,30 %
TRAMP-Z	87	15	68,83 %	42,63 %

Table 2: Results of comparisons valid for the whole company (99 orders)

The comparison of TRAMPAS-1, -2 and TRAMP-Z reveals that TRAMPAS-2 computes the cheapest freight allotments in the shortest time. The higher Roddt in both tables indicates more realized freight consolidation. Exploiting the local knowledge of the regional dispatchers leads to the fact that - after the new load is called in - the "best-qualified" operators are directly applied by the local agents. TRAMP-Z and TRAMPAS-1 quite often deploy the insertion-operator alone. This is caused by the lack of P-PIA-flexibility and by a decomposition strategy where only criteria are considered which are company-wide valid. For the comparisons with the dispatchers, we recorded one week of the manual scheduling process and duplicated the freight assignments with TRAMPAS-2. However, the evaluations are going on.

3. Shipping of Scarce Goods

3.1. Problem Setting

Another application field in the logistical area in which the use of DAI-techniques is very promising is the shipment of goods via a multi-echelon warehouse hierarchy. Logistical objectives typically include improving customer service, guaranteeing quicker deliveries, and for that purpose avoiding stock-outs. In order to accomplish tehse objectives, most authors focus on proactive techniques like forecasting, determining reliable safety stock levels, and optimizing replenishment policies. However, problems like continued shortages of some products are usually caused by hardly foreseeable influences such as supply delays of raw material or intermediate goods, loss of production capacity, lack of quality, or excessive demand[94]. The measures we found in literature cannot completely avoid shortages, and give no hint how to deal with them once they occur. Under the mentioned circumstances, the safety stock is used up and one has to react. Although it may be no longer possible then to improve the common logistical indicative figures, trying to minimize stock-out-costs is worth an effort. In contrast to this, the issue is rarely addressed.

To solve this problem and in parallel judge the applied methods, we simultaneously pursued decentralized and centralized approaches and developed the agents-systems RATAS-1 and -2 as well as a centralized system RAT-Z.

[94] see Schmid (1976), S. 20 ff.

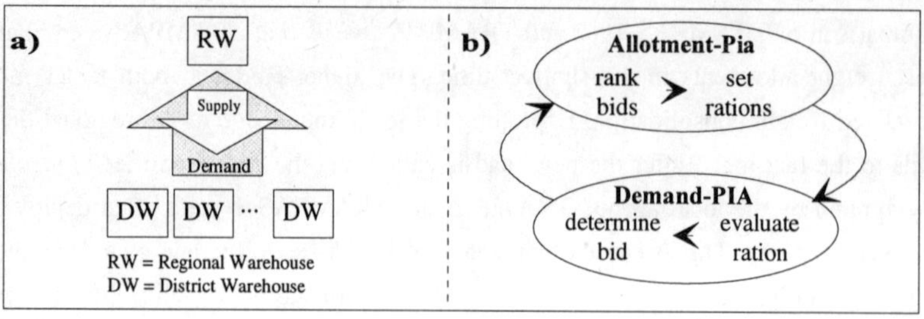

Fig. 4: a) Demand vs. Supply b) Negotiation Cycle

The scenario we look at is characterized by the demands of the (lower level) district warehouses exceeding the stock available at the delivering regional warehouse (see figure 4a). Therefore, it is necessary to set rations for these scarce goods. This is usually the job of a human managing clerk who as a rule relates the size of the rations to the amount requested by the locations. Though this method is quite simple and fair, it is by no means able to guarantee profit maximization.

3.2. Decentralized Approach

In order to achieve the primary goal (profit maximization) the stock-out-costs have to be minimized. Almost all data that can be evaluated for this purpose in a decentralized company are kept locally, including knowledge about the local market, customer structure and behavior, local cost structure, and demand interdependencies. Therefore, a decentralized mechanism seems to be a promising approach. The scenario can ideally be represented by a multi agent system in which each agent is responsible for one depot.

3.2.1. RATAS-1

Determining rations of a scarce good resembles an auction or more generally a market in which one supplier (auctioneer, monopolist) faces several customers. Therefore, a corresponding agent system should pursue an approach in which the agents representing the different depots compete with each other for the scarce goods by bidding higher prices. When within the company each depot is regarded as a profit center and the goods are traded and charged using internal prices[95], this mechanism is easy to implement.

---

[95] see Hertel (1992), S. 96.

This is the basic concept for the prototypical system RATAS-1[96]. It consists of two types of Partly Intelligent Agents. Demand-PIAs (D-PIAs) represent district warehouses (customers). Allotment-PIAs (A-PIAs) look after the interests of regional warehouses (supplier). They compare and rank the incoming bids and assign rations to the D-PIAs.

The D-PIAs use a sophisticated model to estimate the potential stock-out-costs their location would face when receiving a specific small ration. To do so they use probabilities to model the different reactions of customers when their orders cannot (or at least cannot immediately) be satisfied. Costs of lost current profit-contributions, reduced future orders, and of additional activities are evaluated and added up according to the probabilities of the corresponding alternatives. Problems directly connected with this include how to predict which goods can be substituted for the scarce ones and how likely this is? When a customer reduces an order - which are the complementary products that are not requested, too?[97] Since the probabilities of different customer reactions cannot be predicted exactly, the resulting costs have to be viewed as estimates.

Knowing these approximate costs, each D-PIA derives a limit for the premium it is willing to add to the normal price of a scarce good. In the following negotiation cycles, the agents start with low bids and continually increase them until their ration is large enough or until they reach the limit.

Based on the incoming bids, the A-PIA assigns rations of the scarce goods to the next level warehouses. That way it determines intermediate rations and takes turns with the associated D-PIAs who subsequently have the chance to modify their recent offer (see figure 4b). When no D-PIA changes its bid anymore, the intermediate rations are the final ones. For further details see Mertens et al.[98]

In RATAS-1, the A-PIA aims at the single goal of profit maximization considering nothing but the offered price in order to set the rations. The idea behind this mechanism is that, when every agent behaves egoistically, in the end this maximizes the profit of the whole company. The structure of both types of agents is displayed by figure 5. They are implemented in C in the same environment as TRAMPAS (see 2.6) and communicate via message-passing using the Windows DDE-facility.

---

96 see Will (1993).
97 see Böcker (1975), S. 290 ff.
98 see Mertens et al. (1993).

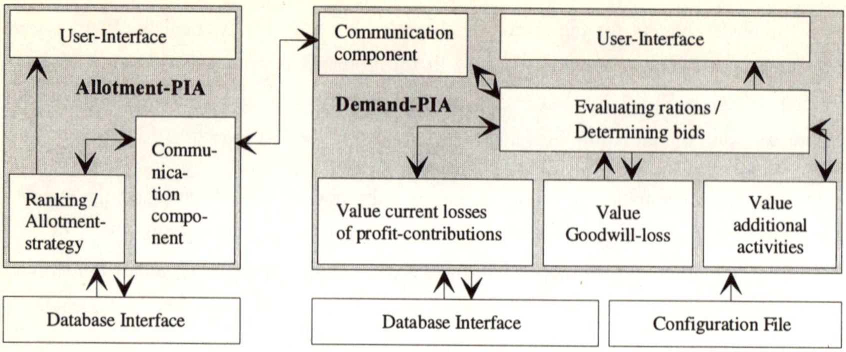

Fig. 5: Agent Structure in RATAS-1

3.2.2. RATAS-2

Concentrating the actions of the A-PIA on a single goal produces good results most of the time but is not sufficient under all circumstances. Once several objectives are pursued in parallel, RATAS-1 is not flexible enough. For instance, it is not possible to set the rations for some regions according to strategical decisions or simply to guarantee a basic supply for every area. In addition to this, the estimated stock-out-costs carry a lot of weight which as a side effect leads to the danger of multiplying calculation- and forecasting-errors.

RATAS-2 tackles these problems by improving the A-PIA while the structure of the D-PIAs and the principles of the negotiation-process remain unchanged. The multiple goal target is pursued with a very flexible mechanism that allows the A-PIA to set some parts of the rations paying less respect to the offered price. The amount of the goods that are handled specially as well as the influence of the bid can be adjusted as one chooses according to the goal structure. It is even possible to copy the strict profit maximization paradigm of RATAS-1.

As a new feature an A-PIA has the option to introduce price intervals for distinct shares of the available goods. Such intervals are tuples

$(\phi_n;\gamma_n)$; $n \in (1..N)$ with		
N = number of intervals,	$\sum_{n\in(1..N)} \phi_n = 100$,	$\gamma_n \in (0..100)$.

An incoming bid has to lie within one of these intervals to be taken into account. Figure 6 illustrates a possible example.

share	interval
10	40
10	20
20	10
60	0

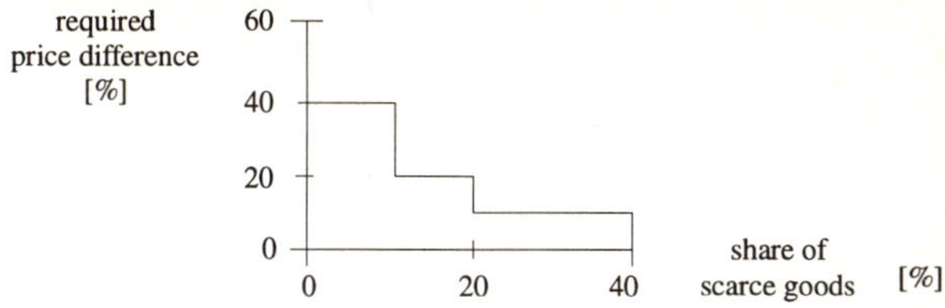

Fig. 6: Price Intervals in RATAS-2

In this example for the allotment of 10 % of the scarce goods the A-PIA considers all bids within 40 % of the highest one equally. For another 10 % this interval comes to 20 %. It is easy to see how flexible this mechanism is. The two extreme (share:interval)-adjustments are (100:0) which corresponds to the profit maximization of RATAS-1, and (100:100) which results in the same treatment of all locations regardless of their bid.

3.3. Centralized Approach (RAT-Z)

When an employee decides upon the rations, this has to be viewed as a centralized solution. Thus, it is an interesting question whether you have to go all the way and implement a distributed system that uses all available local data to determine an optimized solution, or whether centralized IT-support achieves the best cost/benefit-ratio.

A centralized approach works without the feedback mechanisms that characterize decentralized procedures. Thus, it is not possible to conduct such a detailed analysis of market data as the D-PIAs in the RATAS systems do. However, we can incorporate strategic elements that have a similar effect as the price intervals the A-PIA uses in RATAS-2.

RAT-Z is a decision support system for the dispatcher at the regional warehouse who decides upon the ration for the district warehouses. As a first step it examines the incoming orders, compares them to those of past periods. Applying an information-by-exception mechanism it informs the user of improbable rises and proposes changes in the volume of such requests. That way, tactically increased orders shall be identified and prevented.

The strategic feature of RAT-Z allows the user to assign a priority number ranging from 1 to 10 to each depot. Locations with a higher priority receive larger rations than equal treatment would bring them. Starting with initial rations R_i which are determined by treating each location equally, the ration proposals are calculated with the following formula:

$$R_i^{new} = r_i^{new} \cdot \frac{\sum_{i\in(1..n)} R_i}{\sum_{i\in(1..n)} r_i^{new}} \quad \text{with: } r_i^{new} = R_i \cdot \left(1+\frac{p_i}{10}\right) \cdot \frac{n}{n+0{,}1\cdot \sum_{i\in(1..n)} p_i}$$

i: number of a depot

n: number of depots

R_i: ration of depot i

p_i: priority of depot i

This strategy will not increase a ration beyond the originally ordered amount. The user can either confirm the proposed rations or change them. This may be necessary when he or she has new information that requires a different allotment. Of course the system checks the correctness of such changes.

3.4. Results

Tests were conducted in scenarios with three and four competing district warehouses, each of them having a different cost- and customer-structure. In situations where most of the assumptions on which the D-PIAs base their bids are correct, RATAS-1 achieves the profit maximization goal almost perfectly. Most satisfying is that, not only the company as a whole, but also the single locations show good results. A little drawback can be noticed when the stock-out-cost estimations differ from the actual costs. But even then, errors of about 15 % result in deviations from a supposed optimum of less than 5 %.

Since RATAS-2 can emulate RATAS-1, its results should have at least the same quality. It is not easy to judge the performance concerning multiple objectives, though, because it is hard to find the right weights for the different rating criteria.

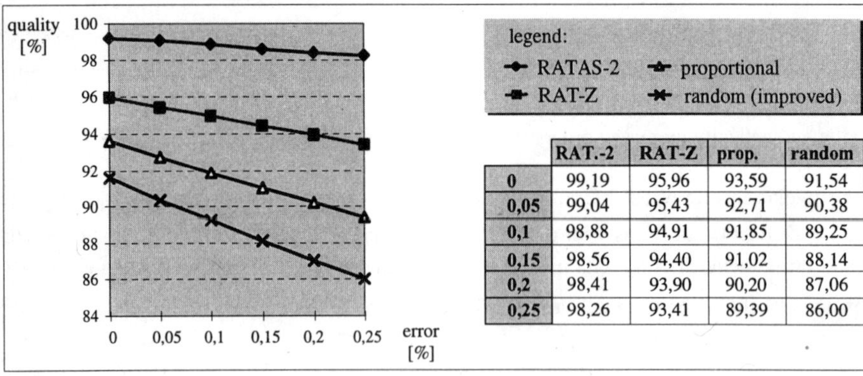

	RAT.-2	RAT-Z	prop.	random
0	99,19	95,96	93,59	91,54
0,05	99,04	95,43	92,71	90,38
0,1	98,88	94,91	91,85	89,25
0,15	98,56	94,40	91,02	88,14
0,2	98,41	93,90	90,20	87,06
0,25	98,26	93,41	89,39	86,00

Fig. 7: Comparison

Let us first take a look at whether the error-sensitivity changes when introducing price intervals. Figure 7 displays the results in a scenario with three warehouses, where one cost estimation is correct, one is too high and one is too low. The A-PIA in RATAS-2 uses (50:10; 50:5) intervals. The two conventional not IT-based approaches are proportional allotment (prop.) and improved random allotment (random). It is obvious that with uncertain input data RATAS-2 achieves significantly better results.

On top of this RATAS-2 is more flexible. To illustrate how specific instructions can be put into action consider the following examples:

- A bicycle-producing company wants to have at least one piece of every model they make at each location. If μ is the percentage of available bicycles that corresponds to the amount which is necessary in order to deliver one to each depot, RATAS-2 would achieve the requested distribution pattern with (μ:100, 100-μ:ν)-intervals, where ν is any number from 0 to 100.

- The company does not trust the stock-out-cost estimations and wants to reduce the influence of expected deviations in advance. Calculating with an average mistake λ, a (100:λ)-interval would be the right answer.

- Both examples can be combined. Then, we would need (μ:100, 100-μ:λ)-intervals.

RAT-Z improves the results a human would achieve, too. But, since it lacks the feedback mechanism, reactions on unexpected situations are not possible. Thus, RAT-Z comes closest to the decentralized approaches when the shortage is induced internally (e. g. production break-down) and not externally (e. g. drastic changes in demand). Including the negotiation, the agent systems take longer to produce their results than the simpler RAT-Z does. However, in contrast to the TRAMPAS-scenario, time is not a critical factor.

4. Conclusion

As our comparison results indicate, agent systems can outperform conventional centralized approaches in solving logistical planning problems. We achieved a similar outcome in an adjacent project dealing with production control[99]. Building more than 300 scenarios we contrasted several decentralized and centralized production control methods using our agent system DEPRODEX (**De**centralized **Prod**uction Control **Ex**pert) and its centralized counterpart

---

99 see Weigelt et al. (1993).

ZEPRODEX. We found out that agents are excellent in avoiding tardiness and in meeting due-dates.

It is our objective to introduce agent systems into practice. Regarding TRAMPAS, we have to tackle some problems concerning the physical communication (the several regional agencies are spatially distributed in Germany). We are inclined to adopt the underlying client/server-architecture (see 2.6) realized at our department and let the agents communicate via ISDN.

In order to attain further results in the field of shipment logistics, we currently work on the more general problem of allocation of goods to warehouses without restriction to shortage situations. Again, we pursue a centralized and a decentralized approach.

Combining the results we will have covered some of the most important aspects of supporting decentralized logistical problems and will be able to judge the applicability of agent systems.

5. References

Adler, P.: Entwicklung mengenorientierter Operatoren für ein dezentrales Dispositionssystem im Bedarfsverkehr bei Speditionen; Diploma Thesis; Nuernberg 1993.

Baehr, Th.: Anpassen eines dezentralen Dispositionssystems für den speditionellen Bedarfsverkehr an Praxisbedingungen und Durchführen verschiedenartiger Vergleiche; Diploma Thesis; Nuernberg 1994.

Bagchi, P.; Nag, B.: Dynamic Vehicle Scheduling: An Expert Systems Approach; International Journal of Physical Distribution & Logistic Management 21 (1991) 2, S. 10-18.

Bodin, L.; Golden, B.L.; Assad, A.A.; Ball, M.O.: Routing and Scheduling of Vehicles and Crews: State of the Art; Computers & Operations Research (1983) 10, S. 63-193.

Böcker, F.: Die Analyse des Kaufverbunds - Ein Ansatz zur bedarfsorientierten Warentypologie; ZfbF (1975) 27, S. 290-306.

Falk, J.; Borkowski, V.; Neumann, R.; Mertens, P.: TRAMPAS: A Knowledge-Based Agent System for Distributed Freight Allotment; in: Balagurusamy, E. (Ed.): Proceedings of the Fourth International Computing Congress (ICC 93); Hyderabad (India) 1993, S. 394-401.

Fischer, K.; Kuhn, N.; Müller, H.-J.; Müller, J.P.; Pischel, M.; Schroth, A.: Verteiltes Problemlösen im Transportwesen; IM Information Management 8 (1993) 2, S. 32-40.

Hertel, J.: Design mehrstufiger Warenwirtschaftssysteme; Heidelberg 1992.

Jaw, J.-J.; Odoni, A.R.; Psaraftis, H.N.; Wilson, N.H.M.: A Heuristic Algorithm for the Multi-Vehicle Advance Request Dial-a-Ride Problem with Time Windows; Transportation Research (1986) 20B, S. 243-257.

Mertens, P.; Falk, J.; Spieck, S.: Unterstützung der Lager- und Transportlogistik durch Teil-intelligente Agenten; IM Information Management 8 (1993) 2, S. 26-31.

Psaraftis, H.N., Dynamic Vehicle Routing Problems: A Taxonomy and Survey, Paper presented at EURO/TIMS, Helsinki 1992.

Schmid, O.: Modelle zur Quantifizierung der Fehlmengenkosten als Grundlage optimaler Lieferservicestrategien bei temporärer Lieferunfähigkeit; Mannheim 1976

Shaw, M.J.; Fox, M.S.: Distributed Artificial Intelligence for Group Decision Support; Decision Support Systems (1993) 9, S. 349-367.

Smith, R.G.: The Contract Net Protocol: High Level Communication and Control in a Distributed Problem Solver; IEEE Transactions on Computers (1980) C29, S. 1104-1113.

Steeb, R.; Cammarata, S.; Hayes-Roth, F.A.; Thorndyke, P.W.; Wesson, R.B.: Distributed Intelligence for Air Fleet Control; in: Bond, A.; Gasser, L. (Eds.): Readings in Distributed Artificial Intelligence; San Mateo 1981, S. 90-101.

Weigelt, M.; Mertens, P.: Production Control with Distributed Knowledge-Based Systems; Journal of Information Science and Technology 3 (1993) 2, S. 200-211.

Will, S.: Entwurf und prototypische Realisierung eines Agentensystems zur Güterverteilung in mehrstufigen Lagerhaltungssystemen bei Engpässen; Study Thesis; Nuernberg 1993.

Organizational Multi-Agent Systems: A Process Driven Approach

R. Unland, St. Kirn, U. Wanka, G.M.P. O'Hare, S. Abbas

Abstract

There exists a need in industrial and business applications to intelligently integrate data, information and knowledge from a diverse range of sources, particularly during product design, or policy formation. Optimizing decision making requires the expertise of many agents, both computational and human, to be combined and coordinated.

The concept of an 'organization' has emerged as central to the structuring of activities of both decentralized human conglomerates and collections of intelligent problem solvers in the multi-agent systems' area. Of late, the idea of integrating these fields has emerged and within this effort one of the most important organizational problems today is that of coordination between and across organizational units. To this purpose, the paper advocates the concept of *organizational multi-agent systems.*

1. Introduction

Today, organizations are faced with rapidly changing markets, global competition, decreasing cycles of technological innovations, world wide (and just in time) availability of information, and dramatic changes in their cultural, social, and political environments. Thus, the ability of enterprises to achieve competitive advantages and to continuously survive in dynamic, even hostile environments largely depends upon their information processing and problem solving capabilities. The keywords of the current discussion such as downsizing of organizational structures, increase of local autonomy and decentralisation, cooperation and team work or business process orientation mention quite well the most important design requirements.

From intra- and inter-organizational networks or virtual organizations we learn that one of the most important problems is that of efficient coordination. These requirements can quite naturally be addressed by methods developed in Distributed Artificial Intelligence (DAI) recently. Hence, in this paper we advocate the approach of so-called *'organizational' multi agent system*. Organizational multi agent systems are quite well suited to

- provide efficient IT support to an organization's "cognitive" skills such as perception, learning, organizational problem solving and communication,

- adapt themselves to organizational aims and objectives, structures, procedures, and constraints,
- actively support business processes through the concept of multi-agent planning.

While the first two points have already been addressed in literature[100] this paper focuses on a particular issue of process orientation, that of automating business process creation through multi-agent planning. The contribution of the paper is threefold:

- It concisely reviews multi-agent planning with respect to business process engineering.
- It advocates a multi-agent planning approach to self organization and cooperative organizational problem solving within and across decentralized organizational subunits.
- It introduces generic operations to support multi-agent plan creation via plan modeling.

The approach presented is new (1) in that it intertwines business process orientation and multi-agent planning and (2), driven by a thorough investigation of organizational requirements, in that it advocates the recently emerged concept of organizational multi-agent systems.

Section 2 introduces the problem through a decentralized banking application, that of the Credit Advisory System (CAS). Section 3 briefly introduces DAI. Sections 4, 5 present a review of planning in multi-agent systems, with particular emphasis on the relationship between multi-agent planning and business process engineering. Section 6 develops towards business process-driven coordination in organizational multi-agent systems and demonstrates the power of our approach through a credit decision scenario. Finally, section 7 discusses the results.

2. Credit Advisory System (CAS)

Our application has been set up to illustrate the cooperation between a variety of local (departmental) information systems that serve local needs in providing information about business processes internal to the respective departments. To realize the potential benefit inherent to business process (re-) engineering consisting in combining these local processes and optimizing them with a global scope an intensive cooperation/negotiation procedure among these autonomous systems has to be established. These kinds of information systems are also called legacy systems and can be viewed as diverse software agents. The recorded processes

---

[100] cf. Kirn (1994) and Kirn & O'Hare (1994)

comprised by these systems correspond with an agent's plans (see section 5). In order to cooperate the agents have to coordinate their plans in a decentralized manner.

In a banking environment products are services and as such can be represented by the (standardized) processes necessary to provide them. Constructing product bundles means the combination of these processes. Therefore an effective support of the customer consultant resp. the bank as a whole is achieved by providing system assistance in constructing such bundles through process operations (see also section 6.1.). Because a description of the whole system (Multi Agent Muensterian Banking Application (MAMBA), what is mainly a compound of a credit and an investment advisory system) would be beyond the scope of this article, we will restrict ourselves in illustrating only the basic concepts of one part, namely the Credit Advisory System (CAS).

This system provides a financial consultant with advise as to how a particular customer credit ought best to be arranged. The system architecture takes its bearings from real bank organizations with their respective departments by modeling each competence center as an agent. By cooperation a solution has to be worked out, that takes into consideration both the individual aims of the customer and the departments involved and higher level aims and guidelines of the bank as such. Organized like profit-centers our individual agents are autonomous but benevolent in their cooperation behavior. The necessary coordination of the participating subunits is ensured by negotiations, that on the one hand are driven by the desire to reach one's aims and on the other are controlled by a benevolent attitude towards each other to enable the arrival at the global aims.

Such a system takes a stereotypical customer profile and specializes it through consultation to capture accurately the respective peculiarities. Based upon this and additional product specific information provided by the customer, like payback pattern, available securities and so forth, the CAS will seek to recommend a particular credit arrangement. The criteria by which this is proffered is one of fulfilling the requirements given by the individual whilst at the same time minimizing the risk of the loan and maximizing the profits of the bank in question.

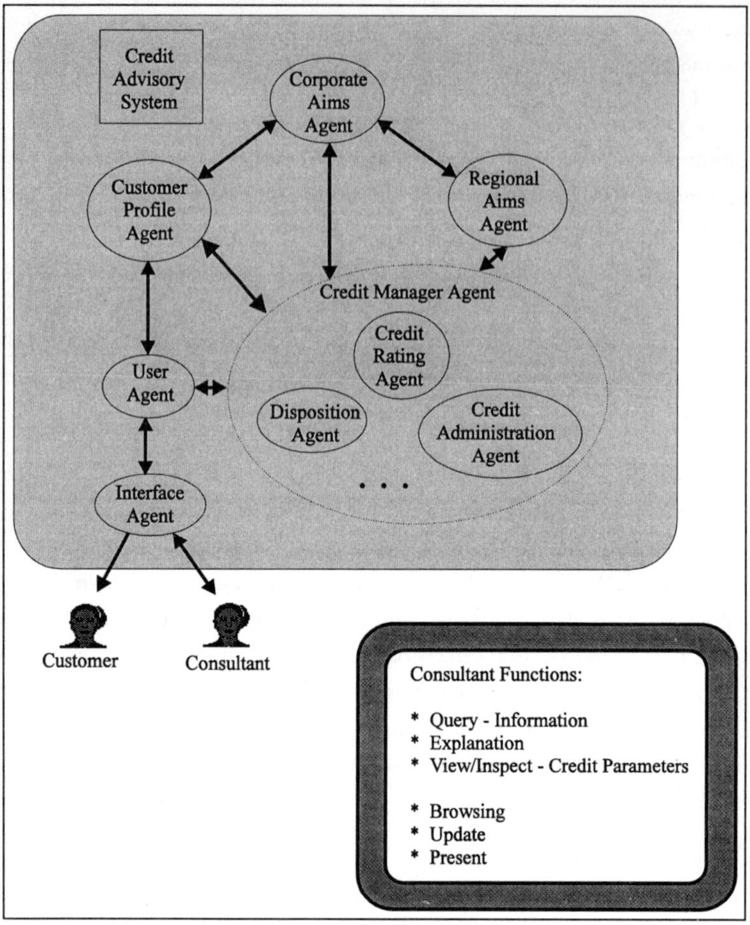

Fig. 1: Credit Advisory System (CAS)

The evaluation of such circumstances is highly complex and involves several discrete areas of expertise. Fig. 1 provides a high level picture of the constituent agent interactions. Abb. 2 provides a more detailed view of two of the agents, namely those of the Customer Profile Agent and the Credit Rating Agent. The charge of the former is to keep the customer profile up to date with respect to the corporate aims and to the information acquired about the customer during the consultation process. This profile is to be exported to other agents that make use of it through instanziating certain variables according to the respective values recorded for the customer in question. The job of the latter is to make sure that the customer is creditable and to arrange a distribution of the securities for the credit that meet the requirements of the bank. So each possible security must first be requested and then be assessed by determining a variety of values (i.e. declaration of value, risk rating, potential win / loss, etc.) in order to enable the optimal decision for which securities ought to be accepted and what their respective share should be.

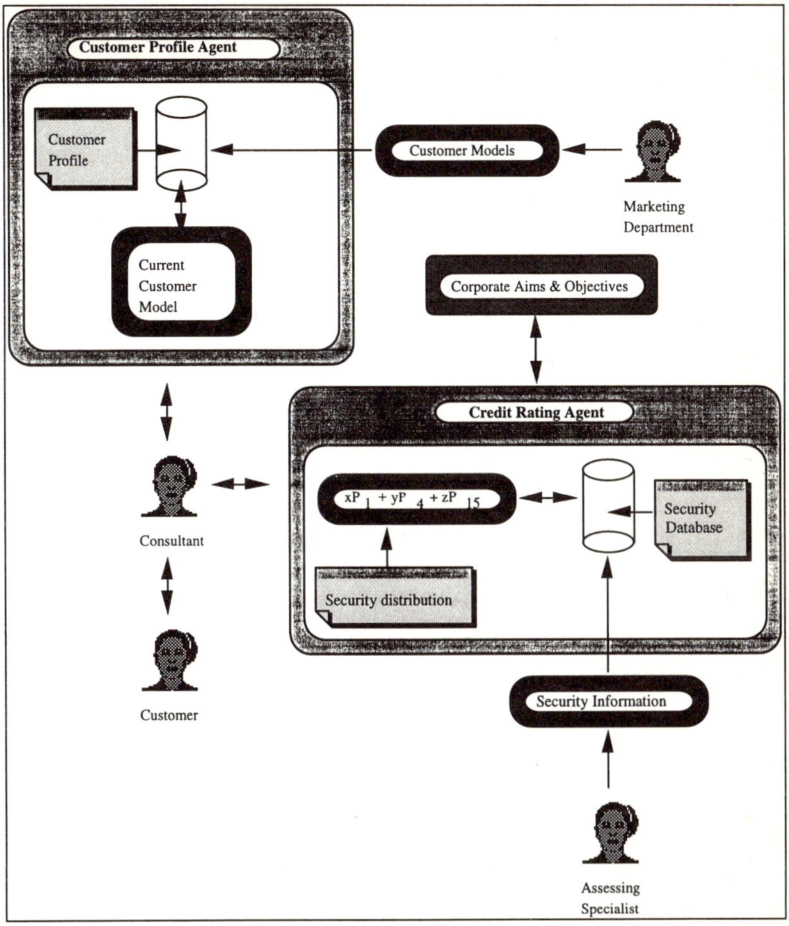

Fig. 2: The Customer Profile and Credit Rating Agents

Drawing from this credit advisory example the following organizational concepts play a key role for the design of information systems that are to support collaborative business procedures:

- **Fractalization:** Emerging from increased decentralization and autonomy (not only) the future banking organization will increasingly involve intelligent and self referencing departments (organizational fractals), which are equipped with self organization skills thus being able to recursively form complex, well-organized organizational bodies. Organizational fractals exhibit intelligent local and global coordination skills. Thus, fractalization makes large organizations extremely flexible and adaptive. It also (re-) implements learning capabilities into them.

- **Business Process Orientation:** The shift from structural to process oriented organizations aims to describe, to analyze, and to model organizational procedures on the different levels of an enterprise's information processing system. Further, the formal representation of business processes provides for an automated or at least semi-automated control of business procedures through computer based technology.

- **Computerized Organization:** Self referencing, self control, and self organization skills require extensive coordinate capabilities of each organizational unit. Going far beyond today's concept of workflow management such systems must be capable to control fully decentralized organizational procedures, and to flexibilize the coordination management of business processes as such. These issues presuppose a deep integration of the organizational and machine based information processing systems of an enterprise[101].

3. Distributed Artificial Intelligence : A Brief Review

Distributed Artificial Intelligence (DAI) represents a departure from the centralized approach advocated by mainstream Artificial Intelligence (AI). It seeks to develop intelligent systems by distributing intelligence (or expertise) across a community of semi-autonomous automated intelligent agents[102]. According to Bond and Gasser the field of DAI can be divided into the branches of parallel artificial intelligence, distributed problem solving and multi-agent systems [103].

The DAI system's agents are often physically and logically distinct and are typically capable of reasoning, planning, communicating and cooperating[104]. Agents may perform cognitive functions, react to stimuli, contain symbolic plans, or possess natural language capabilities. Shoham points out that: *"An agent is an entity whose state is viewed as consisting of mental components such as beliefs, capabilities, choices, and commitments."*[105]. An agent is thus regarded as an entity, that functions continuously and largely autonomously, with little guidance or external intervention. An agent functions in an environment which is typically highly dynamic and unpredictable, within which other agents coexist and perform.

---

[101] cf. Matsuda (1992) and Steiner et. al. (1990).
[102] cf. O'Hare and Jennings (1994).
[103] cf. Bond and Gasser (1988).
[104] cf. Hern (1988).
[105] cf. Shoman (1993).

Multi-agent systems bear many similarities with distributed systems in general. The inherent concurrency they exhibit is frequently incorporated into models and subsequent implementations using tried and tested software engineering techniques like Object Based Concurrent Programming[106]. They also bear many similarities with human organizations. However, a key distinction between them is that organizations usually have got a key motivation for their very existence (e.g., maximizing profit). Consequently these organizations exhibit a clearly defined framework within which departments and workgroups have to operate, and they provide a strict portfolio of services with an associated set of business procedures. In current multi-agent systems such procedures are modeled and controlled in an implicit manner in which they become inextricably entwined within low level actions and conversational primitives. In order to support business processes we need to develop mechanisms by which they are able to explicitly create, model and perform such business procedures. Further, a need exists for such patterns of behavior to be aggregated into higher level entities which become subject to scrutiny.

4. Planning in Multi-Agent Systems

Planning is one of the most thoroughly investigated fields within AI. In AI planning, there is usually a set of goals given together with a starting state and a set of allowable actions in a planning environment. The planning task is to find a sequence of actions that fulfills the respective constraints and that allows the system to achieve all of the desired goals. Well-known AI planning systems are STRIPS[107], and NOAH[108]. However, AI planning is not applicable to typical multi-agent settings because of its far too restrictive assumptions[109].

A multi-agent plan coordinates the activities of multiple executing agents[110]. Multi-agent planning refers to the process of creating a multi-agent plan (see Abb. 5). It may be performed by one agent alone, or by several agents in close cooperation. In distributed planning we distinguish goal driven planning (plans are constructed from scratch) from plan coordination, where existing plans are to be coordinated through cooperative activities of plan modeling.

---

[106] cf. Masini et. al. (1991) and Yonezawa (1990).
[107] cf. Fikes & Nilson (1971).
[108] cf. Sacerdoti (1977).
[109] cf. v. Martial (1992).
[110] cf. Bond & Gasser (1988).

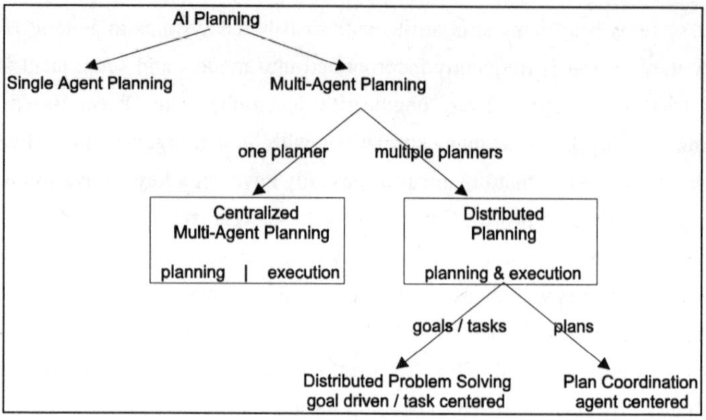

Fig. 3: Taxonomy of AI Planning Paradigms[8]

Assumptions about agents are:

- We distinguish departmental agents from individual agents. Departmental agents represent autonomous, self-contained organizational units (organizational "fractals"). They are allowed to engage the department into a particular task, they provide the departmental interface to its environment, and they act as a coordinating agent[111] within their organizational unit.

- Agents are intelligent, autonomous problem solvers. They have their own goals, resources, and knowledge. Some of their goals and resources are inherited from the organization Formal goals may (positively, negatively) interact with their private goals.

- Agents may incorporate the actions of other agents as part of their own plans (multi-agent planning). This requires the agents to exchange their plans before execution in order to allow other agents greater access to their anticipated behavior.

- Within fractalized systems there is no overall planning task to be solved in closed cooperation. Each agent wants to solve its local problems and to achieve its local aims. Thus, coordination requires them to interact and may be supported through the possibility to negotiate the distribution of benefits achieved as a result of cooperation.

- The agents in an organizational multi-agent system are benevolent, i.e. they tell the truth about their plans, and they are willing to cooperate in order to improve the outcome of the whole system, or to resolve conflicts within the system. Thus, the agents have a cordial relationship and are not hostile towards one another.

---

111 cf. v. Martial (1992).

Assumptions about plans are:

- The actions of plans require resources.
- Plans may contain temporal information. The actions of a plan are not necessarily sequential. They are even not necessarily partially ordered. Plans may contain concurrent and overlapping actions.
- Plans are created and executed in the same environment. They may involve positive and negative interactions. These interactions may occur within and across plans.
- The plans which are exchanged among agents may be partial, or not fully expanded.
- Plans may be specified on different levels of abstractions.

Most DAI research is concerned with the distribution of tasks among agents which *then* have to be coordinated. In organizational multi-agent systems we are less concerned with task allocation, but rather with the problem of how to coordinate decentralized activities *after* task allocation has been completed (i.e., plan coordination). This involves that different types of operations on plans must be supported. Going beyond current DAI research organizational multi-agent systems need to support a broad range of meta level activities such as plan creation, plan analysis and evaluation (e.g., the context in which plans are executed, time constraints, resources involved, organizational constraints, etc.). A key issue in plan coordination are plan interactions. We know, that the characterization of plan interactions can be built on a formal logical framework based on an activity-based characterization of actions[112]. This allows for the representation of concurrent actions in multiple agent plans, temporal relationships among actions, and plans at multiple levels of abstraction.

5. Multi-Agent Planning vs. Business Process (Re-) Engineering

We are now able to evaluate multi-agent planning with respect to the coordination requirements in process-oriented organizational settings. A process (e.g., a business process or organizational procedure) refers to a set of interrelated activities (e.g., a sequence) which are performed by decentralized actors in a real world setting. Business process (re-) engineering refers to the human activity of modeling business processes. It typically aims to establish smart organizational procedures which then are to be represented formally (e.g., through graphs, petri nets). Formal representations of business processes are also referred to as workflows in

[112] cf. v. Martial (1992).

current literature. They enable organizational designers to apply formal manipulations to them, and they also provide for an automated triggering and control of business processes (workflow management). However, we prefer the term *(business) process model* instead of workflow. Business process model is better suited for standard terminology in data modeling and knowledge representation as well as with the very purpose and nature of what type of operations can be performed on it. As we will see in section 6.1., these operations go far beyond what current workflow management provides.

Going back to multi-agent planning we now learn that a multi-agent plan refers more or less to what organizational designers would call a "business process". Thus, representing a multi-agent plan in a "graph-like" notation means to consider a multi-agent procedure as a structured sequence of the leaf nodes of that graph. The paths from the root node to the leaf nodes tells us how a procedure has been expanded through a sequence of stepwise refinements. Thus, the (automated) process of creating a multi-agent plan is quite similar to the (human driven) creation of a workflow. From that viewpoint the task of plan generation within a multi-agent system can quite easily be compared with the task of business process engineering within a human organization. However, in order to apply multi-agent planning to business process orientation we need to introduce an adequate organizational coordination scenario for multi-agent systems:

- **Multi-agent plans:** Multi-agent plans represent organizational procedures within a multi-agent system. They may be available through recent experiences, or they may be constructed dynamically with respect to a particular request.

- **Individuals:** Individual agents plan and act on their own. Individual plans comprise a set of individual activities (i.e., each individual plan refers to a different organizational plan!).

- **(Informal) groups:** The term "informal" within an organizational multi-agent system equals exactly what current DAI refers to as a multi-agent organization.

- **Formally established organizational units:** Each organizational unit comprises a set of local (organizational) plans, which can be processed to (organizational) node plans. Local plans are typically created through centralized multi-agent planning, where the departmental agent acts as a local coordinator. Coordination within such organizational units represents the *vertical dimension* of multi-agent coordination.

- **Networking:** The departmental agents of each organizational unit communicate the set of currently active node plans to their acquaintances in order to create global plans. The planning procedure involves distributed planning with the departmental agents acting as autonomous actors. This requires them to coordinate their node plans (together with the underpinning local plans) with respect to global plans. Thus, plan coordination typically needs to be performed top down as well as bottom up. Coordination across organizational units represents the *horizontal dimension* of multi-agent coordination.

It becomes increasingly visible that the creation of multi-agent plans is central to the approach of organizational multi-agent systems. In contrast to traditional multi-agent systems where, at request, plans are constructed from scratch, organizational multi-agent systems involve a set of pre-existing plans. These plans must be involved in plan construction *iff* their preconditions are fulfilled. This, in turn, requires organizational multi-agent systems to be equipped with a set of operators for multi-agent plan modeling and, in particular, for plan modification.

6. Coordination of Cooperating Problem Solvers: A Process-Driven Approach

6.1. Plan Construction Through Plan Modeling

Today the ability of an enterprise to achieve competitive advantages largely depends upon its capability to innovate its internal processes[113]. It is well understood also that the set of processes available to a company together with its possible combinations represent the potential set of products it is able to bring to the market. Hence, flexibility of production arises not only from the processes as such, but also from the ability of an organization to flexibly combine and modify them. Thus, before developing a set of mechanisms that are able to support coordination within and among decentralized, more or less autonomous organizational units we have to investigate which operations on process models need to be performed. We have divided these operations into four categories and because of limited space we can just give an idea of what this operations are expected to do by naming two of them for each category. We also omit examples for any of these operations, since the reader should easily be able to illustrate them by oneself through examples from one's own experience. On that basis we then are able to develop formal representations of business processes together with the respective coordination tools.

In the following presentation, process models are represented by upper case letters, while representations of single actions are represented by lower case letters.

Modification of Process Models

- A is transferred into A´.

[113] cf. Warnecke (1993). p 113

Modifications are necessitating a version management for process models.

- A inherits the characteristics of a higher process model B

  There are elements b of B, that are exported to A by B when A is called.

Abstractions on Plans and Actions

- A refines B

  There is one element $b \in B$ which is replaced by A.

- B generalizes A under view V with respect to function F

  Suppose, V is a database-like view onto plan A (examples: actors being involved in A, cost structure of A). Then, V extracts the respective information from A and maps it onto B through a function F.

Interactions among Process Models

- B calls A and halts its execution until A completed

  Most simplistic kind of a mutual dependency.

- A and B interact without synchronization.

  That may be the case, when A is able to modify parameters of B without being able to interfere directly with the execution of B.

Interactions between Processes and their Environment

- B is triggered by an event produced in A

  Simple form of a situated plan, e.g., characteristic for modeling of event triggered processes[114].

- In a certain situation both A and B are executable.

  Semantics: $A \wedge B$

---

[114] cf. Hoffmann et. al. (1992) and Keller et. al. (1992).

At this point it is important to understand that the operations mentioned above may not only be performed in isolation but can also be combined into complex aggregates (see section 6.2.). All that is required then, is to create a set of combination rules in order to establish a well-defined semantics of aggregated operations.

6.2. Example: Plan Refinement in CAS

For our planning procedure there are two dimensions we have to model appropriately.

- Process dimension:

  First of all we have to represent processes that are actions and knowledge about these actions i.e. temporal constraints or their ordering with respect to certain conditions. Formally processes consist of two sets. The first set, A, contains the actions that the respective process is made of and the second set, COND, is filled with constraints for the actions or the relationships (sequential / parallel) between them.

  process = (A, COND)

  There are two kinds of actions: Actions that are atomic with respect to their domain and actions that have to be refined (made more concrete) in order to become operational.

  The planning procedure mainly consists of repeated refinements of actions that are part of a certain process and are not yet atomic. The repetition stops when a process is build only out of atomic actions.

- History dimension:

  So the second dimension we have to model is the history of our planning procedure. It could be visualized by a tree that represents processes at various levels of abstraction with the nodes being actions and the edges showing the refining relationships from more abstract to a more concrete ones. So the leafs of our tree might be viewed as the most operational actions reached by this phase of planning.

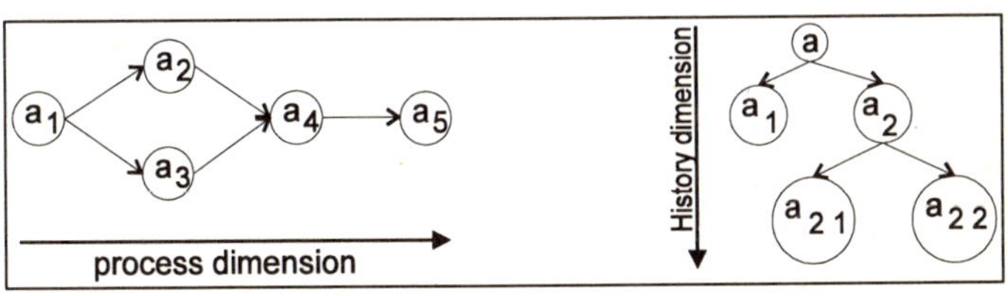

Fig. 4: Process Dimensions

We have no *static* planning i.e. first the plan is being developed and afterwards it is executed (separation of planning- and runtime) but we do have *dynamic* planning i.e. planning and execution is intervened. Therefore in the latter case it is possible to have the refinement procedure made dependent on the actual situation at runtime.

A plan representing processes that fulfills the requirements stated above is defined as follows:

$$plan = (A, HIS, COND) \text{ with } HIS = A \times A$$

Set A contains all actions included in our plan (nodes in the resp. tree), the set HIS consists of tupels representing the refinement relation or history dimension between those actions (edges in the resp. tree) and the set COND is composed of all the temporal constraints that are important to model the process dimension.

Let p = (A, HIS, COND) and p' = (A', HIS', COND') be plans then the refinement of action a by the plan p' is defined by

$$\text{refine}(a, p')(p) = (A \cup A', HIS \cup HIS' \cup \{(a,a') \mid a' \in A' \wedge \text{root}(a',p')\}, COND \cup COND')$$
$$\text{with root}(a', p') \Leftrightarrow \neg\exists a'' \in A' : (a'', a') \in HIS'$$

To make it more clear the planning procedure will be explained by refining a plan describing necessary actions to be executed by the Credit Advisory System that was introduced in section 2.

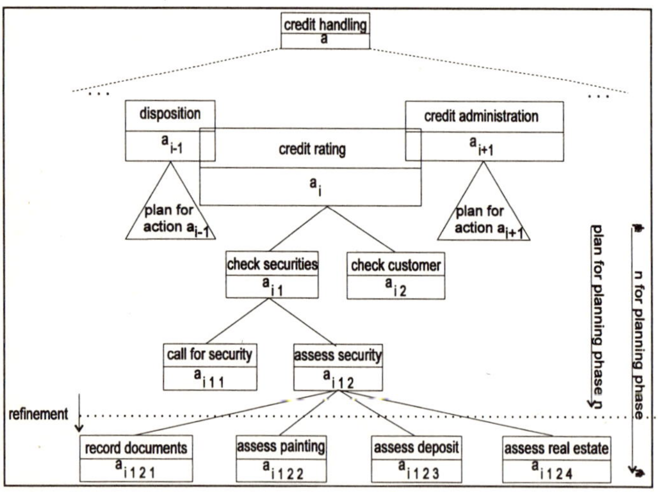

Fig. 5: Plan Refinement

In order to perform a comprehensive task, e.g., a credit application, that exceeds the capabilities of a single agent, a group of agents has to cooperate with each other. This is illustrated in Abb. 5 by the overlapping rectangles which represent the respective tasks or actions of the disposition agent, the credit rating agent and the credit administration agent. The agent we will focus on is the credit rating agent, a subagent of the departmental agent credit manager. We will not elaborate on the necessary consulting process between different agents, but on the mode a single agent produces his local plan for the actions he is able to perform himself.

At planning phase n the top part of the plan presented in fig. 5 has been constructed.

For our example we will concentrate on the actions a_{i11} a_{i12}. The first one is atomic and can be realized by a system generated letter, while the second is not atomic in the credit domain. The second action may be refined by the action a_{i121} and depending on the kind of security the customer did provide dynamically by actions a_{i122}, a_{i123}, a_{i124}. Because dynamics and context-sensitivity of plan refinement is beyond the scope of this paper, we will not elaborate on this. For our example and the following definitions we assume static planning. Therefore, the action a_{i12} could be refined by the action a_{i121} and the three alternative checking procedures a_{i122}, a_{i123} and a_{i124} specialized to the respective kind of security (picture, real estate or deposit) the customer provided.

The following predicate SEQ(a, b) stands for a sequence of the actions a and b, the predicate PRE(a, c) stands for a precondition c that must be fulfilled in order to make action a executable.

Let $a_{i12} \in A$ and p = (A, HIS, COND) be the plan before the refinement. The non atomic action a_{i12} is to be refined by the plan p' = ({a_{i121}, a_{i122}, a_{i123}, a_{i124}}, ∅, {SEQ(a_{i121}, a_{i122}), SEQ(a_{i121}, a_{i123}), SEQ(a_{i121}, a_{i124}), PRE(a_{i122}, picture(security_object)), PRE(a_{i123}, deposit(security_object)), PRE(a_{i124}, real_estate(security_object))}).

So refine (a_{i12}, p') (p) =

(A∪{a_{i121}, a_{i122}, a_{i123}, a_{i124}}, HIS∪{(a_{i12}, a_{i121}), (a_{i12}, a_{i122}), (a_{i12}, a_{i123}), (a_{i12}, a_{i124})}, COND ∪{ SEQ(a_{i121}, a_{i122}), SEQ(a_{i121}, a_{i123}), SEQ(a_{i121}, a_{i124}), PRE(a_{i122}, picture(security_object)), PRE(a_{i123}, deposit(security_object)), PRE(a_{i124}, real_estate(security_object))}).

7. Conclusions

This paper addressed the question of how coordination in decentralized, process-oriented organizations can be efficiently supported through modern information technology. Addressing the issue of cooperative organizational problem solving within such settings we advocated a

Distributed AI-based approach to system design. As a starting point the paper introduced the decentralized Credit Advisory System. Drawing from the organizational requirements imposed by the application we reviewed the different concepts of multi-agent planning, which bear a lot of similarities with the concept of business process orientation. As a result of that review we suggested concentrating future analysis on the similarities between multi-agent plans and workflows, where workflows are formal representations of business processes. Taking this approach has allowed us to apply multi-agent planning as a tool to achieve, at least partially, automated business process (re-) engineering. On this basis the paper proceeded to the modeling and modification of multi-agent plans. We then introduced two sets of interaction types (interactions among process models, interactions among a process model with its environment) together with two sets of modeling operations (modifications, abstractions), which perform on process models. The depth of this approach was demonstrated by a credit application example in which we show how a multi-agent system creates a multi-agent plan through plan refinement instead of doing it from scratch like current multi-agent systems.

By this way the contribution of this paper can be summarized as follows:

- It provides a concise review of multi-agent planning with particular respect to business process (re-) engineering.
- It provides a set of operators which can be applied to business process models. By these operators a multi-agent system can be enabled to create and manipulate business process models and to adapt its own behavior according to the rules and procedures described by these models.

These results contribute in making Distributed AI methods productive for such applications like business process orientation and enterprise integration. Further, the results of the paper are new in that they provide a significant contribution towards deeper integration of organizational theory and the design of distributed and cooperative information systems.

Acknowledgments

This work was funded in part through an SERC Studentship awarded to S. Abbas; through the British Council and the DAAD Anglo-German Academic Research Grant (ARC, 313-ARC-VII-93/89/scu) entitled Multi-Agent INtentionality (MAIN); and through a Research Grant donated by the German Research Foundation (DFG, Un 94/1-1).

References

Bond, A.; Gasser, L.: Readings in Distributed Artificial Intelligence, Morgan Kaufmann Publishers, San Mateo, CA., 1988.

Fikes, R.E.; Nilsson, N.: STRIPS: a new approach to the application of theorem proving to problem solving, Artificial Intelligence, 3(3-4), pp. 189-208, 1971.

Hern, L. E. C.: On Distributed Artificial Intelligence, The Knowledge Engineering Review, Cambridge University Press, 1988.

Hoffmann, W., Kirsch, J.; Scheer, A.-W.: Modellierung mit Ereignisgesteuerten Prozeßketten (Methodenhandbuch, Stand: Dezember 1992). Universität des Saarlandes, Institut für Wirtschaftsinformatik, Januar 1993.

Keller, G.; Nüttgens, M.; Scheer, A.-W.: Semantische Prozeßmodellierung auf der Grundlage "Ereignisgesteuerter Prozeßketten (EPK)", Universität des Saarlandes, Institut für Wirtschaftsinformatik, Januar 1992.

Kirn, St.; O'Hare, G. M. P.: Organisational Intelligence:A Distributed AI Perspective, in: Kirn, St., and O'Hare, G. M. P, Towards The Intelligent Organization: The Coordination Perspective, Springer-Verlag, 1996 (Forthcoming).

Kirn, St.: Supporting Human Experts Collaborative Work: Modelling Organizational Context Knowledge in Cooperative Information Systems, In: John H. Connolly, Ernest Edmonds (eds.): CSCW and AI. Springer Series on CSCW, pp127-139, 1994.

Malone, T. W.; Crowston, K.; Lee, J.; Pentland, B.: Tools for inventing organizations: Toward a handbook of organizational processes, CCS WP #141, Sloan School WP #3562-93. Massachusetts Institute of Technology, Sloan School of Management, Cambridge, Mass., May 1993.

v. Martial, F.: Coordinating Plans of Autonomous Agents, Lecture Notes in Artificial Intelligence, No. 610. Springer-Verlag, Berlin, Heidelberg. Germany 1992.

Matsuda, T.: Organizational Intelligence: Its Significance as a Process and as a Product, In Proceedings of the International Conference on Economics/ Management and Information Technology 92, Tokyo, Japan, August 31-September 4, pp219-222, 1992.

Masini, G.; Napoli, A.; Colnet, D.; Leonard, D.; Tombre, K.: Object Oriented Languages, The A.P.I.C. Series, Harcourt, Brace, Jovanovich, Publishers, 1991.

O'Hare, G.M.P.; Jennings, N., (eds.): Theoretical Foundations of Distributed Artificial Intelligence, Sixth Generation Computer Technology Series, Wiley Inter-Science, 1995.

Sacerdoti, E.D.: Structure for Plans and Behavior, New York, Elsevier Publishers, North-Holland, 1977.

Shoman, Y.: Agent-Oriented Programming, Artificial Intelligence, 60 pp51-92, 1993.

Steiner, D.; Mahling, D.; Haugeneder, H.: Human Computer Cooperative Work, In: Proceedings of the 10th International Workshop on Distributed Artificial Intelligence. MCC Technical Report ACT-AI-355-90, Austin, Texas, 1990.

Warnecke, H.-J.: Revolution der Unternehmenskultur, Springer-Verlag, 1993.

Yonezawa, A., (ed.): ABCL An Object-Oriented Concurrent System, MIT Press, Cambridge, Mass., 1990.

Development and Simulation of Methods for Scheduling and Coordinating Decentralized Job Shops Using Multi-Computer Systems

Oliver Holthaus, Otto Rosenberg, Hans Ziegler

Abstract

This paper presents a new simulation methodology for scheduling and coordinating decentralized job shops using multi-computer systems. The parallel working subsystems of an integrated production system are distributed across a network of computers. Utilizing the special structure of parallel processor architectures new coordination and scheduling rules for job shops are designed and evaluated. The simulation experiments show that the performance of conventional scheduling rules is significantly improved using the developed coordination approach. Furthermore the run-time of the distributed simulation model comes closer to real-time response of job shop simulations.

Keywords: Job Shop Scheduling, Dispatching Rules, Coordination Rules, Distributed Simulation, Multi-Computer Systems.

1. Introduction

The scheduling or sequencing problem can be stated as follows: N jobs must be processed by M machines or work stations within a given time period to optimize some objectives. Each job consists of a specific set of operations which have to be processed according to a given technical precedence order (routing). An operation may require a deterministic or a stochastic processing time. The production system consists of M subsystems each of them may comprise some identical parallel working machines. If the precedence order of the operations is identical for all jobs the problem is called *flow shop scheduling problem* as opposed to a *job shop scheduling problem* where the jobs may have different sequences of operations. If all jobs are available at the beginning of the scheduling process the problem is called *static;* if the set of jobs may change over time the problem is called *dynamic*. In a *deterministic* problem all parameters are known with certainty. If at least one parameter is probabilistic the problem is called *stochastic*. The aim of the planning process is to find a schedule for processing all jobs to optimize one or several goals (for instance, *minimizing mean flow time* or *minimizing the number of tardy jobs*). For efficient planning and controlling of production operations scheduling has to be performed quickly, if possible at real-time.

Prior research focused on static deterministic scheduling problems. In theory it is possible to determine optimal schedules for static sequencing problems. In practice the computation of optimal solutions is not possible since these problems belong to the class of *NP-hard problems*[115]. Therefore, the existence of algorithms with a computation time polynomially bounded in the problem size is very unlikely. The time requirements for calculating optimal processing orders for typical problems in reality would be too time consuming. In the last decades many heuristic methods have been developed to solve deterministic scheduling problems[116]. For scheduling dynamic stochastic job shops a variety of dispatching rules has been proposed and simulation models have been formulated to analyze their efficiency under various conditions and with respect to different goals[117].

Despite of their importance in reality decentralized scheduling rules based upon an efficient coordination of the subsystems up to now have found only scarce attention by researchers. Since this seems to be one of the major weaknesses of existing production planning and control systems, we have concentrated on the development of dynamic stochastic job shop scheduling models, the design of new efficient rules for solving these problems, and the analysis of their performance using distributed simulation models on multi-computer systems. Based on empirical data the performance of conventional scheduling rules has been analyzed and new improved scheduling rules for dynamic stochastic job shops have been developed. Utilizing the special structure of parallel computers new coordination and scheduling rules for achieving efficient coordination of decentralized and parallel working subsystems of an integrated production system are designed and evaluated with regard to economical and technical criteria. Furthermore, the application of parallel computers for planning and controlling the daily production of a manufacturing system by real-time simulation is studied.

Section 2 characterizes the dynamic stochastic job shop scheduling problem in detail. Section 3 presents some traditional dispatching rules and an approach for the decentralized coordination of scheduling rules. Section 4 shows the basic structure of a distributed simulation model for job shops. Section 5 analyzes the distributed simulation model and the coordination mechanism. Section 6 summarizes the essential results.

2. Characterization of the Dynamic Stochastic Job Shop Scheduling Problem

The model of the job shop scheduling problem is based on the following assumptions[118]:

---

[115] cf. Garey & Johnson (1979), Rinnooy Kan (1976)

[116] cf. Baker (1974), Blazewicz, Ecker, Schmidt & Weglarz (1993), French (1982)

[117] cf. Haupt (1989), Ramasesh (1990)

[118] cf. Haupt (1989), Ramasesh (1990)

Each subsystem comprises a set of identical machines. All machines are continuously available, this means breakdowns or interruptions for maintenance are not considered. Each machine processes only one job at a time. Each job can be processed by only one machine at a time. Each operation started has to be completed without interruption, i.e., job preemption is not allowed. The technological order of the operations of a job is fixed. The processing times are independent of the job order. Set-up times or transportation times are included in the processing times. The jobs arrive in the shop continuously in time. Processing times, release times and routings are stochastic.

The following notations are used:

N: number of jobs [-]

M: number of machines [-]

r_i: release time of job i [tu] (tu = time units)

k_i: number of operations of job i [-]

p_{ij}: processing time of the j-th operation of job i [tu]

p_i: total processing time of job i [tu]; $p_i = \sum_{j=1}^{k_i} p_{ij}$

m_{ij}: machine on which the j-th operation of job i has to be processed [-]

d_i: due date of job i [tu]

d_{ij}: operation due date of the j-th operation of job i [tu]

C_i: completion time of job i [tu]

F_i: flow time of job i [tu]; $F_i = C_i - r_i$

$\overline{F}$: mean flow time [tu]; $\overline{F} = (1/N)\sum_{i=1}^{N} F_i$

$F_{\max}$: maximum flow time [tu]; $F_{\max} = \max\{F_i | 1 \le i \le N\}$

T_i: tardiness of job i [tu]; $T_i = \max\{0, C_i - d_i\}$

$\%T$: percentage of tardy jobs [%];

$\%T = 100 \cdot NT / N$, NT = number of tardy jobs [-]

$\overline{T}$: mean tardiness [tu]; $\overline{T} = (1/N)\sum_{i=1}^{N} T_i$

T_{max}: maximum tardiness [tu]; $T_{max} = \max\{T_i | 1 \le i \le N\}$

We are looking for job sequences (schedules) that optimize some objectives. In the following we consider objectives based on flow time and due dates, chosen as substitutes for economic goals[119].

Minimization of mean flow time $\overline{F}$ and *minimization of maximum flow time* F_{max} are defined by the times necessary to complete the jobs. The minimization of mean flow time tends to minimize the costs of capital while the minimization of maximum flow time is used if there are costs which increase with the maximum time for job completion. The due date based objectives *minimization of the percentage of tardy jobs, minimization of mean tardiness* and *minimization of maximum tardiness* are defined by the spans of time between the due dates and the completion times of late jobs. Minimization of mean tardiness is equivalent to minimization of costs caused by tardy jobs, for instance penalties per days of delivery delay. The minimization of maximum tardiness is reasonable if the penalties for tardiness increase more than proportional with the length of the delays.

3. Job Shop Scheduling and Coordination Rules

In dynamic stochastic job shops jobs arrive continuously over time. The release times, routings and processing times of the jobs are stochastic. For dynamic stochastic scheduling problems it is neither theoretically nor practically possible to compute optimal schedules in advance because only for jobs currently in the shop processing sequences on the various machines can be determined. The two basic objectives of scheduling dynamic stochastic job shops are to process the jobs as fast as possible and to complete them on time. With respect to these objectives job sequences are determined using decentralized *scheduling rules*.

3.1. Scheduling Rules

As soon as a machine becomes available, it has to be decided which of the waiting jobs (if there is any in the queue) should be processed next. The way a machine is selecting the job to process next from the set of waiting jobs is called *priority, scheduling,* or *dispatching* rule. Typical priority rules are for instance[120]:

FIFO (*first in, first out*): The jobs are processed in the order they arrive at the machine.

---

[119] cf. Haupt (1989)
[120] cf. Baker (1984), Blackstone, Phillips & Hogg (1982), Haupt (1989), Russell, Dar-El & Taylor (1987)

SPT (*shortest processing time*): Highest priority is given to the job with the shortest processing time.

MOD (*modified operation due date*): The modified operation due date is the maximum of the operation due date and the earliest possible completion time of the operation. The job with the smallest modified operation due date will be processed next.

S/OPN (*slack per number of operations remaining*): Highest priority is given to the job with the smallest ratio of slack to number of operations remaining, where the slack of a job is defined by the difference of the job due date and the earliest possible completion time of the job.

NINQ (*number of jobs in the queue of its next operation*): The job whose next operation has to be processed by the machine with the smallest queue of waiting jobs is selected for processing.

COVERT (*cost over time*): Highest priority is given to the job with the largest ratio of estimated costs for tardiness to processing time.

The *local* priority rules FIFO, SPT, MOD and S/OPN only require information about the jobs currently waiting at the machine under consideration, whereas the *global* scheduling rules NINQ and COVERT are based on information about jobs in other queues or other machines. Using simulation models, the relative performance of the different scheduling rules under various conditions can be analyzed[121].

3.2. Coordination Rules

In general, the schedule for each machine m is determined by evaluating the set of jobs currently waiting in its queue. The determination of the schedule for machine m is not influenced by the schedules of other machines $\hat{m}$, $\hat{m} \neq m$. Obviously, these M *isolated* solutions, which have been determined without considering the actual states of the connected machines, do not necessarily lead to a good solution for the overall production system. Better performance can be achieved by coordinating these M schedules, i.e., considering not only the status of a given machine m, but also the status of all machines $\hat{m}$ which *precede* machine m in the processing of some jobs. A rule describing such activities of coordination between the machines is called *coordination rule*. We will next present a newly developed coordination

[121] cf. Baker (1984), Blackstone, Phillips & Hogg (1982), Conway (1965a), Conway (1965b)

rule, called *look ahead job demanding* (LAJD). This rule is based on look ahead information[122] about machine idle times and a mechanism for demanding and supplying jobs.

The rule LAJD can be described as follows:

If the *work in stock* of a machine m (ws_m) falls below a specific *work in stock bound* (wsb), machine m initiates a job demand inquiry to all other machines $\hat{m}$. The work in stock of machine m is defined as the sum of processing times of jobs waiting in the queue of machine m plus the remaining processing time of the job currently served by machine m. If there are jobs in the queue of machine $\hat{m}$ which after having been processed by this machine have to be processed by machine m, machine $\hat{m}$ offers these jobs to machine m. Among the jobs offered, machine m chooses the job which will arrive at the earliest possible time after machine m will become idle. After the selection of this job the corresponding machine $\hat{m}$ is instructed to process this job next. If a machine $\hat{m}$ receives processing instructions from different machines at the same time, the machine chooses one instruction randomly and informs the corresponding machine m that the requested job will be processed next. The other machines receive a refusal of their processing instruction. If there are no jobs offered to machine m or machine m receives a refusal of its processing instruction, machine m starts a new job demand after a specified time period, for instance after 10% of the minimum processing time of a job. Contrary to the first definition of LAJD[123], where the coordination is initiated once a machine starts the processing of the last waiting job, the coordination is already started by a machine m as soon as ws_m falls below the specified parameter wsb.

4. A Distributed Simulation Model for Job Shops

In this section we present the basic structure of a distributed simulation model for the event-oriented simulation[124] of dynamic stochastic job shops.

---

[122] cf. Itoh, Huang & Enkawa (1993), Koulamas & Smith (1988), Nawijn (1985), Nawijn (1990), Rosenwein, Stone & Wahls (1991), Zeestraten (1990)

[123] cf. Holthaus, Rosenberg & Ziegler (1993)

[124] cf. Askew, Carpenter, Chalker, Hey, Moore, Nicole & Pritchard (1988), Fujimoto (1990), Mattern & Mehl (1989), Misra (1986), Nicol (1992), Papaspyropoulos & Maritsas (1989), Philipps & Cuthbert (1991), Scheiber (1990)

4.1. General Structure of the Simulation Model

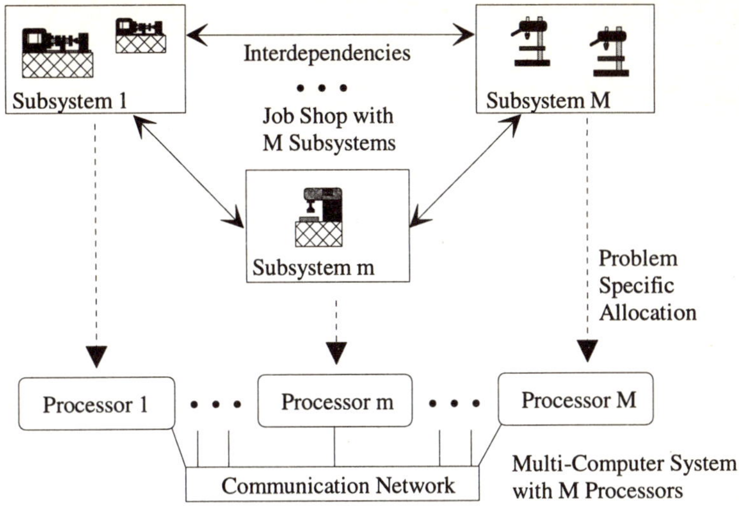

Figure 1: General Structure of the Distributed Simulation Approach

The distributed simulation model for dynamic stochastic job shop scheduling utilizes the parallelism existing in a real job shop. This parallelism is used directly by placing each subsystem (or set of subsystems) of the simulated job shop on one processor of the multi-computer system. Figure 1 shows the general structure of this approach. The multi-computer system comprises M processors (for instance, transputers[125]) connected by an interconnection network and communicating through messages[126]. In the simulation model coordination is realized by communication between processors (here: transputers).

4.2. Components of the Simulation Model

Figure 2 shows the detailed structure of the simulation model that maps a job shop with M subsystems on a multi-computer system with P processors ($P \leq M$).The simulation model consists of one *control processor* and a set of *simulation processors*.

[125] cf. Mitchell, Thompson, Manson & Brookes (1990)
[126] cf. Hoare (1985)

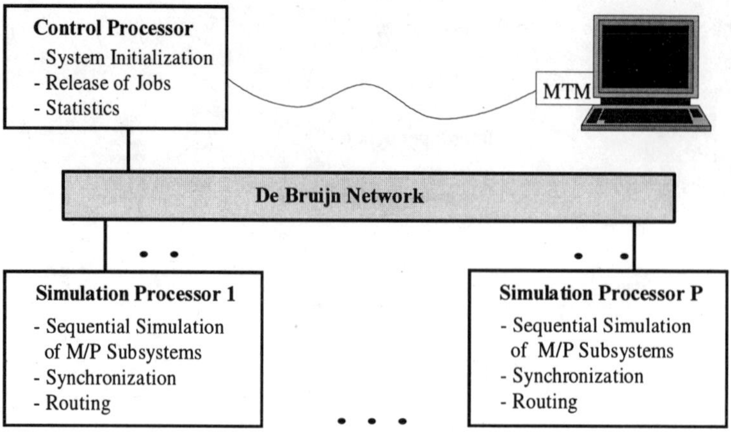

Figure 2: Special Structure of the Simulation Model

The control processor releases the jobs into the system according to empirical data or theoretical probability functions. After receiving information about the completed jobs the control processor evaluates them for data analysis. Each simulation processor uses a special process to sequentially simulate a set of subsystems/machines. This process simulates the activities for all machines within the set. Typical activities are: selecting a waiting job for processing on a machine available for operation, simulating the processing of jobs of the allocated machines and transmitting a processed job to the next machine which belongs to the same processor, or initiating its transfer to a machine allocated to a different processor. Each processor is able to communicate with all the other processors using routing processes and messages which are routed through a *de Bruijn* interconnection network[127]. Special timing processes synchronize simulation times.

4.3. Physical Configuration of the Simulation Model

The presented simulation methodology has been designed and implemented on the *Parsytec Supercluster SC320* of *the Paderborn Center of Parallel Computing* ($(PC)^2$) using the *ANSI C Toolset*. The SC 320 is a multi-computer system containing 320 T800-transputers, separated in 20 clusters with 16 processors each. Network control units are applied to dynamically configure any network with a maximum degree of four. A de Bruijn network of dimension k configured for the simulation model contains $P = 2^k$ nodes. The set of nodes V and set of edges E are defined as follows:

---

[127] cf. Leighton (1992)

$V = \{x_k x_{k-1} \ldots x_1 | x_i \in \{0,1\}\}$ and

$$E = \{\{x_k \ldots x_2 y, y x_k \ldots x_2\} | x_k \ldots x_2 y \in V\} \cup \{\{x_k \ldots x_2 y, \bar{y} x_k \ldots x_2\} | x_k \ldots x_2 y \in V\},$$

with $\overline{0} = 1$ and $\overline{1} = 0$. Figure 3 shows a de Bruijn network of dimension 3 (8 simulation processors) with one control processor (CP).

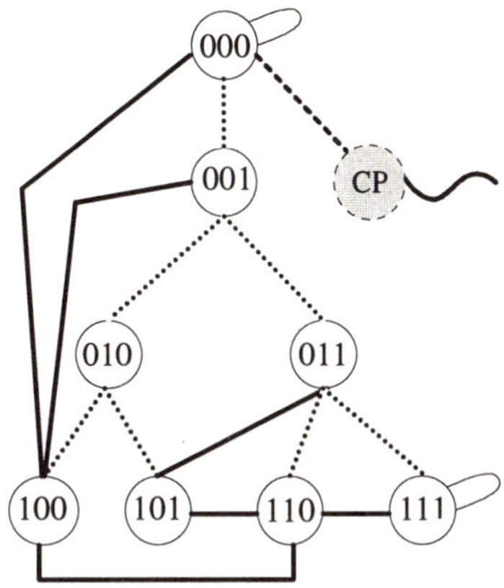

Figure 3: De Bruijn Network of Dimension 3

De Bruijn networks have a maximum degree of four, a diameter of $\log P = k$, and contain a binary tree. Based on this binary tree (dotted lines) a synchronization mechanism has been developed to ensure consistency in simulation time and event order. The synchronization of P processors requires $2 \cdot \log P = 2k$ steps.

5. Results of the Simulation Experiments

A variety of production systems with up to 256 subsystems has been simulated and analyzed using the distributed simulation model and transputer networks with 4 - 64 processors. The performance of conventional scheduling rules and the developed coordination rules has been investigated. In the following sections a short representative selection of our computational results is presented.

5.1. Analysis of the Scheduling and Coordination Rules

In each simulation run 4000 jobs were released into the shop. Only the jobs indexed from 1001 to 3000 were used for data analysis. Processing times and routings were uniformly and interarrival times were exponentially distributed. To determine the due date we weighted the total processing time with a due date factor c: $d_i = r_i + c \cdot p_i$. In the simulation experiments different scheduling rules with and without coordination rule LAJD were studied.

The simulation results prove the efficiency of the coordination rule LAJD which reduces the mean flow time $\overline{F}$. The scale of mean flow time reduction and the effect on maximum flow time depends on the shop utilization and the work in stock bound *wsb*. The scale of improving $\%T$, $\overline{T}$, and T_{max} is also effected by the size of the due date factor c. We next analyzed how the efficiency of LAJD depends on *wsb*. As a representative example we selected the scheduling rules SPT and COVERT and a shop utilization of 90%.

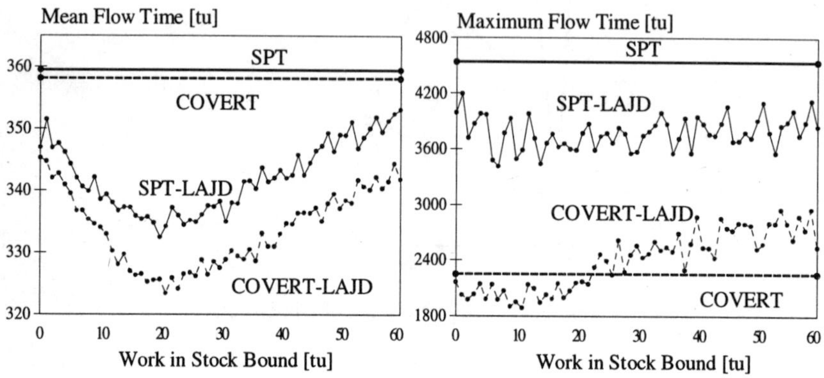

Figure 4: $\overline{F}$ and F_{max} in Dependence of wsb

Figure 4 shows how $\overline{F}$ and F_{max} depend on *wsb*. The parameter *wsb* was increased from 0 tu to 60 tu with a step size of 1 tu. For these experiments the processing times were chosen randomly between 10 and 20 tu. On $wsb \in [0,20]$ tu, $\overline{F}$ decreases in *wsb*. Best performance was observed for *wsb* between 10 and 30 tu, whereas for *wsb*-values above 30 tu the reduction was diminishing with increasing *wsb*. Considering F_{max} and SPT, the improvement of the maximum flow time is independent of *wsb*, whereas with regard to COVERT the coordination yields reduced F_{max}-values up to a *wsb* of about 20 and then tends towards increasing F_{max}-values.

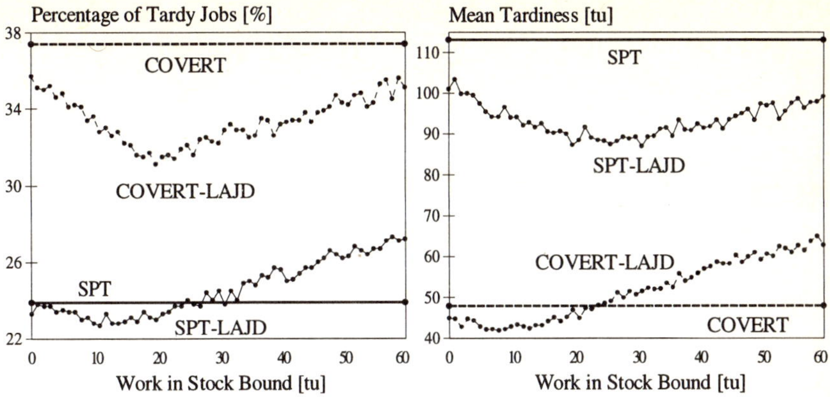

Figure 5: $\%T$ and $\overline{T}$ in Dependence of wsb

Figure 5 shows how $\%T$ and $\overline{T}$ depend on *wsb*. We used a due date factor of $c = 4$. COVERT-LAJD performed significantly better than COVERT with respect to $\%T$ within the whole analyzed range of *wsb*. With SPT the largest reductions were realized in the *wsb*-range [10,20], whereas over 25 tu the $\%T$-values were increasing by coordination with increasing *wsb*. Considering the $\overline{T}$-values SPT-LAJD yields lower values than SPT within the whole analyzed range of *wsb*. For COVERT-LAJD this statement is valid only for *wsb* up to 25 tu. For *wsb*s exceeding this bound the use of COVERT-LAJD results in higher values of $\overline{T}$ in relation to the use of COVERT.

5.2. Analysis of the Distributed Simulation Model

Our method of allocating the subsystems/machines to the processors depends on the number of subsystems in the job shop and the size of the processor network. In case of uniform distributed routings and P processors, the machines are allocated to the processors by placing machine j on processor p if $j \bmod P \equiv p$. In case of non-uniform distributed or empirical routings, clustering algorithms[128] have to be used to determine an allocation minimizing the interdependencies between the processors.

Figure 6 shows that the time required for synchronization depends on the number of processors. 5000 times synchronizing a network of P processors require about $5.1 \cdot \log P$ seconds. Except for the constant factor, which depends on the size of data to transmit and the transmission rate between two processors, the theoretical time for synchronization is achieved in practice.

---

[128] cf. Bock (1974), Vogel (1975)

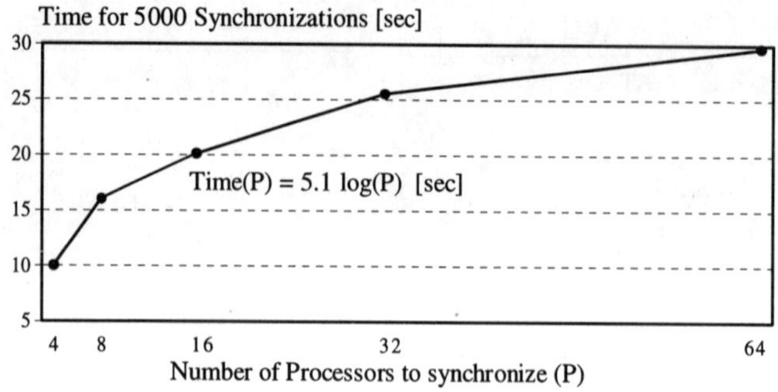

Figure 6: Time Requirements for Synchronization

To analyze the time requirements of the distributed simulation model job shops of different sizes have been simulated on transputer networks with varying numbers of processors. We now present the execution times for simulating job shops with 256 subsystems.

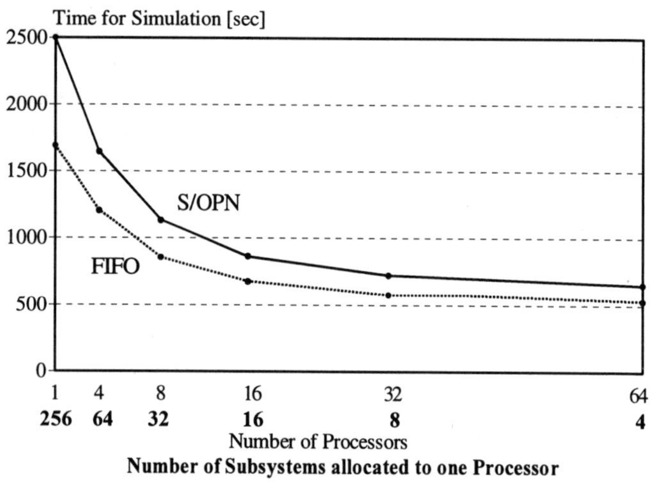

Figure 7: Time Requirements for Simulation

Figure 7 illustrates the execution times of the simulation model as a function of the number of processors and the number of subsystems allocated to one processor using the scheduling rules FIFO and S/OPN. In comparison to sequential simulation (placing all 256 subsystems on one processor) the use of additional processors results in a reduction of time requirements. A network of 4 or 8 simulation processors yields the largest increase in speedup. Networks of 16 and 32 transputers produce further speedups, whereas a 64-processor network insignificantly reduces the execution time compared to a 32-processor network. The different execution times of the priority rules FIFO and S/OPN can be explained by differences in the time required for priority calculations.

The small execution time reduction using a 64-processor network as opposed to a 32-processor network is explained by the fact that the calculation time reduction of the additional processors is almost compensated by increased communication and synchronization time. These small speedup improvements have been noticed every time when less than 8 subsystems were allocated to one processor. A variety of simulation experiments analyzing smaller job shops has shown similar behavior. For every size of a production system there exists an ideal range for the number of processors that minimizes execution time.

6. Summary

We have presented a distributed simulation model for dynamic stochastic job shop scheduling. The simulation model contains a set of simulation processors and one control processor which were connected through a special communication network. Using the special structure of parallel computers a coordination rule for achieving an efficient coordination of the decentralized subsystems has been designed and analyzed. A large number of simulation experiments has demonstrated the efficiency of the coordination rule LAJD. Flow time and due date based objective values could be improved simultaneously. The analysis of execution times has shown that depending on the number of processors and the number of subsystems allocated to one processor different speedups could be achieved. Considering simulations critical in time, for every size of a production system there exists an ideal range for the number of processors that minimizes execution time.

Acknowledgement: The authors are indebted to Assistant Professor Ulrich Thonemann, Stanford University, Departement of Industrial Engineering, for many helpful comments and suggestions for improving the language and grammar of this article.

References

Askew, C.R.; Carpenter, D.B.; Chalker, J.T.; Hey, A.J.G.; Moore, M.; Nicole, D.A.; Pritchard, D.J.: Monte Carlo Simulation on Transputer Arrays; Parallel Computing 14 (1988) 6, pp. 247-258.

Baker, K.R.: Introduction to Sequencing and Scheduling; New York 1974.

Baker, K.R.: Sequencing Rules and Due-Date Assignments in a Job Shop; Management Science 30 (1984) 9, pp. 1093-1104.

Blackstone, J.H.; Phillips, D.T.; Hogg, G.L.: A State-of-the-Art Survey of Dispatching Rules for Manufacturing Job Shop Operations; International Journal of Production Research 20 (1982) 1, pp. 27-45.

Blazewicz, J.; Ecker, K.; Schmidt, G.; Weglarz, J.: Scheduling in Computer and Manufacturing Systems; Berlin 1993.

Bock, H.H.: Automatische Klassifikation; Göttingen 1974.

Conway, R.W.: Priority Dispatching and Work in Process Inventory in a Job Shop; Journal of Industrial Engineering 16 (1965a) 2, pp. 123-130.

Conway, R.W.: Priority Dispatching and Job Lateness in a Job Shop; Journal of Industrial Engineering 16 (1965b) 4, pp. 228-237.

French, S.: Sequencing and Scheduling: An Introduction to the Mathematics of the Job-Shop; Chichester 1982.

Fujimoto, R.: Parallel Discrete Event Simulation; Communications of the ACM 33 (1990) 10, pp. 31-53.

Garey, M.R.; Johnson, D.S.: Computers and Intractability: A Guide to the Theory of NP-Completeness; San Francisco 1979.

Haupt, R.: A Survey of Priority Rule-Based Scheduling; OR Spektrum 11 (1989) 1, S. 3-16.

Hoare, C.A.R.: Communicating Sequential Processes; London 1985.

Holthaus, O.; Rosenberg, O.; Ziegler, H.: Verteilte Simulation dezentraler Werkstatt-fertigungssysteme; Information Management 8 (1993) 2, S. 6-12.

Itoh, K.; Huang, D.; Enkawa, T.: Twofold Look-Ahead Search for Multi-Criterion Job Shop Scheduling; International Journal of Production Research 31 (1993) 9, pp. 2215-2234.

Koulamas, C.P.; Smith, M.L.: Look-Ahead Scheduling for Minimizing Machine Interference; International Journal of Production Research 26 (1988) 9, pp. 1523-1533.

Leighton, F.T.: Introduction to parallel Algorithms and Architectures: Arrays, Trees and Hypercubes; San Mateo, California 1992.

Mattern, F.; Mehl, H.: Diskrete Simulation - Prinzipien und Probleme der Effizienzsteigerung durch Parallelisierung; Informatik-Spektrum 12 (1989) 4, S. 198-210.

Misra, J.: Distributed Discrete Event Simulation; ACM Computing Surveys 18 (1986) 18, pp. 39-65.

Mitchell, D.A.P.; Thompson, J.A.; Manson, G.A.; Brookes, G.R.: Inside the Transputer; Oxford 1990.

Nawijn, W.M.: The optimal Look-Ahead Policy for Admission to a Single Server System; Operations Research 33 (1985) 3, pp. 625-643.

Nawijn, W.M.: Look-Ahead Policies for Admission to a Single Server Loss System; Operations Research 38 (1990) 5, pp. 854-862.

Nicol, D.: Conservative Parallel Simulation of Priority Class Queueing Networks; IEEE Transactions on Parallel and Distributed Systems 3 (1992) 3, pp. 294-303.

Papaspyropoulos, G.T.; Maritsas, D.G.: Parallel Discrete Event Simulation with SIMULA; Parallel Computing 15 (1989) 12, pp. 359-373.

Philipps, C.I.; Cuthbert, L.G.: Concurrent Discrete Event-Driven Simulation Tools; IEEE Journal on Selected Areas in Communications 9 (1991) 3, pp. 477-485.

Ramasesh, R.: Dynamic Job Shop Scheduling: A Survey of Simulation Research; Omega International Journal of Management Science 18 (1990) 1, pp. 43-57.

Rinnooy Kan, A.H.G.: Machine Scheduling Problems; The Hague 1976.

Rosenwein, M.B.; Stone, R.E.; Wahls, E.T.: Constrained 'Look-Ahead' Manufacturing; International Journal of Production Research 29 (1991) 9, pp. 1845-1851.

Russell, R.S.; Dar-El, E.M.; Taylor, B.W.: A comparative Analysis of the COVERT Job Sequencing Rule using various Shop Performance Measures; International Journal of Production Research 25 (1987) 10, pp. 1523-1540.

Scheiber, J.: Simulation und Prozeßvisualisierung auf Transputersystemen; in: Simulationstechnik, Tagungsband, 6. Symp. in Wien, Hrsg.: Breitenecker, F.; Troch, I.; Kopacek, P.; Braunschweig 1990, S. 407-411.

Vogel, F.: Probleme und Verfahren der numerischen Klassifikation; Göttingen 1975.

Distributed Environments for Evolutionary Algorithms by means of Multi-Agent Applications

Herbert Kopfer, Thomas Utecht, Christian Bierwirth

Abstract

Advanced modeling of control and optimization in management science often leads to a computational complexity which cannot be handled by traditional algorithms and computer systems. On this background the paper develops a general approach to combine the power of distribution and parallelism in natural systems and modern distributed and parallel computing systems. The link between these topics is reached by the concept of multi-agent systems. We show how to build a genetic agent system upon a base model of distribution. Computational performance of this system is presented by a sample application to production scheduling and a runtime analysis of distributed and parallel processing.

Keywords: evolutionary algorithms, multi-agent systems, production scheduling, distributed computing

1 Introduction

In recent years many decision problems from the domain of management science were approached and solved by some classes of evolutionary algorithms (EAs). Within such fields as production, inventory, distribution and organization we find a broad range of management applications for computational paradigms that were already developed during the last two decades, compare e.g. the overviews by Alander (1995) and Nissen (1995). These paradigms lead to most promising new approaches which fit the complex demands arising from optimization, configuration and forecasting. A collection of current applications can be found in Biethahn et al. (1995). The probably most important feature of EAs is the explicit introduction of distribution. In order to combine the power of distributed problem solving and strategies from natural systems we outline a model for handling EAs by means of multi-agent systems.

Section 2 gives a brief review on multi-agent systems and its extension to distributed agents. Complex attributes of distribution lead to a Base Model of interaction between agents in a distributed environment. Section 3 sketches the formulation of evolutionary algorithms in terms of agent systems, which enables these kinds of algorithms to make use of the functionality of distributing agents as provided by the Base Model. Section 4 reports on the application of a distributed EA to a class of production scheduling problems. Scheduling performance and distributed runtime analysis are discussed for a number of benchmark problems.

2 Distributed Computing Environment

The actual state in Distributed Computing Environments (DCE) is represented by a combination of Remote Procedure Calls (RPC) and concurrently running leight-weighted processes (multi threaded processes), compare Open Software Foundation (1992). Setting up on this state a general environment for multi-agent applications - implementable on operating systems supporting concurrency (Solaris 2.3, Mach 2.6, OS/2, Windows NT, OSF/1) - is outlined in this section. Here, agents are typically implemented by threads and communication is carried out via shared memory or message passing.

2.1 Multi-Agent Systems

An agent is the basic component in a set of independently acting agents constituting a *multi-agent system.* In order to solve common application problems, agents cooperate with other concurrent agents in the set.

Cooperation requires either the exchange of messages or is based on shared data. The power of multi-agent systems comes from agent action and interaction. Each action of an agent is either cooperation via communication or is independent and therefore concurrent to other agents' actions.

Many approaches have been developed to describe the way of acting and interacting in multi-agent systems. Some authors propose a knowledge based approach to model the behavior of agents. Weigelt and Mertens (1992) introduce *Partly Intelligent Agents* (PIA) where each agent follows its internal goal with respect to the current information about the environment. Other authors focus on the ability of agents to react flexibly on events of a changing environment. Nevertheless in all approaches the challenge is to find a suitable organization of many agents, whereas a single agent executes well known algorithms.

2.2 Distributed Agents

To distribute a multi-agent system in a network of processing nodes, e.g. a workstation cluster, communication has to be done by exchanging messages in order to attain efficiency and scalability of an implementation. An actual global state (time, data) cannot be determined because of the lack of shared memory. An agent still should be implemented by a thread. Next it should communicate with other agents in a way which is independent from locations. Therefore agents communicate in a transparent way. Beside *transparency* there are some more attributes attributes we have to comply with. These attributes are *autonomy, separation, flexibility* and *heterogeneity*. Each attribute can be examined from different viewpoints in a distributed system. So beneath *transparency of location* we may have *transparency of service* meaning that we do not have to care how a service is provided. The service provider itself may have to react flexibly on a possible event (i.e. power down) affecting its service quality. With these attributes in mind we build a model of distributed agents in a workstation cluster depicted as the *Base Model.*

According to Enslow's model of decentralization (compare Enslow 1978) as described briefly by Sloman and Kramer (1987) the Base Model can be classified as follows: From an agent's viewpoint complete distribution (concerning control, data and processors) is achieved with the only exception that heterogeneous processors are not supported.

2.3 Base Model

Our model of distribution is developed in a straightforward manner from the general idea of real world teamwork. That is why we like to introduce it in terms of team, office, mailport, notice-board, agent and message.

A team consists of an arbitrary number of agents each belonging exactly to one office. In the simplest case we have only one office and therefore all agents belong to this office. An office administers the agents themselves and provides further services for communication and cooperation between agents. These services are represented by different types of communication objects which are mailports, notice-boards and agents. For addressing any of these objects an office has a hierarchically ordered (according to the type of objects) name space.

A message within the Base Model consists of a structured addressing part and a data part of variable length. An agent is the only active object within our model that generates messages based upon its needs and sends them to a communication object by adding the office and name of the recipient. An involved office processes a message according to the type of the addressed communication object. In case of a mailport the message is simply stored in the mailport preserving the order of messages. If a notice-board is addressed, the previous message in the notice-board will be replaced by the current one. When a communication object of type agent is addressed the office starts a new instance of the corresponding agent. This instance gets the message sent as its initial input.

Let us summarize the usage of communication objects: "Sending a message to an object" means transporting information to a passive object (mailport or notice-board) or to an active object (agent that is starting to "live" upon receiving a message). The sending agent of a message which is addressed to a communication object of type agent (i.e. the creator of a job) gets an identification number in return to its request. Using this identification the sending agent can wait for the job to finish and it can receive an answer message.

In order to realize a distribution of agents an initially existing office opens further offices at different locations. Now the team of agents operates in a distributed environment. Compared to the case of only one office this extension is transparent from an agent's view. The addressing field of a message still contains the entries of office and object name. In contrast to the simple case (one office) the office now does not need to be the own one. Because a new agent is created by sending a message this occurrence is still transparent.

Beneath communicating by exchanging messages an agent has the ability to migrate to another office. Clearly, its local state (local variables, point of execution in its program) does not change, but its environment (office, global variables) does. Migration always happens independently from the name spaces of the involved offices to regard the autonomy of an agent.

A distributed system must be able to react flexibly to an unexpected event, e.g. a total failure of an office or a message addressed to a so far unknown object. The Base Model manages these kinds of events by sending appropriate messages to predefined communication objects which are integrated into the model itself. So the predefined communication objects represent a default behavior for unexpected events. This behavior can be changed to specific application needs by replacement of some of the predefined objects.

2.4 Implementation

For building our distributed computing environment a three-layered implementation architecture is used. The idea is to become increasingly specific from the bottom layer up to the top layer which is in fact the real world application itself.

The bottom layer implements the Base Model and is named the Base System. Above this layer a more specific Interface Layer is used to provide additional support for a specific class of applications. Here we focus on a class of "population-based agent systems" - a term that is made more precise in the next section. Finally the third layer represents the application itself. Figure 1 gives a snapshot on the layer model distributed on four workstations (processing nodes).

For implementing the Base System we have chosen the Mach 2.6 and Solaris 2.3 operating systems. The Base System is accessible by using a library depicted as Parnet Library which represents the programming interface to our Base Model., compare Utecht (1994).

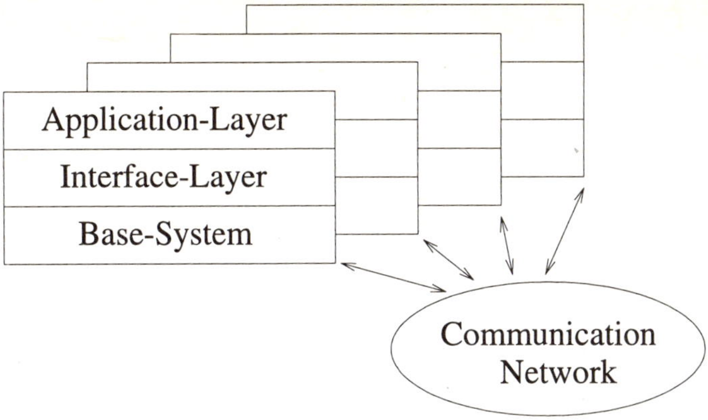

Figure 1: Layer model.

Diverse Tests	Results
Local message transfer rate (128 - 1024 Byte) (independent from message size, varying)	2500 - 3500 Messages/s
Remote messages transfer rate (128 - 1024 Byte) (results are varying)	200 - 500 Messages/s 40 - 400 Kbyte/s
Average turnaround time for a local empty job (independent from size of parameter)	2.4 ms
Average turnaround time for a remote empty job (1024 Byte request, 20 Byte reply)	7.4 ms
Migration of a thread (small amount of local data)	250 Migrations/s

Table 1: Communication performance of the Base Model implementation.

We measured the performance of the implemented Base Model in terms of message throughput, message latency and turnaround time for asynchronous jobs. Table 1 gives a rough overview of the performance achieved so far. All tests were made using two "low-end workstations" of type Sparc Classic (50 Mhz Micro-Sparc Processor, roughly comparable to Intel 486,

66 Mhz) connected via Ethernet. According to the limited bandwidth of our network the measurements match with comparable results of Schill (1993).

3 Distributed Problem Solving

A major research direction in "distributed problem solving" focuses on search and optimization techniques that are inspired by the natural evolution of species, compare e.g. Schwefel and Männer (1990), Männer and Manderik (1992), and Davidor et al. (1994). Following a modern classification, the class of Evolutionary Algorithms contains the paradigms of Evolutionary Programming, see Fogel et al. (1966), Genetic Algorithms, see Holland (1975), Evolutionary Strategies, see Rechenberg (1973) and Schwefel (1977), and Genetic Programming, see Koza (1992). A common property of these paradigms is to perform a population based search by a multitude of individual searchers and not by a sequential step by step process of single search trials. By adopting the biological principles of replication, variation, and selection the global state of an EA-based system can meet high quality solutions of an optimization problem even without centrailzed control.

The difference between EA search strategies and multi-agent systems relies on the fact that all involved agents follow the same program. Such a program is an agent's life routine of alternating individual search and communicating with other agents. The effectivity of shared search arises from specific cooperation and competition schemes which are modelled according to the modern understanding from natural processes. The set of agents participating search is called a population. We therefore suggest to refer to these paradigms as *population-based agent systems*.

3.1 Population-Based Agent Systems

The most frequently observed difficulty in the application of population-based agent systems to optimization arises from *premature convergence*, i.e. search stagnates early resulting in suboptimality, compare e.g. Goldberg (1989). In such a state all agents have similar characteristics which confines any cooperation to at best very small rates of improvement. A promising approach to avoid this phenomenon comes from spatially distributed populations. Isolating agents in space requires the use of specific communication structures.

In spatially distributed populations communication of agents is restricted to a small number of nearby agents. Hence global premature convergence is alleviated at the expense of local convergence. In this situation the propagation of slowly changing local environments of agents anticipates a reasonable way out. The force of adaptation under modified environmental conditions increases the odds of crucial cooperation from generation to generation. Therefore we developed a novel approach which moves the adaptation action from the population-based agent system to single agents neighborhood environments. In this approach agents are able to change behavior usefully as a function of immediate local environmental changes.

We borrowed the basic ideas of our model from the phenomenon of social hierarchies and individual behavior, which can be found in natural populations, for a detailed description see Mattfeld et al. (1994). The model incorporates the three most pertinent individual attitudes observed in human communities which bring about three different patterns of social-like agent behavior.

The initial attitude of agents is to act *cooperatively* within their environments. An elitist attitude follows a *conservative* behavior pattern. Finally a critical attitude causes a more *risk-prone* behavior of an agent. The actual behavior of each agent is rewarded or punished in terms of social interaction. Again we classify three simple responses which are defined by reinforcements. An agent can be *pleased, satisfied* or *disappointed.* The success of the actual behavior carried out may change its attitude and therefore changes its habit in a similar situation within the near future.

In most cases a cooperative agent will be satisfied and therefore does not change its attitude. If pleased by success of its habit, next time it will tend to act conservatively trying to keep its previous performance level. With the elitist attitude an agent can only become satisfied or disappointed. In case of disappointment it will change back to cooperation. Failing on cooperative behavior brings up a critical attitude of the agent towards its neighborhood environment. It will then tend to more risk-prone behavior. This critical attitude is kept as long as a disappointing response is still received. If the agent is satisfied by the result of its behavior, it may change to cooperation again. In rare cases a risk-prone agent receives a pleasing response and eventually changes to conservative behavior.

3.2 Application to Evolutionary Algorithms

The EA paradigms fit well into our understanding of a population-based agent system. We now demonstrate its application to Genetic Algorithms (GA). The main components of a GA are:

- **(a)** A genetic representation which encodes the reachable points of the search space. Each valid instantiation of such a representation scheme describes the characteristics of a feasible solution which can be explored by agents.
- **(b)** A fitness evaluation function which assigns each agent a real-valued number according to the quality level of its actual solution.

(c) A selection procedure which builds up communication links between agents with respect to their level of fitness and to the predefined population structure.

(d) Genetic operators which generate unexplored points in the search space from the encoded solution of one agent (mutation) or the encoded solutions of two distinct agents (crossover).

Let us now focus on the question of how to incorporate our model of agent behavior outlined in the previous section into a GA-based agent system. To simplify matters we consider a population structure where agents reside on a torodial square grid. Communication of agents is restricted to the "North", "South", "West" and "East" neighbors. The selection procedure - component (c) - is carried out locally by a ranking scheme of 40%, 30%, 20% and 10% from the best to the worst fit neighbor. Whenever an agent generates a new solution which is at most 1% worse than the actual solution, it replaces the old by the new solution.

In order to implement individual agent behavior we transform the metaphor of social attitudes into a *local recombination strategy* as introduced by Gorges-Schleuter (1992). The cooperative attitude corresponds to *crossover* with one of the neighbors. The critical attitude corresponds to a mutation. Conservative behavior tries to save a reached state, i.e. the agent performs the non-active operation sleeping to avoid replacement by a new solution. Figure 2 shows these operations in boldface.

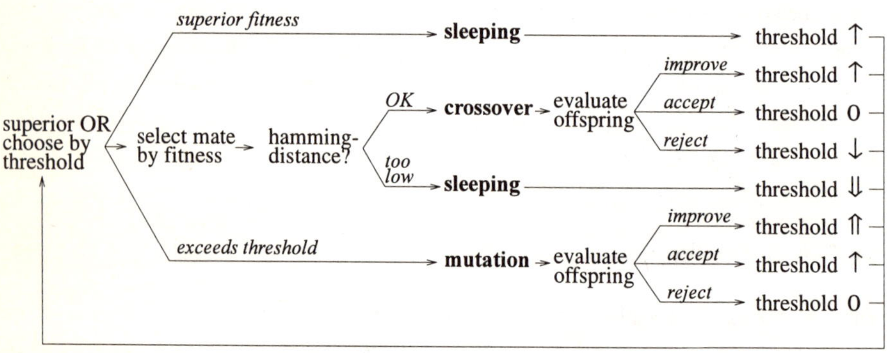

Figure 2: Control model of local recombination.

First an agent looks at the fitness of its neighborhood. If its fitness is superior to all neighbors, the conservative behavior will cause the agent to sleep. An inferior agent states its behavior in the actual generation probabilistically from a threshold. Initially the threshold is set to 1, which enforces crossover. Decreasing the threshold increases the probability of mutation. In case of crossover the hamming distance between the encoded solutions of an agent and its selected mate solution is evaluated. If two solutions differ in less than 1% of their characteristics it is not worthwhile to try a crossover. Again, the agent sleeps, but now because of a different reason. If crossover or mutation is carried out, the generated solution is evaluated. It either dominates the fitness of the actual solutions of both parents (improve), or the acceptance rule decides whether the agent replaces the new solution (accept/reject).

Summing up all distinct operations we count 8 responses which are tied to reinforcements of the threshold. We modify the threshold by rules of plausibility. The symbols "$\Uparrow \Downarrow \downarrow \uparrow$" express the degree of change of the threshold. This rule set attempts to adjust the behavior of each single agent towards the environment of its actual neighborhood. In our implementation a setting of (+0.02, +0.05, 0, -0.02, -0.20, +0.15, +0.05, 0) performed well. This setting reacts adaptively to local convergence with a strong decrease of the threshold.

3.3 Implementing GA-Based Agent Systems

In order to distribute population-based agent systems in a workstation cluster we use the functionality of the Base System. Actually this step is executed by the Interface Layer. This section briefly outlines how the interface handles communication between agents. But let us first become aware of the advantage of formulating distributed search strategies in terms of multi-agent systems. It enables applications to carry over the attributes of distribution by inheritance from the Base Model. From the application's viewpoint no difference arises from using a single workstation or a whole cluster. Of course, in the latter case we get enhanced performance by parallel processing.

In the literature diverse models of spatial GA populations are proposed, compare Gorges-Schleuter (1992). The basic idea of these models is to structure populations by discrete topologies. This feature isolates population members according to a measure of space or time. Thus initially fixed areas of local communication result for all agents of the population. The Interface Layer provides most of the common communication topologies as a service to the application.

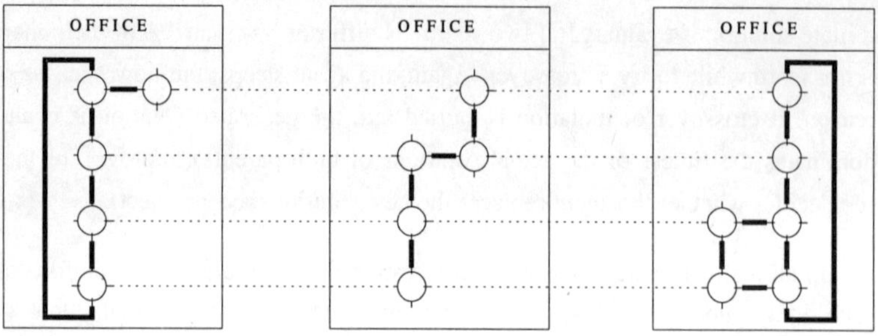

Figure 3: Torodial mapping of agents.

Consider for example the quadratic torus population structure of 16 agents in Figure 3. Each agent is connected to 4 neighbors. The Interface maps the agents on the cluster with respect to a static load balancing and a minimal number of links across the network. The distribution of 16 agents yields a slightly different work load for 3 offices. In case of a synchronized population dynamics (generation progress is step by step) a uniform work load is preferable, because the longest computing time of a generation step determines the overall progress. To achieve an alleviation for heavy loaded offices the mapping tends to maximize their number of local links (bold lines).

For each agent four mailports are exclusively used to receive information from its neighborhood. Sending of information to neighbors is oriented via the four directions of the compass rose and therefore does not require to specify offices. Thus, from agents point of view, communication areas are completely transparent.

4 Application to Production Scheduling

In order to validate our distribution model this section develops a GA for a general production scheduling problem going by the terms of *n-job m-machine* job shop. The problem is briefly described by three components:

The manufacturing system: We consider a manufacturing system of m dedicated machines $M_1 \ldots M_m$, i.e. a machine cannot substitute other machines. Further we assume the system to be idealistic, i.e. no machine breakdown occurs and passing times of tasks between machines are neglected. Tasks do not require a setup time, hence machines are available if they are not busy.

The production program: A production program covers n jobs $J_1 \ldots J_n$ that are released at predetermined points in time. Each job J_i defines a technological precedence constraint τ_i = $(o_{i\phi_i(1)} \ldots o_{i\phi_i(m_i)})$ of processing m_i operations with determined processing times by the machines

$M_{\phi_i(1)} \ldots M_{\phi_i(m_i)}$. Hence, if $\phi_i(k) = j$, M_j is the k-th machine that processes J_i. No job has to be processed twice by the same machine and it does not necessarily have to be processed by all machines.

The measure of performance: Scheduling a production program in the manufacturing system means to determine a table of starting times of all operations with respect to release times and precedence constraints. We consider the performance measure of minimizing the makespan of the entire program. If C_i gives the completion time of J_i we can calculate the makespan by $C_{\max} = \max_{1 \le i \le n} C_i$.

We now turn to the description of the job shop specific GA-components (a), (b) and (d) of section 3.2. A more general description of this approach can be found in Bierwirth (1995). In our model n denotes the number of jobs J_i. If m_i denotes the number of tasks of J_i, a permutation with repetition of three jobs containing $m_i = 3, 4, 3$ tasks, is for example given by

$$(J_1, J_2, J_2, J_1, J_3, J_1, J_2, J_3, J_2, J_3)$$

Here J_2 has to be processed on all four machines whereas J_1 and J_3 have to be processed only by three of them. If we consider operations as tasks on machines the above permutation with repetition is interpreted as a task sequence

$$(T_{11}, T_{21}, T_{22}, T_{12}, T_{31}, T_{13}, T_{23}, T_{32}, T_{24}, T_{33})$$

Reading it from left to right, a task T_{ij} of job J_i has to be scheduled on machine $M_{\phi_i(j)}$ as determined by the technological order τ_i. Assume that technological constraints τ_1 = (o_{11}, o_{13}, o_{12}), $\tau_2 = (o_{21}, o_{22}, o_{23}, o_{24})$ and $\tau_3 = (o_{32}, o_{33}, o_{34})$ are given. This leads to tasks orders (T_{11}, T_{21}), (T_{22}, T_{31}, T_{13}), (T_{12}, T_{23}, T_{32}) and (T_{24}, T_{33}) for the machines M_1, M_2, M_3 and M_4 respectively. Notice that this technique allows a unique transformation of every n-permutation with m_i-repetitions into a feasible symbolic solution in terms of processing orders for machines. Thus we can use the permutation scheme as a genetic representation of the job shop problem, i.e. as GA-component (a).

Any instantiation of the representation describes a possible state of an agent. In order to evaluate its state (the fitness of the current permutation) the agent calculates a minimal makespan for the represented solution using the GA-component (b). The agent considers the resulting $C_{\max}$ value as its present fitness (maximizing fitness means minimizing the makespan). In order to achieve high quality solutions it is indispensable to incorporate local-search techniques for the job shop problem into genetic search, compare Pesch (1994) and for a description of our hybridization approach Mattfeld (1996).

Finally we focus on GA-component (d) which represents the cooperation scheme of agents. In case of a mutation actually no cooperation takes place. A mutation performs a random exchange of two arbitrary tasks in a given n/m_i permutation. According to the GA paradigm co-operation of agents is temporarily restricted to pairwise mating. In analogy to natural genetics the process is called *crossover*. This operator builds up new instantiations of the representation scheme based on the states of two cooperating agents. Crossover ensures to pass a balanced mix of encoded characteristics in offspring solutions with respect to the n/m_i permutation structure. A description of such kind of technique - derived from a generalization of the well known *Order-Crossover* for simple permutations can also be found in Bierwirth (1995).

5 Computational Validation

The local-genetic recombination strategy, shown in Figure 2, was embedded into a population-based agent system as described in section 3.2. The resulting distributed algorithm was implemented by use of the Parnet Library to run on a variable number of UNIX workstations in parallel, see section 2.4. We refer on this program as *Parallel Genetic Algorithm + Social Behavior Patterns* (PGA+SBP). Parallel computing action was synchronized, hence the quality of PGA+SBP solutions is independent from the degree of parallelism. All computations were executed on a cluster of 20 Sparc-Classic machines connected via Ethernet.

5.1 Scheduling Performance

PGA+SBP has been applied to a suite of 13 job shop benchmarks. It includes the three famous Muth-Thompson problems (mt-problems) and the ten most difficult problems of the benchmarks suite provided by Applegate and Cook (1991). A short description of the benchmarks is listed in Table 2. The solution complexity of the problems ranges from the relatively easy to solve mt-problems to the much more difficult abz-problems. It can be seen from the column "Status" that beside the abz-problems only problem la29 is still open, i.e. the best known solution is not proved to be optimal. PGA+SBP is parameterized according to the assumed complexity of a problem instance. The torus-population size was set to 100 (10x10) and 144 (12x12) while termination occurred after 100, 150, 300 or 400 generations respectively.

PGA+SBP were run for a total of 30 iterations on each problem. Computational results in terms of the average makespan ($C_{max}^{average}$) and the best found makespan (C_{max}^{best}) appear in Table 2 as well. Notice that these results were achieved by use of a powerful improvement heuristic for makespan evaluation as remarked in section 4. The column "Trials" refers to the average number of fitness evaluations in a single run. These values are approximately 20% smaller than the maximal numbers of trials (generations times torus size). This is caused by "sleeping" of agents, hence agents avoid the computationally expensive makespan evaluation in about one of five generations.

n-Job/*m*-Machine Benchmarks					PGA+SBP Results			Parameters	
Name	*n*	*m*	Status	Known	$C_{max}^{average}$	C_{max}^{best}	Trails	Generat.	Torus size
mt06	6	6	solved	55	55.0	55	7628	100	10 x 10
mt10	10	10	solved	930	947.5	930	10935	150	10 x 10
mt20	20	5	solved	1165	1188.2	1165	11738	150	10 x 10
la21	15	10	solved	1046	1061.5	1053	24956	300	10 x 10
la24	15	10	solved	935	948.0	938	25335	300	10 x 10
la25	15	10	solved	977	989.1	977	25733	300	10 x 10
la27	20	10	solved	1235	1265.7	1236	24797	300	10 x 10
la29	20	10	open	1153	1214.4	1184	47881	400	12 x 12
la38	15	15	solved	1196	1222.4	1201	24026	300	10 x 10
la40	15	15	solved	1222	1243.5	1228	25013	300	10 x 10
abz7	15	20	open	665	684.6	672	45812	400	12 x 12
abz8	15	20	open	670	697.9	683	44664	400	12 x 12
abz9	15	20	open	686	712.6	703	45004	400	12 x 12

Table 2: PGA+SBP scheduling results for 13 job shop benchmark problems.

The solutions generated by PGA+SBP are close to the best known solutions in all runs. The best generated makespan of each problem instance maximally differs by 31 units (la29) from the best known solution whereas the average deviation counts only 7.6 units. Four benchmarks were solved to optimality by PGA+SBP.

5.2 Runtime Performance

To validate the computational performance we choose three problems, of different solution complexity, in particular mt06, mt19, and la27. Runtime performance of PGA+SBP (population size = 100 agents, generations = 100) on a varying number of workstations (1-20) is presented in Table 3. The work load of a single workstation varies according to unbalanced mappings of agents as shown in the second line of the table.

No. of Workstations	1	2	4	6	8	10	12	14	16	18	20
Agents/ Workstation	100	50	25	16-17	12-13	10	8-9	7-8	6-7	5-6	5
Problem					Runtime in sec.						
mt06	133	88	45	35	29	22	21	18	16	14	12
mt10	621	313	157	116	90	71	65	57	51	43	38
la27	2428	1174	664	452	354	278	244	222	202	171	144

Table 3: PGA+SBP runtimes for a small, moderate and large-scale benchmark problem.

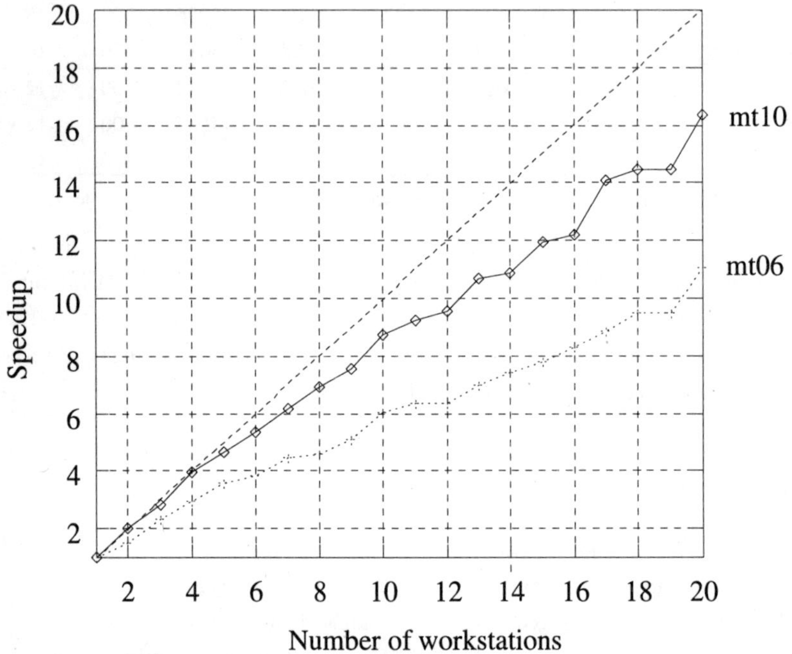

Figure 4: Speedup for 2 job shop problems.

The speedup for mt06 and mt10 is charted in Figure 4. Because the speedup for la27 nearly matches the mt10-curve within the range of 20 available workstations it is not displayed.

Due to their complexity the examples show a reasonable speedup. Obviously, mt10 shows a better speedup in comparison to mt6 because the quotient of communication (equal in terms of the number of messages for both problems) to computation load (less expensive fitness evaluation for the smaller problem) decreases strongly. But within the range of 20 workstations a saturation of scalability does not happen even for the small problem. A slight staircase shape can be seen clearly in both curves. This is caused by a similar work load on the heaviest loaded workstation, e.g. 5-6 agents share one station while using a total of 17, 18 or 19 workstations.

6 Conclusions

The idea of distributed problem solving - based on a team of agents and on the computational power of a workstation cluster - leads to the development of a Base Model. Its implementation makes an universally and easy to use Distributed Computing Environment available. The adaptation of Genetic Algorithms to concepts of distribution and to the complex needs of production scheduling showed at least the following results:

- A cluster of 20 workstations suffices the communication demand of GAs. Hence a specialized parallel computing device is not needed.
- The solution quality does not suffer from distribution as shown by the computational validation.
- The autonomy of distributed agents comes closer to the driving force of population based algorithms than a traditional artificially serialized implementation.

These results underline the importance of recent research in distributed problem solving and machine learning for management science and operations research.

Acknowledgements

This research is supported by the Deutsche Forschungsgemeinschaft (Project Parnet). Furthermore, we like to thank Dr. Dirk C. Mattfeld for many helpful discussions and Dr. Kevin R. Caskey for editorial assistance.

References

Alander, J.T. (1995): An Indexed Bibliography of Genetic Algorithms in Operations Research, Technical Report No. 94-1-OR, University of Vaasa

Applegate, D.; Cook, W. (1991): A Computational Study of the Job-Shop Scheduling Problem, ORSA Journal on Computing 2, 149-156

Bierwirth, C. (1995): A Generalized Permutation Approach to Job Shop Scheduling with Genetic Algorithms, OR Spektrum 17, 87-92

Biethahn, J.; Nissen, V. (eds.) (1995): Evolutionary Algorithms in Management Applications, Springer-Verlag, Berlin Heidelberg

Davidor, Y; Schwefel, H.P., Männer, R. (eds.) (1994): Parallel Problem Solving from Nature III, Springer-Verlag, Berlin Heidelberg

Enslow, P.H. (1978): What is a distributed Data Processing System?, Computer (January), 13-21

Fogel, L.J.; Owens, A.J.; Walsh, M.J. (1966): Artificial Intelligence through Simulated Evolution, John Wiley/NY

Goldberg, D.E. (1989): Genetic Algorithms in Search, Optimization and Machine Learning, Addison Wesley, Reading/MA

Gorges-Schleuter, M. (1992): A Comparison of Local Mating Strategies in Massively Parallel Genetic Algorithms, in Männer and Manderick (eds.) 553-562

Holland, J.H. (1975): Adaptation in Natural and Artificial Systems, The University of Michigan Press, Ann Arbor

Koza, J.R. (1992): Genetic Programming, MIT Press, Cambridge/MA

Männer, R.; Manderick, B. (eds.) (1992): Parallel Problem Solving from Nature II, North-Holland, Amsterdam

Mattfeld, D.C.; Kopfer, H.; Bierwirth, C. (1994): Control of Parallel Population Dynamics by Social-Like Behavior of GA-Individuals, in: Davidor et al.(eds.) 16-25

Mattfeld, D.C. (1996): Evolutionary Search and the Job Shop, Physica-Verlag, Berlin Heidelberg

Nissen, V. (1995): An Overview of Evolutionary Algorithms in Management Applications, in Biethahn and Nissen (eds.), 44-97

Open Software Foundation (1992): Introduction to OSF DCE, Open Software Foundation, Cambridge/MA

Pesch, E. (1994): Learning in Automated Manufacturing, Physica-Verlag, Berlin Heidelberg

Rechenberg, I. (1973): Evolutionsstrategie. Optimierung technischer Systeme nach Prinzipien der biolo-gischen Evolution, Fr. Fromman Verlag, Stuttgart

Schill, A. (1993): DCE - Das OSF Distributed Computing Environment, Springer-Verlag, Berlin Heidelberg

Sloman, M.; Kramer, J. (1987): Distributed Systems and Computer Networks, Prentice-Hall, Englewood Cliffs/NJ

Schwefel, H.P. (1977): Numerische Optimierung von Computer-Modellen mittels der Evolutionsstrategie, Birkhäuser-Verlag, Basel

Schwefel, H.P.; Männer, R.(eds.) (1990): Parallel Problem Solving from Nature I, Springer-Verlag, Berlin Heideberg

Utecht, T. (1994): Schnittstelle des PARNET-Basissystems, Technical Report, University of Bremen

Weigelt, M.; Mertens, P. (1992): Theorie und Anwendungen von Agenten-Systemen in der Produktionssteuerung, Working Paper No. 12, University of Erlangen-Nürnberg

Application Section

Multi-Layered Development of Business Process Models and Distributed Business Application Systems - An Object-Oriented Approach -

Otto K. Ferstl, Elmar J. Sinz

Abstract

The paper presents a comprehensive and integrated approach for business process modeling and for the specification of distributed business application systems. The approach is based on a framework of business systems which consists of three layers: (1) business process model, (2) business application systems, and (3) computing systems. This framework is used to manage the complexity of a business system and to address the different actors and abstractions of actors within a business system (e.g. persons and machines, application systems, and computing systems). The linkage of the layer of business application systems to both the layers of business processes and computing systems helps to specify the distribution of business application systems in a natural way. Object-oriented concepts are used as universal enabling techniques.

Keywords: business system, business process, business application system, business object, business transaction, coordination mechanism, semantic object model (SOM)

Contents

1. Introduction

This paper presents a new approach to business process modeling and to the specification of distributed business application systems. The approach is based on a multi-layered framework which consists of three layers: (1) business processes, (2) corresponding business application systems, and (3) computing systems to execute the application systems. All three layers may be distributed, employing multiple cooperating actors. Actors are persons and machines (e.g. production machines, transport systems, assembly lines, and computers). The layer of the business application systems is explicitly linked to the layer of the business processes. The initial structure of the specification of a business application system can even be derived directly from the corresponding business process model.

Throughout the paper, we take a system-oriented viewpoint on *business systems* (e.g. companies, business units and departments). From an outside view, a business system is considered open and goal-oriented. The inside view of a business system is developed by a stepwise decomposition which uses two different criteria:

- Production and delivery relationships lead to a decomposition into cooperating business processes. The relationships between the business processes follow the client/server principle. In the role of a server, a business process produces and delivers its outcome to one or more client processes. Each business process can act in both roles.
- Control relationships lead to a decomposition into a controlled subsystem which produces and delivers the outcome of business processes, and a controlling subsystem which is called the business information system. It works as the *nervous system* of a business system (see Ferstl & Sinz (1994)). A business information system consists of automated and non-automated sub-systems. An automated sub-system is called a *business application system*; a non-automated sub-system is part of the personnel organization.

In the following chapters the approach is outlined in detail. Chapter 2 introduces the concept of distributed systems and specializes the concept into distributed business systems, distributed business application systems, and distributed computing systems according to the layers mentioned above. Chapter 3 explains our approach to business process modeling especially focusing on the coordination principles within business processes. Based on the architecture of distributed business systems we develop in chapter 4 an architecture of distributed business application systems and link both layers. In this way we are able to provide a unified approach to business process modeling as well as to the specification of distributed business application systems.

2. Distributed Systems

In general, a *distributed system* is characterized by the following properties (see also Enslow (1978)):

a1) From an outside view, the system is a black box and pursues a set of joint goals.

b1) The system consists of multiple autonomous components which cooperate in pursuing these goals. There is no component which has global control of the system.

Property (a1) requires that a distributed system be an *integrated system*, consisting of interacting components. Isolated components do not pursue joint goals. Property (b1) refers to the autonomy of the cooperating components. This means that the components generate separate concurrent processes while executing their tasks. Concurrent processes communicate by exchanging messages and service packages.

The definition of a distributed system is applicable to business systems, business application systems, and computing systems. For example, a *distributed business system* consists of multiple interacting business processes, each of them pursuing joint enterprise goals.

In the case of *distributed business application systems* and *distributed computing systems*, the definition given above can be extended:

a2) The distribution of the system into multiple components is invisible to any user of the system. This feature is called *system transparency*.

b2) The components of a distributed system are loosely coupled. Each component is autonomous and encapsulates both structure and behavior.

Figure 1 shows the difference between loosely coupling and tightly coupling of components. While *loosely coupled components* have their own memory and communicate by exchanging messages via a communication channel, *tightly coupled components* communicate by sharing a common memory (see Gray & Reuter (1993) and Martin, Pedersen & Bedford-Roberts (1991)).

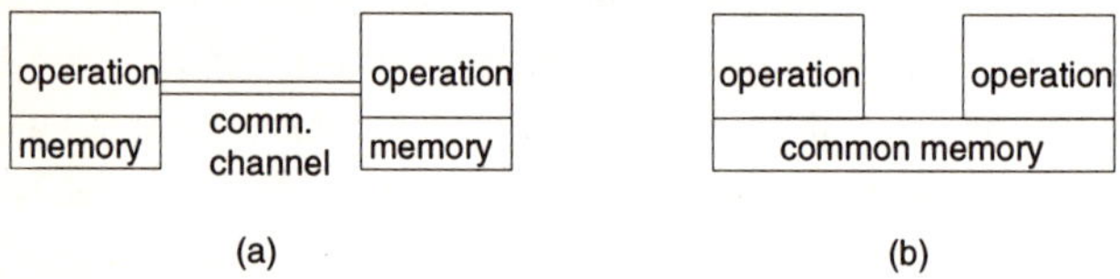

Fig. 1: Loosely coupled (a) and tightly coupled components (b)

A system can have different degrees of distribution. Shifting the coupling of components from loose to tight decreases the system's degree of distribution. On the other hand, splitting tightly coupled components into loosely coupled components increases the system's degree of distribution.

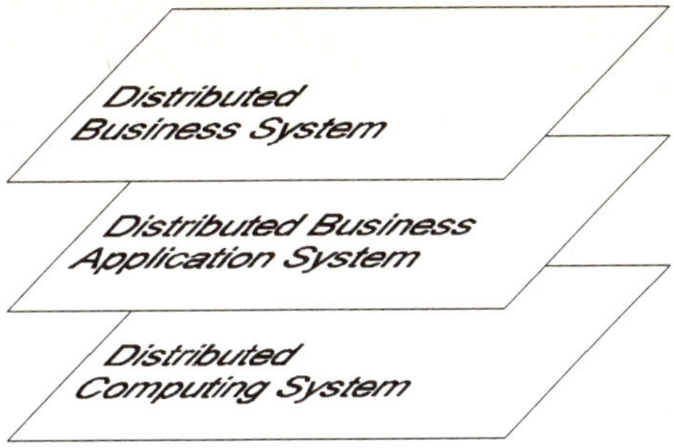

Fig. 2: Conceptual framework for distributed systems

Throughout this paper the specification of distributed systems follows the conceptual framework shown in figure 2. It distinguishes three layers of specification:

- 1st layer: Specification of a *distributed business system* as a set of cooperating business processes. Each business process can be decomposed into loosely coupled sub-processes, thereby becoming distributed.

The purpose of a business application system is to automate or to semi-automate tasks of a business process. The whole business process may be supported by multiple interacting application systems. Identifying the scope of these business application systems within a business process model leads to the second layer of specification.

- 2nd layer: Specification of a *distributed business application system.* At this layer, the domain-related components of an application system are divided into sub-components for communication, application, and data management. Assuming that all sub-components at this layer are loosely coupled leads to the domain-related specification of a business application system with a maximum degree of distribution (see fig. 9).

Starting with a domain-related specification with a maximum degree of distribution, the coupling of the components can be shifted from loose to tight according to specific design goals. This change leads to a domain-related specification of a business application system with a convenient degree of distribution. Finally, the resulting components utilize the virtual machines specified at the third layer.

- 3rd layer: Specification of a *distributed computing system*, consisting of virtual machines. These machines are actors for the components of the distributed business application system. Examples of virtual machines are operating systems, database management systems, user-interface management systems, and application-independent class libraries. They run on computers and communication networks.

Object-oriented techniques promise to be suitable for the specification of distributed systems on all three layers. This is because these techniques specify loosely coupled, autonomous components in a natural way. This paper concentrates on the object-oriented specification of the first and second layer as well as the transition between these layers. The third layer is conceptually integrated, but not outlined in this paper.

3. Business Process Modeling

There are various meanings of the term business process in literature and practice (see Ferstl & Sinz 1993b). The definition of business processes used here follows the approach of the *Semantic Object Model (SOM)* (see Ferstl & Sinz (1990), Ferstl & Sinz (1991), Ferstl & Sinz (1993a), and Ferstl, Sinz, Amberg, Hagemann & Malischewski (1994)). Within the SOM approach, business process modeling is embedded as part of a comprehensive analyis and design method for business systems. The SOM approach covers three major steps:

- *Enterprise planning*: Identification of a company's universe of discourse, its environment, its services, its goals and objectives[129], its success factors, and its value chains.
- *Business process modeling*: Identification of main processes and service processes. Main processes contribute directly to the company's goals, service processes provide their outcome to main processes or other service processes. Relationships between business processes follow the client/server model. A client process engages a service process to deliver a certain service.
- *Specification of business application systems*: The purpose of a business application system is to automate some part of a business process. Application systems are identified and separated within the set of business processes and are specified using an object-oriented notation.

3.1. Meta Model for Business Process Modeling

This section of the paper concentrates on business process modeling based on the meta model shown in figure 3. The purpose of a business process is to produce different kinds of services and to transmit the services to the clients of the business process. Therefore, the specification of a *business process* consists of the following elements:

---

[129] We use the term *goal* to denote the intended final state of an object, pursued by the execution of a task. The term *objective* refers to the corresponding quality aspects, aimed by the execution of the task.

- Specification of the *services* the business process deals with.

- Specification of a *business object* and a set of *business transactions* which produce and transmit the services. Concerning the delimitation of the universe of discourse, *internal objects* and *external object* are distinguished. From a static viewpoint, a transaction builds a communication channel between two business objects. From a dynamic viewpoint, a transaction controls and executes the exchange of service packages and messages, respectively.

- Each transaction is associated with exactly two *tasks*. These tasks can be regarded as drivers of a transaction. One task provides and pushes a particular service package or message, and the corresponding task pulls it. The tasks carry out a protocol which is necessary to transmit a service package or a message from a server to a client.

  The tasks of a transaction are assigned to the business objects which are connected by the transaction. In this way, an object is associated with a set of tasks, each task driving a particular transaction. From the viewpoint of a business object, tasks can be regarded as the object's operations.

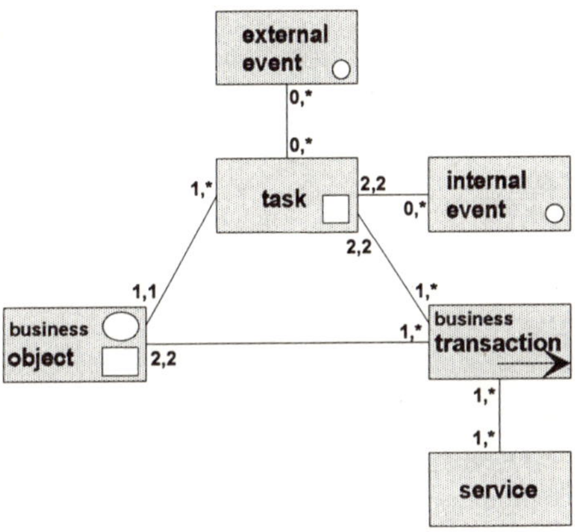

The meta model shows

- the meta objects used for business process modelling,
- the relationships between these meta objects using a (min,max) notation, and
- the symbols used for graphical represantation of business process models

Fig. 3: Meta model of business process modeling

- In addition to the transactions, two kinds of *events* are used to control the execution of tasks. *Internal events* connect tasks within an object. *External events* define environmental pre-conditions for the execution of tasks.

Business processes are too complex to be presented in a unitary form. Therefore, two different views on business processes are used for representation. These views can be derived from the meta model.

- The first view is called the *interaction schema* and focuses on the static structure of a business process. It contains objects and transactions in their roles as communication channels.
- The second view is called the *task-event schema*[130] and presents the dynamic behavior of a business process. It consists of tasks, internal events, external events, and transaction-bound events.

3.2. Coordination of Business Objects

A business process described according to the meta model above can be refined recursively to a more detailed level. This is done by decomposing business objects as well as business transactions. Decomposition of objects and transactions uncovers the basic coordination mechanisms between objects (see fig. 4):

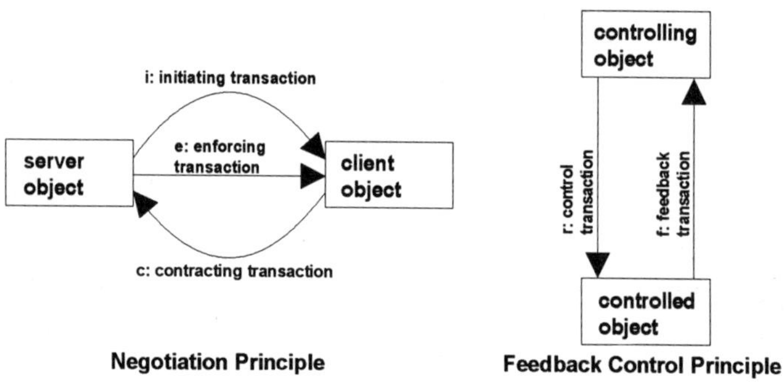

Fig. 4: Basic coordination mechanisms between objects

- *Negotiation principle*: Applying the negotiation principle, a business transaction between two objects is decomposed into a sequence of sub-transactions: (1) an initiating transaction, (2) a contracting transaction, and (3) an enforcing transaction. During the execution of an *initiating transaction*, the objects learn to know each other and exchange information on deliverable services. Within the *contracting transaction* both

[130] Task-event schemata are based on the petri-net concept and can be formally translated into petri-nets.

objects agree to a contract on the exchange of a service. The purpose of the *enforcing transaction* is to exchange the service between the objects.

- *Feedback control principle*: Applying the feedback control principle, an object is decomposed into two sub-objects and two transactions, together establishing a feedback control loop. The controlling sub-object prescribes objectives or sends controlling messages to the controlled sub-object by a *control transaction*. A *feedback transaction* closes the feedback control loop by reporting to the controlling object.

3.3. Example: The Business Process Distribution

In the following, the business process *distribution* is examined to illustrate the coordination of business objects. At the initial level, this business process consists of three components: (1) an internal object *distributor*, (2) an external object *customer*, and (3) a transaction *service* which models the service delivery from distributor to customer. Figure 5 shows the interaction schema and the task-event schema belonging to this level of detail.

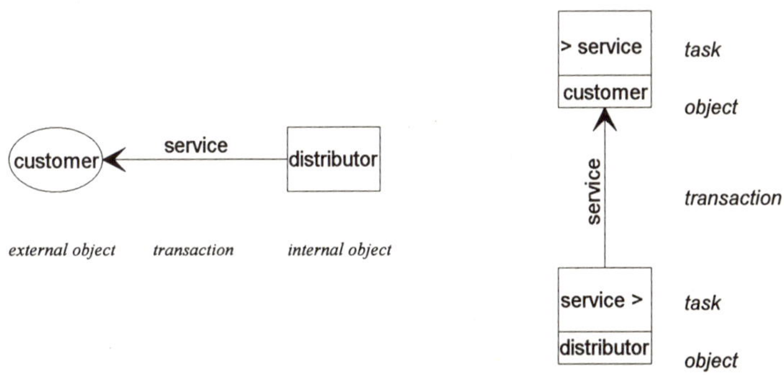

Fig. 5: Interaction schema (left) and task-event schema (right) of business process *distribution* (1st level)

In the task-event schema, the initial task names are derived from the transaction name. For example, the task names *service>* (say "send service") and *>service* (say "receive service") are derived from *service*.

The second level consists of a refinement of the initial level. Here the *service* transaction is decomposed to uncover the coordination between *distributor* (server object) and *customer* (client object). As the two objects negotiate about the delivery of a service, the transaction is decomposed according to the negotiation principle into the sub-transactions *i: price list* (initiating), *c: order* (contracting), and *e: service* (enforcing transaction). Because the sub-transactions are executed sequentially, the task-event schema corresponding to the interaction schema is determined implicitly (see fig. 6).

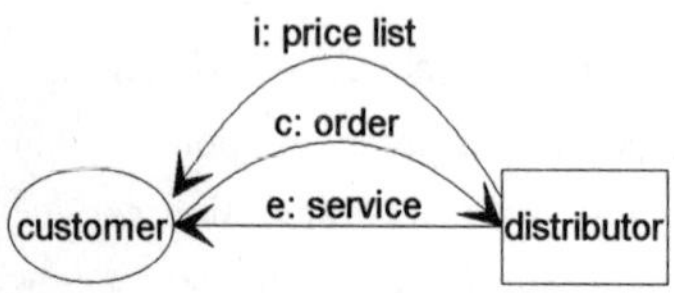

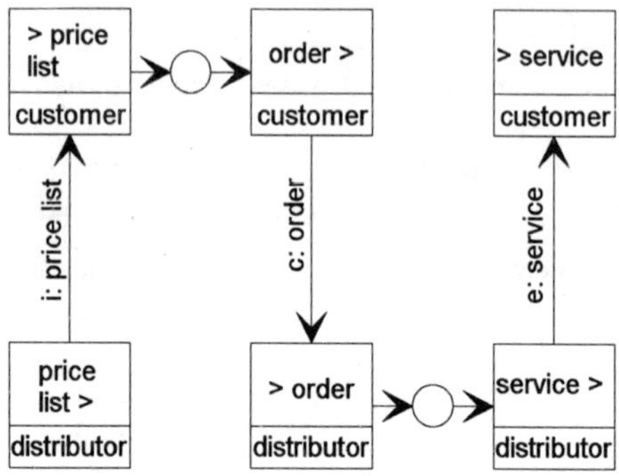

Fig. 6: Interaction schema (left) and task-event schema (right) of business process distribution (2nd level)

At the third level, the object *distributor* is decomposed according to the feedback control principle. This leads to the sub-objects *sales* (controlling sub-object) and *servicing system* (controlled sub-object). At the same time the sub-transactions *price list*, *order*, and *service* are re-assigned to the sub-objects. The *sales* sub-object deals with *price list* and *order*; the *servicing system* sub-object manages the *service* transaction.

In addition, the decomposition of the *distributor* object introduces the sub-transactions *r: service order* (control transaction) and *f: service report* (feedback transaction) from *sales* to *servicing system* and from *servicing system* to *sales* respectively. The purpose of *service order* is to connect the *order* sub-transaction to the *service* sub-transaction. Since the sequence of tasks cannot be fully derived from the interaction schema at this level of detail, the task-event schema shows additional information (see fig. 7).

Fig. 7: Interaction schema (left) and task-event schema (right) of business process *distribution* (3rd level)

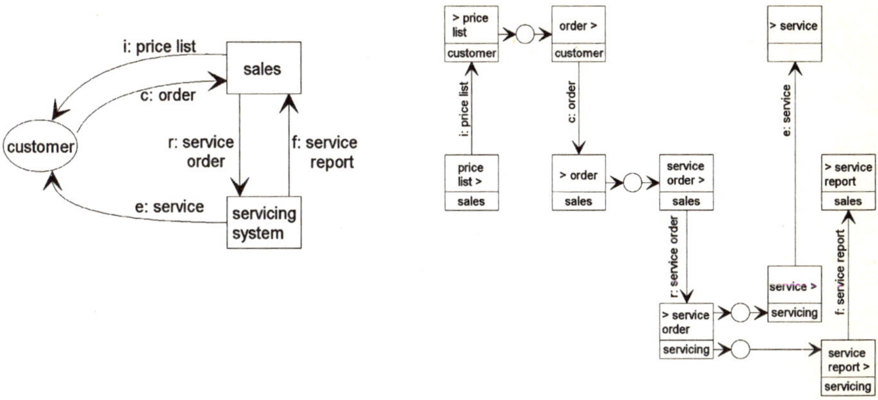

The next decomposition leads to the fourth level (see fig. 8). First, the *e: service* transaction is decomposed into the sequence *e: delivery* and *e: cash up*. The *cash up* transaction is decomposed again according to the negotiation principle into the sequence *c: invoice* and *e: payment*. An initiating transaction is omitted here because the business objects already know each other. The contract of the *invoice* transaction refers to the amount of payment, not to the obligation to pay in principle.

As a result of this refinement, several other decompositions become necessary. The business object *servicing system* is decomposed into *store* and *finances*, responsible for products and payments respectively. *r: service order* is decomposed into the parallel transactions *r: delivery order* and *r: debit*. On the other hand, *f: service report* is decomposed into the parallel transactions *f: delivery report* and *f: payment report*.

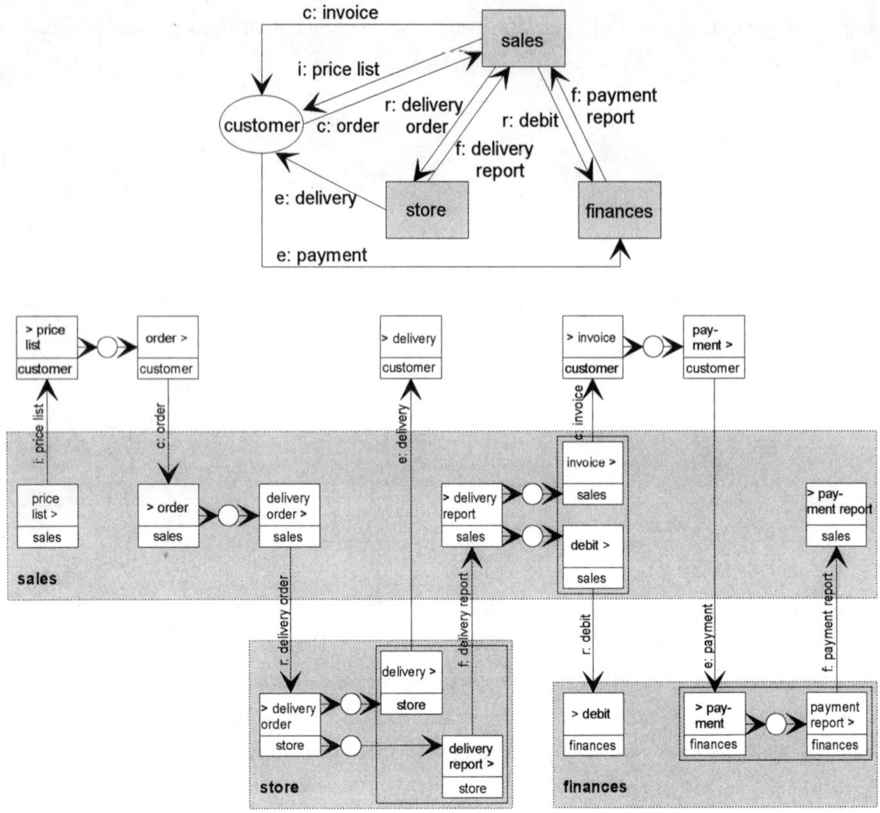

Fig. 8: Interaction schema (above) and task-event schema (below) of business process *distribution* (4th level)

4. Object-Oriented Specification of Distributed Business Application Systems Based on Business Process Models

A business process model as developed in the previous chapter provides a solid platform for an object-oriented specification of distributed business application systems. The corresponding conceptual framework, which is part of the SOM approach, has been outlined in chapter 2 and will be detailed below (see fig. 9).

Following this approach, business systems, business application systems, and computing systems are specified at the corresponding layer as distributed systems with a specific client/server architecture at each layer:

- Within a distributed business system, servers deliver clients with requested services.
- A distributed business application system consists of domain-related components for application, data management, and communication and client/server relationships between these components.
- A distributed computing system provides virtual machines which are connected by communication channels. These virtual machines may also establish a client/server architecture.

As proposed throughout this paper, the specification of a distributed business application system consists of a sequence of design steps, each step corresponding to one layer of the following conceptual framework:

1. Identifying the business application system within a business process model,
2. specifying the domain-related architecture of the distributed business application system according to the application/data management/communication concept, and
3. specifying the physical architecture of the distributed business application system which consists of computers and communication networks.

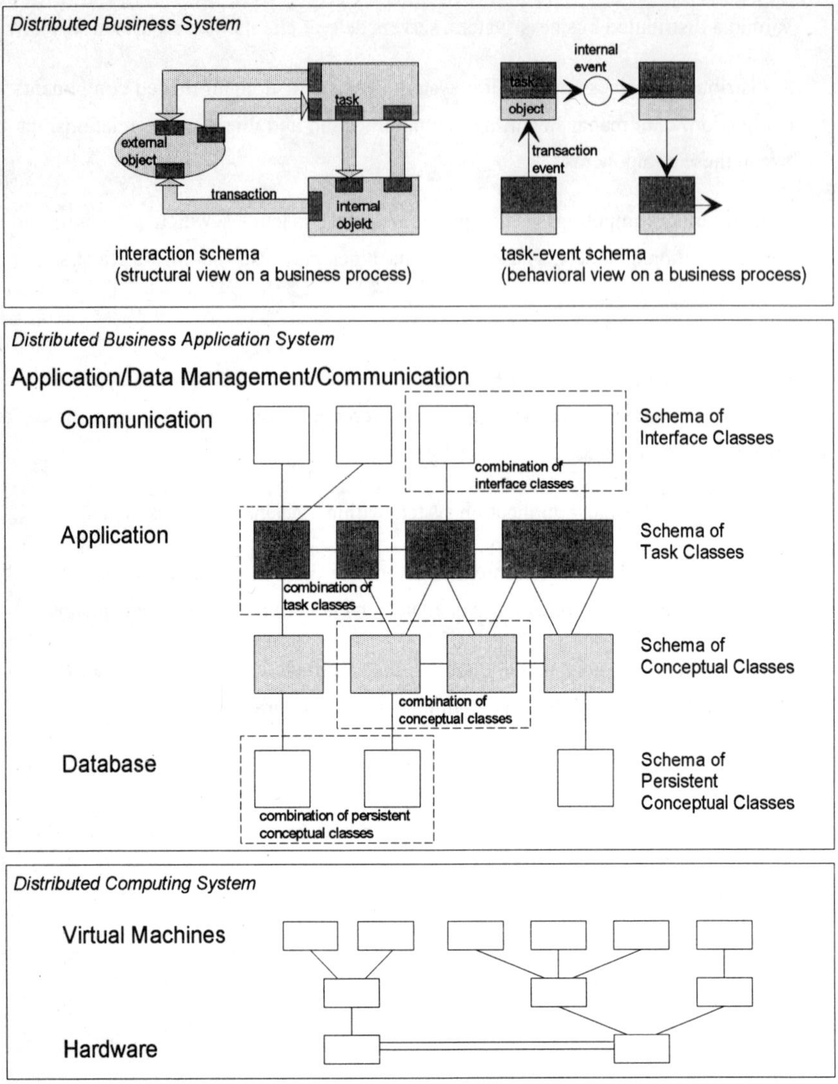

Fig. 9: Conceptual framework for the specification of distributed business application systems

The design of a distributed business application system is influenced by various design goals. Each design step focuses on specific design goals. Since all the goals are mutually dependent, the design of a distributed business application system constitutes a simultaneous decision problem, which is resolved through a sequence of design steps. The design steps and the associated design goals are explained in the following sections.

4.1. Identification of a Business Application System within a Business Process Model

The first layer of the conceptual framework shown in figures 2 and 9 specifies a distributed business system as a set of business processes. The interactions between these business processes constitute the *client/server architecture of the business system.* When a business process is decomposed into its sub-processes, the interactions of these sub-processes follow the client/server concept in turn.

A business application system automates or semi-automates some part of a business process. Therefore, the first design step of specifying a distributed business application system is to identify the scope of the application system within the interaction schema and the task-event schema of a business process model.

The design goal of this design step is to support business objects with *joint goals and objectives* by one application system. Following this guideline, the business process *distribution* should be supported by three application systems:

- a *sales* application system,
- a *store* application system, and
- a *finances* application system.

The scope of these application systems is shaded within the interaction schema and the task-event schema of the detailed business process model (see fig. 8).

4.2. Specification of the Domain-Related Architecture of a Distributed Business Application System

The second layer of figures 2 and 9 specifies the domain-related architecture of a distributed business application system. At this layer, an application system is decomposed into its domain-related components according to the application/data management/communication architecture.

Using the SOM approach, the application/data management/communication architecture of a distributed application system is specified by four schemata:

- The *application* sub-system is specified by the schema of conceptual classes and the schema of task classes. Conceptual classes establish the domain-related basis of a business application system. Task classes specify the cooperation of conceptual classes when executing a task.

- The *communication* sub-system is specified by the schema of interface classes.
- The *data management* sub-system is specified by the schema of persistent conceptual classes.

The *schema of conceptual classes* consists of specifications of classes with attributes and operations (see fig. 10). The classes are connected by *is_a*, *interacts_with*, and *is_part_of* relationships (see Ferstl & Sinz (1990)).

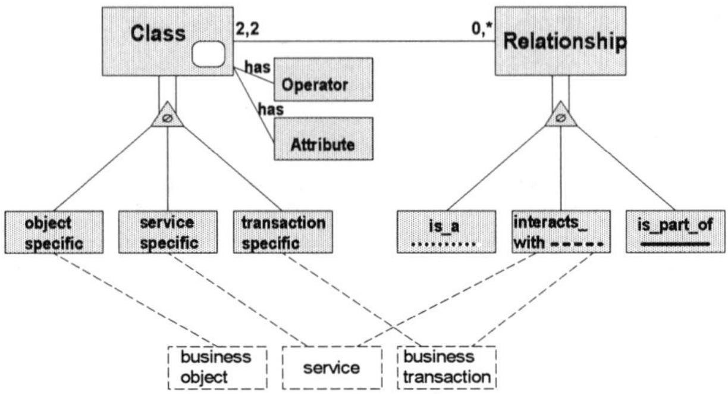

Fig. 10: Meta model of the schema of conceptual classes

According to the meta model shown in figure 10, an initial schema of the conceptual classes can be derived using the interaction schema and the task-event schema of the business process *distribution* at the most detailed level (see figure 8). Dashed rectangles and lines show the relationships between a business process model and a schema of conceptual classes. Business objects, service specifications, and business transactions lead to classes and *interacts_with* relationships. *is_a* and *is_part_of* relationships cannot be derived from the business process model at this stage. Existence dependencies between the instances of the classes are visualized from left to right by graphical placement of the class symbols. The resulting initial schema of conceptual classes is shown in figure 11.

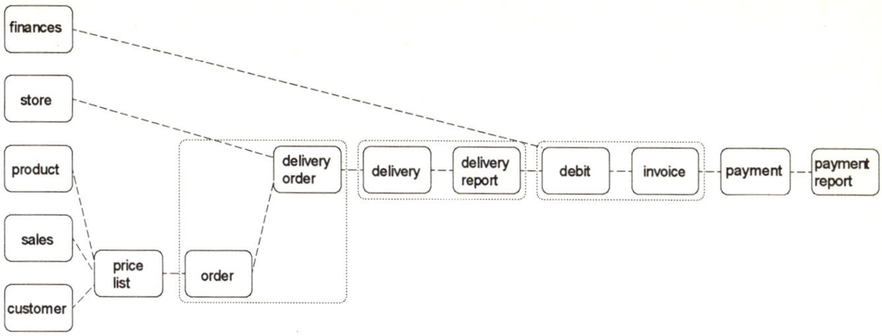

Fig. 11: Conceptual class schema derived from business process *distribution*

The schema of conceptual classes has to be completed by assigning attributes and operations to the class definitions, finding *is_a* relationships between classes, decomposing class definitions using *is_part_of* relationships and specifying the complexity of *interacts_with* relationships. These aspects are beyond the scope of this paper (see Ferstl & Sinz (1990)).

The *schema of task classes* specifies for each task the cooperation of conceptual classes during the execution of a task. The initial schema of task classes can be derived from the task-event schema of the business process model. Each task within the scope of the business application system leads in general to a separate task class (see fig. 8). Details of the specification of task classes are not explained here (see Ferstl & Sinz (1990)).

The *schema of interface classes* specifies interfaces for human-computer communication and computer-computer communication. Human-computer interfaces are used to implement semi-automated tasks, computer-computer interfaces are used to connect different application systems.

The *schema of persistent conceptual classes* specifies classes whose instances are persistent even when the execution of a task has been finished. Therefore, these instances have to be stored in a database. The attributes of the schema of persistent conceptual classes result from a projection onto the attributes of the schema of conceptual classes. In addition, each class specifies access operations onto these attributes.

The initial schemata as constructed above constitute the basis for the design step at the second layer of the conceptual framework. The design goal of this step is to remove *domain-related redundancy and inconsistency*. This is done by combining particular classes within the initial schemata. Combining two classes shifts their coupling from loose to tight and reduces the application system's degree of distribution.

The initial schemata represent a business application system with a maximum degree of distribution related to the decomposition of a given business process model. Applying this design step repeatedly leads to a desirable degree of distribution with respect to redundancy and consistency.

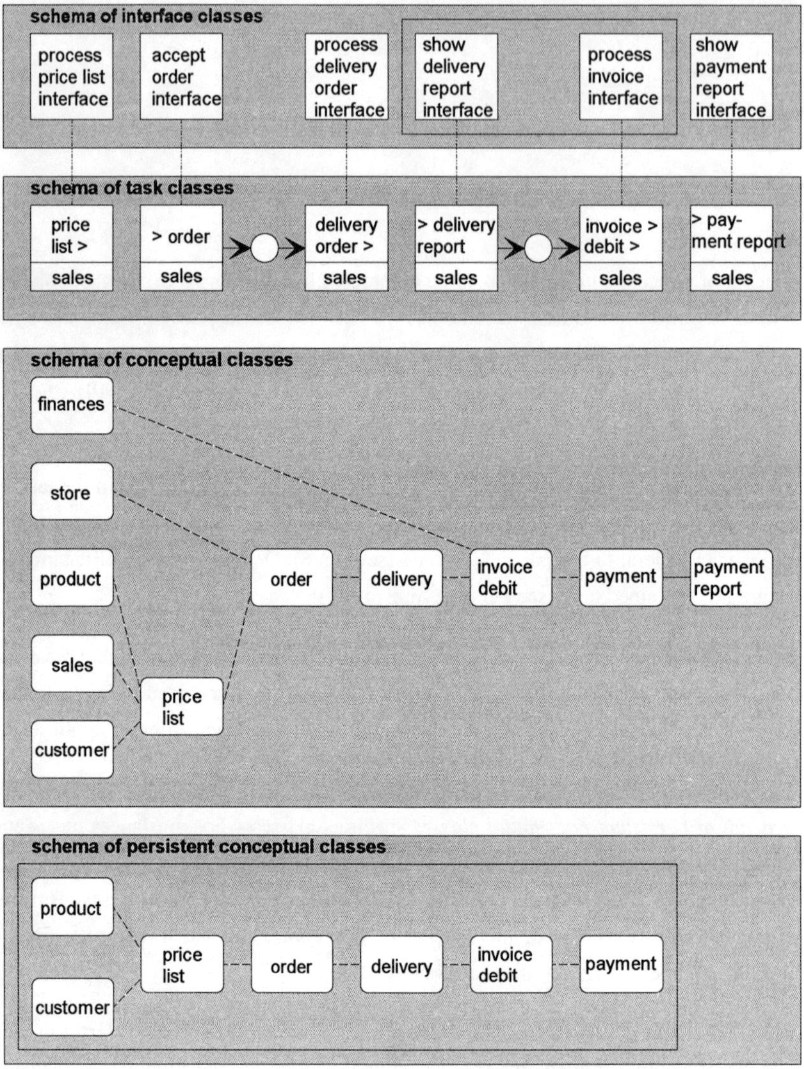

Fig. 12: Components of the domain-related architecture

Figure 12 shows the resulting schemata after applying the design rules:

- Assigning attributes and operations to the conceptual classes in figure 11 uncovers that some classes show (nearly) the same attributes and operations. To avoid redundancy and inconsistency, these classes should be combined. Refering to figures 11 and 12, the classes *order* and *delivery order* are combined to *order*; *delivery* and *delivery report* are combined to *delivery*; and *debit* and *invoice* are combined to *invoice/debit*.

- The structure of the initial schema of task classes is shown above in figure 8. It contains a task class for each task of the business object *sales*. To avoid redundancy and inconsistency again, the tasks *invoice>* and *debit>* have been combined (see figure 11). This is because the tasks perform nearly the same function (redundancy), and to ensure the *invoice* and *debit* are sent to *customer* and *finances* at the same time (consistency).

- The initial schema of interface classes provides an interface class for each task class (see fig. 12). Here, the *show delivery report* interface and the *process invoice* interface are combined. This avoids redundancy when processing invoices on delivered products by a person using the application system.

- Assuming that the conceptual classes *finances*, *store*, and *sales* have no persistent attributes, and that *payment report* can be derived from *payment*, leads to the initial schema of persistent conceptual classes shown in figure 12. If it is required to manage the referential integrity constraints between the classes by a database management system (consistency), the classes have to be combined into a single database schema.

4.3. Specification of the Physical Architecture of a Distributed Business Application System

The third layer of figures 2 and 9 specifies the physical architecture of a distributed business application system. At this layer, the domain-related components of the second layer are assigned to virtual machines, which in turn are assigned to lower level virtual machines.

Virtual machines are actors for the domain-related components of the second layer. Examples of virtual machines are database management systems which support persistent conceptual classes, user-interface management systems which support interface classes, and other application-independent class libraries.

The design goal of this step focuses on the criteria *capacity and performance of virtual machines*. This goal is achieved by a convenient mapping of domain-related components into virtual machines. In this context it may be necessary to reduce the number of components and relationships at the domain level. This is done by a further combination of domain-related classes. In contrast to the design step at the second layer, classes of different schemata may also be combined.

The design step at the third layer is highly dependent on the specific hardware and software platform and therefore cannot be described in general.

5. Conclusion

This paper focuses on distributed business systems. It considers a distributed business system to be a set of business processes, coordinated by negotiation and feedback control principles. The decomposition of a business system is directed by the outcome of the business processes and follows the client/server concept.

Business application systems are regarded as actors for business processes. The linkage of business processes to business application systems ensures compatible structures at both layers. An initial structure of a business application system can even be derived from the corresponding business process model. The structuring of a business application system follows the paradigms of (1) the coordination principles in business processes, (2) the application/data management/communication structure, and (3) the client/server concept. It is noteworth that the object-oriented paradigm and the client/server concept is valid over all three layers of the SOM approach.

The specification of a distributed business application system remains challenging. We hope that the approach outlined in this paper contributes to turn the specification of a distributed business application system from an intuitive trial and error process to a systematic system engineering procedure. This is the most important prerequisite for total quality management at a high level of maturity.

References

Enslow, P.H.: What is a 'Distributed' Data Processing System? In: IEEE Computer, Vol. 11, No. 1, January 1978, 13 - 21

Ferstl, O.K.; Sinz, E.J.: Objektmodellierung betrieblicher Informationssysteme im Semantischen Objektmodell (SOM). In: Wirtschaftsinformatik Band 32, Heft 6 (1990), 566 - 581

Ferstl, O.K.; Sinz, E.J.: Ein Vorgehensmodell zur Objektmodellierung betrieblicher Informationssysteme im Semantischen Objektmodell (SOM). In: Wirtschaftsinformatik Band 33, Heft 6 (1991), 477 - 491

Ferstl, O.K.; Sinz, E.J.: Der Modellierungsansatz des Semantischen Objektmodells (SOM); Bamberger Beiträge zur Wirtschaftsinformatik, Nr. 18, Bamberg, 1993

Ferstl, O.K.; Sinz, E.J.: Geschäftsprozeßmodellierung; In Wirtschaftsinformatik Band 35, Heft 6 (1993), 589-592

Ferstl, O.K.; Sinz, E.J.: Grundlagen der Wirtschaftsinformatik. 2. Auflage, Oldenbourg, München 1994

Ferstl, O.K.; Sinz, E.J.; Amberg, M.; Hagemann, U.; Malischewski, C.: Tool-Based Business Process Modeling Using the SOM Approach. Proc. IFIP World Computer Congress, Hamburg 1994

Gray, J.; Reuter, A.: Transaction Processing: Concepts and Techniques. Morgan Kaufmann, San Mateo, California 1993

Martin, B.E.; Pedersen, C.H.; Bedford-Roberts, J.: An Object-Based Taxonomy for Distributed Computing Systems. In: IEEE Computer, Vol. 24, No. 8 (1991), 17 - 27

Acknowledgement:

This work is partly supported by the Deutsche Forschungsgemeinschaft (DFG), contract No. Si 481/1-3.

Computer Support for Distributed Information Management Tasks (CUVIMA)

Elgass, P.; Krcmar, H.; Ludwig, B.; Schönwälder, S.[131]

Abstract

This article presents an overview of the research results of the project CUVIMA. This interdisciplinary project combined aspects of the research areas "information management", "computer aided team", "conversation structuring" and "object-orientation". CUVIMA identified "information systems planning" and "business process planning" as representatives of highly interesting, quite complex and exceptional distributed information management tasks. These tasks are not only suitable for implementing computer support in a computer aided team environment, but also allow the use of computer-based conversation structuring for a more efficient problem solving process within groups. Object-orientation was used for the analysis phase and as the implementation method.

1. Introduction

This article presents an overview of the results of the research project CUVIMA[132], Computer Support for Distributed Information Management Tasks. The article outlines the goals and research approaches used. Results of the project are presented by explaining the CUVIMA tool concept and architecture followed by a description of the concepts and prototypes of CONSUL, PROPLAN and ISPLAN.

2. Research Propositions of CUVIMA

Within the overall framework of the research program "Distributed Systems in Business", CUVIMA has three goals and provides contributions in these areas:

---

[131] The authors of this article are listed in alphabetical order and contributed equally to this article. Acknowledgement: C. Krcmar for review of the manuscript.

[132] The project is funded by the the Deutsche Forschungsgemeinschaft within the research program "Verteilte DV-Systeme in der Betriebswirtschaft". CUVIMA is the acronym of "Computer Aided Team-Werkzeugprototypen für verteilte Informationsmanagementaufgaben".

1. development of concepts for computer support tools for distributed tasks (e.g. business process planning and information systems planning) in information management, prototype implementation and evaluation,

2. evaluation of the usability of conversation structuring for the improvement of computer aided team tools and,

3. evaluation of the suitability and efficiency of object-oriented software development for business-oriented software, especially the use of object-oriented database representation.

CUVIMA is an interdisciplinary project, as it combines the research areas "information management", "object-orientation", "computer aided team" and "conversation structuring" (see figure 1).

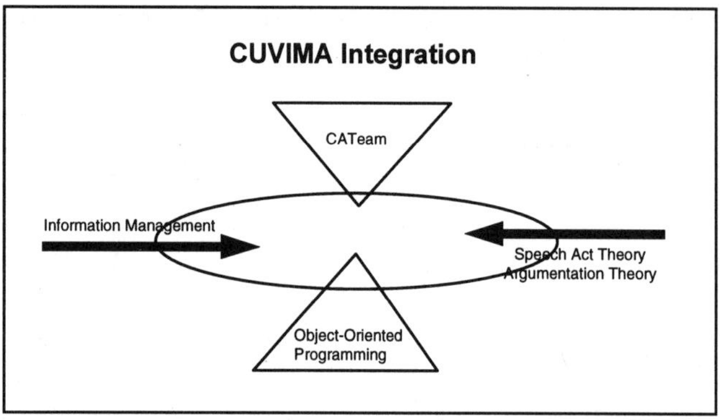

Figure 1: Conceptual aspects of CUVIMA Integration

The following paragraphs provide the rationale for choosing the two specific information management tasks, "business process planning" and "information systems planning". This explanation will then be used to support the argument that an interdisciplinary approach was required to reach the goals of the project.

For this project, two different tasks in information management were chosen: "strategic planning of information systems" and "business process planning". These were chosen for a number of reasons:

1) they are useful for practical and theoretical analysis,

2) they represent a wide range of tasks, and

3) they are concerned with multifaceted and complex problems and are usually performed in project teams which follow a typical team process with a sequence of classic and distributed meetings with individual work interspersed.

Additionally, both tasks are distributed over time and space as well as they are performed by groups of individuals. The two tasks are structured and formalised to a different degree. Various methods have been developed to support them. Creativity is involved to a different degree in each of the tasks. Although tool support for these tasks exists, it certainly does not fulfill all needs[133] especially aspects of distribution in the problem solving phase.

There are a number of reasons why an interdisciplinary approach was required for the study. As information management tasks are often performed as team processes, we needed to interpret the support for distributed[134] information management tasks as a support for a team performing them. This explains the need to integrate the content aspects of information management with the process aspects of Computer Aided Team (CATeam) or Computer Supported Co-operative Work (CSCW). Within group work there is a lot of discussion and ongoing debate about how much structured conversation and what kind of action is useful. For purposes of this study, we integrated group work and conversation structuring, speech act theory (SAT)[135], and argumentation theory[136]. In order to answer the third research proposition about the usability of an object-oriented implementation in that context, it was essential to integrate the research area "object-orientation"[137].

3. Research Approaches

In order to fulfill the goals, CUVIMA was divided into three sub-projects which were directly linked to the research propositions:

1. CONSUL (CONversation Structuring UtiLity) focuses on conversation structuring,
2. PROPLAN (business PROcess PLANning) focuses on computer based business process planning,
3. ISPLAN (strategic Information System PLANning) focuses on computer based strategic planning of information systems.

---

133 See Krcmar, 1992a. Krcmar, 1992b.

134 Within CUVIMA the word distribution is not used in the technical sense, but as a term that describes the distribution of tasks such as group planning processes.

135 See Searle, 1969; Kunz/Rittel ,1970.

136 See Reuter/Werner 1983; Austin, 1962; Habermas, 1981.

137 Due to space limitations, research results about object-orientation and prototype evaluation will be reported elsewhere.

Object-orientation is anchored within all sub-projects as an integrative cross-project task. All sub-projects are designed and implemented object-oriented.

We used different research approaches: literature review, expert interviews, prototype implementation, industrial co-operation and prototype evaluation. This mixture of approaches was used because of the varying levels of research work that had been reported within each area and because of the heterogeneity of the goals we followed.

CUVIMA was divided into three major phases: analysis, implementation, and evaluation. During the first phase, a literature review was performed and expert interviews about the two Information Management tasks (PROPLAN and ISPLAN) and the Conversation Structuring Utility (CONSUL) were conducted. They were conducted to identify the crucial issues and requirements for concept design and prototype implementation. During the second phase of the study, the tools CONSUL, PROPLAN and ISPLAN were implemented. We decided to develop three stand-alone single-user tools in an object-oriented programming language[138] with the notion of integrating them later. The experience in CATeam research Hohenheim[139] provided the requirements for supporting these tasks in a management environment. The third phase was aimed at evaluating the tools in order to demonstrate the usability of the concepts and their implementation. Tests were performed within the department and in co-operation with industry.

4. Research Results

4.1. Tool Concepts

As a consequence of integration and distribution considerations, the tool concept of CUVIMA separates two layers of tools (see figure 2). With domain specific tools such as PROPLAN and ISPLAN, specific tasks are supported. Generic group tools support generic group tasks or processes such as voting, ranking and conversation structuring (CONSUL). The generic tools serve as basis for group tasks of the domain specific tools even though they do not supply all functional primitives. Both layers perform their own data handling and consequently provide their own functional classes. Each domain specific tool has a distributed and a non-distributed part which depends on the structure of the task or process itself and is typical for client/server environments. The generic group tools are distributed by default as they support group tasks or processes.

---

[138] See Taylor, 1990.
[139] See Krcmar, 1992a.

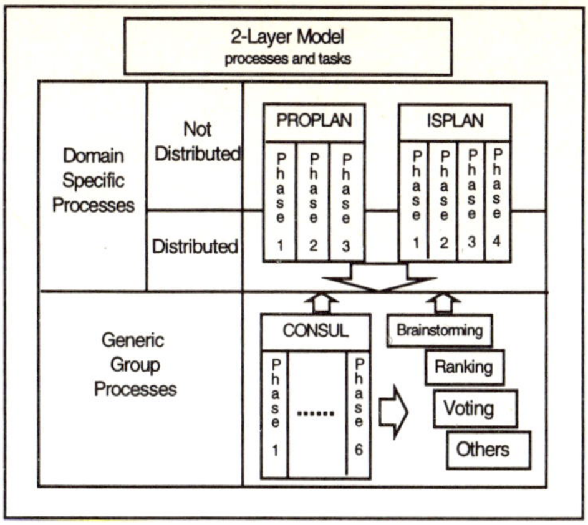

Figure 2: 2-Layer Model

The advantages of the layered model are the flexibility within the individual tools and also the flexibility in connecting and combining domain specific tools with general tools. One tool can be changed without affecting another.

4.2. CONSUL

Group discussions and problem solving are generic tasks needed for constructive and efficient team work. Therefore, CONSUL (CONversation Structuring Utility)[140] is a tool concept supporting group based problem solving by structuring conversation. It can be used for computer-based discussions without having an artificial or human group facilitator. Methods are chosen and implemented which streamline this effort and rely on the self-organization of teams using language.

4.2.1. CONSUL Concept

The CONSUL concept is based on several argumentation theories[141] and focuses on computer-based discussions and problem solving. The CONSUL concept provides a model for group negotiations and agreements (see figure 3). The negotiation and agreement process is divided into four phases.

---

[140] See Ludwig, 1994b.
[141] See Toulmin 1958; Kunz/Rittel 1970; Habermas, 1989.

Phase I: Constitution: This is the entry point of the discussion where the problem itself and one or more issues concerning that problem are stated by the group members.

Phase II: Solving: Problem solving alternatives are entered, discussed, and information exchange on possible alternatives takes place among the group members.

Phase III: Ranking: This phase is used for an individual ranking of the different.

Phase IV: Ranking of Ranking: Putting together the different rankings of the individual group members, the whole group ranks the different rankings for a final group result.

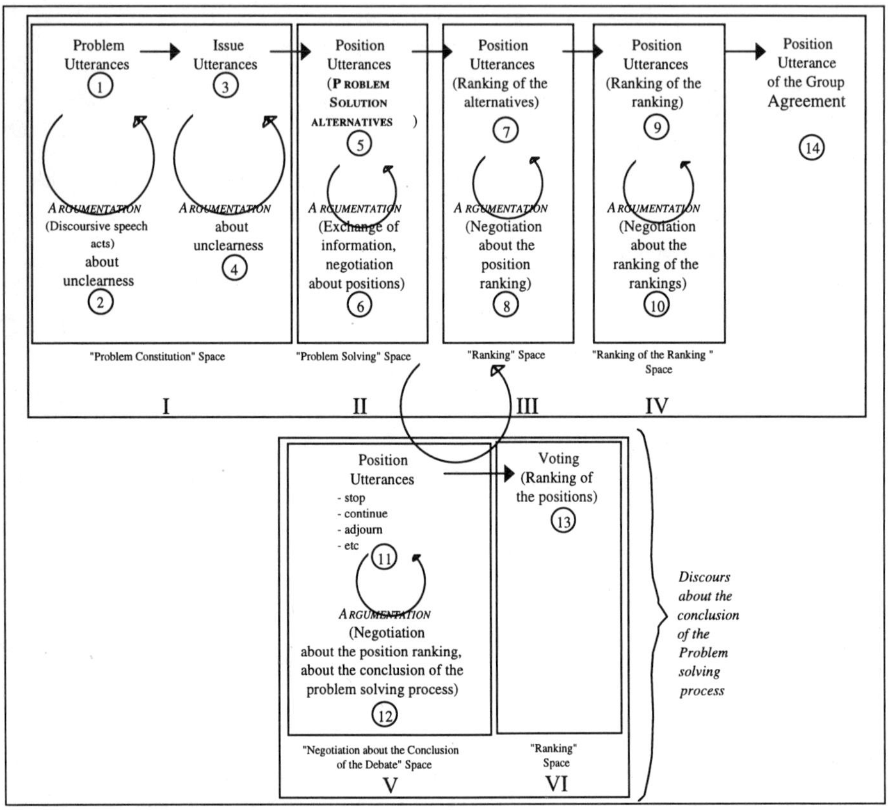

Figure 3: Discussion and problem solving process

Parallel to phases I to IV, the phases V and VI take place. They support discussions about ending a particular phase. Phase V supports a discussion about an ending for each phase (I-IV) and phase VI allows a ranking of different opinions about the endpoint. It is important point to stress that phases V and VI support the group in finding the final point of discussion without any group mediator (group facilitator).

The main differences to common IBIS[142]-based concepts are the refinement of the argumentation process and the support of the problem-solving process. In addition, compared to other conversation structuring tools (e.g. ConversationBuilder[143], Coordinator[144]), the CONSUL concept and tool allow the users to modify the discussion and problem solving process.

4.2.2. CONSUL Prototype

The CONSUL prototype is a client/server-based tool which provides support for the process of problem solving explained above. CONSUL is divided into an administrative and an user part. The administrative part is used to prepare the process, making it a combination of flexible and universal tools. In the user part the group members work in a computer-based discussion or problem solving meeting.

a) CONSUL Administration

Even though CONSUL itself can be used in group discussions without a mediator, someone has to prepare CONSUL for use within meetings. One derived design issue was flexibility and ease of use. Flexibility is the ability to insert, delete and change speech acts and speech act sequences to allow easy adaptation. As an example, speech acts cannot be translated directly from one language to another as they might have different meanings within two different languages. Therefore, a CONSUL administrator can use speech act templates provided by CONSUL as a reference or can modify, delete, or add new ones. CONSUL provides editors for speech act and speech-act-sequence modelling. The Speech-Act-Protocol-to-Phase-Assignment-Editor is used to assign speech act sequences to phases. The person preparing the group discussion can use this editor for defining the phases.[145] First, he defines the phases and then assigns a speech act sequence (protocol) to each phase. This is also possible by using the protocols provided by CONSUL or the definition of new speech act sequences using the speech act editor and the speech-act-sequence editor.

The Speech-Act-Sequence Editor allows adding, modifying and deleting speech acts and also speech act sequences. First, a speech act sequence has to be selected and then one or more already existing speech acts will be assigned to it. In this way, it is possible to create a tree with

---

[142] IBIS is the acronym of Issue Based Information System

[143] See Kaplan, 1992.

[144] Coordinator (Version 2.0 1990) is a software product from Action Technologies.

[145] The administrator can modify or adapt the phase model described above. CONSUL tools allow free definition of phases but CONSUL comes with the phase model described above and its use is recommended.

multiple levels that build a speech act sequence. To change speech acts the speech act editor must be used. The speech act editor is initiated by the speech-act-sequence editor and allows the insertion, change, and deletion of speech acts. CONSUL provides a couple of utilities that can be used to support computer-based group work. For example, a utility for graphical ranking and voting[146] which is required in phase V and VI of the developed negotiation and problem-solving process mentioned above and which was used for ISPLAN and PROPLAN.

b) Using CONSUL

After either choosing or defining the pre-delivered phases, speech act sequences, and speech acts a group discussion can be started. The users do not see the different editors explained above. They use CONSUL as a medium for group discussions. Although CONSUL can be integrated within domain specific tools such as ISPLAN, PROPLAN, or others, it can also be used alone without a domain specific tool. In either situation, the CONSUL interface remains the same.

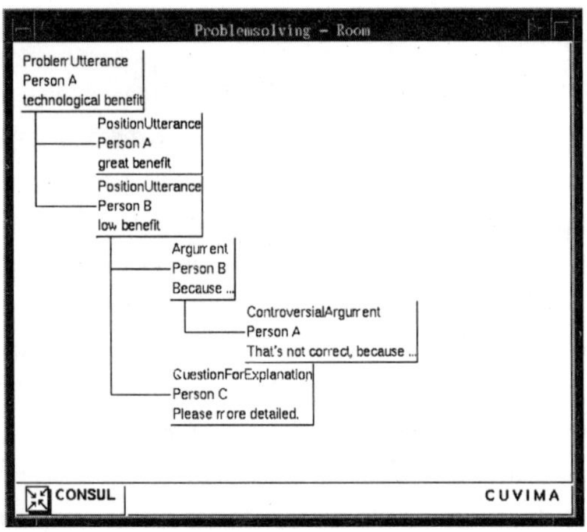

Figure 4: CONSUL - problem solving space

Based on the phases and the speech act sequences, the user follows the given path of conversation structuring that finally leads to a commonly accepted group discussion result. The user browses his way through one or many discussion trees and adds his speech acts. Within a discussion tree, any group member can browse through the tree and see the utterances made so far. Figure 4 illustrates a small example of a group discussion with CONSUL, using the prob-

[146] Ludwig, 1994b.

lem solving space[147]. The top left node contains the problem utterance: In our example, person A has a problem with the evaluation of the technological benefit of a project portfolio. Therefore, the user inserted the new problem utterance. In the next step, person A inserted his position, identifying "great benefit". Then, person B inserted his position, which identifies only "low benefit", and B adds in the next step an argument for this position. Person A then adds a controversial argument with "That's not correct, because ...". Finally, person C does not understand the position of person B and inserts a QuestionForExplanation speech act with the content "Please more detailed.".

Open questions on the CONSUL concept and prototype

Argumentation theory is still an under-researched area, especially with regard to the definition of suitable speech acts and speech act sequences. There is hardly any empirical knowledge about the design of speech acts and how they can be used efficiently for group discussions. It is also unclear if and how felicity conditions for speech act sequences should be supported. Another problem we are facing is how the problem solving process derived in the CONSUL concept will be accepted in real group meetings. Partial answers to these questions are found through the empirical evaluation of CONSUL[148].

4.3. PROPLAN

Even though business process reengineering (BPR) is a widely discussed topic in many companies and serveral tools exist supporting BPR, 50-70% of the reengineering projects fail[149] because of three fundamental flaws shown through our analysis[150]. The first flaw is the lack of team orientation. Second, the focus is often geared toward activities instead of the interfaces between the activities and therefore the communication and information relationships between people. Third, there is a lack of an integrated method which enables the planners to transform an informal into a semiformal and a formal feasible process model.

PROPLAN tries to overcome these shortcomings by providing a computer-based concept for supporting business process planning.

---

147 The problem solving space is the user environment for the discussions.
148 See Ludwig, 1994b.
149 See Hammer/Champy 1993.
150 See Krcmar/Schwarzer 1994.

4.3.1. PROPLAN Concept

The analysis mentioned above consisted of two parts and was catapulted by the search for reasons for the high failure rate in business process reengineering projects. The first part was the analysis of the corresponding literature and the second part was the interview of experts in different branches of business[151].

To get an in-depth view and understanding of process planning in practice, we interviewed[152] experts from banking, industry, and consulting. The key results of the interviews[153] were:

1. For the definition of business processes, various approaches are taken. These approaches represent different combinations of analytical methods, reference processes and creative techniques. Another important point is field experience and creativity of competent employees of companies or external consultants.

2. Process structuring is done in many different ways and relies heavily on experience and creativity. It seems that the usage of analytical methods is insufficient because conventional methods derive processes from already existing structures within an organization. The methods used by the interviewed persons were reference processes, creative techniques and a combination of both. In some cases, the existing work-flow is taken as the basis for reengineering an existing structure.

3. Companies are aware of the necessity of process modelling and controlling but do not have action plans for implementation.

The literature study and the interviews lead to a detailed 3-phase model[154] into which methods from the areas conversation structuring and CSCW were integrated (see figure 5). The three main phases are process definition, structuring, and logic.

Phase I: Process Definition

Business process planning is a strategic task that needs adequate information to achieve a suitable result. The quality of the result depends very much on the information used to define the strategic processes. Therefore, methods like critical success factor analysis and strategic environmental factor analysis will be used.

---

[151] The research approach taken was a qualitative, empirical research method namely a verbal interview with a semi-structured interview guide.

[152] The research approach taken were qualitative, empirical interviews. We interviewed experts from different branches with different business processes in a semi-structured, verbal interview.

[153] See Elgass, 1994a.

[154] See Elgass, 1994b.

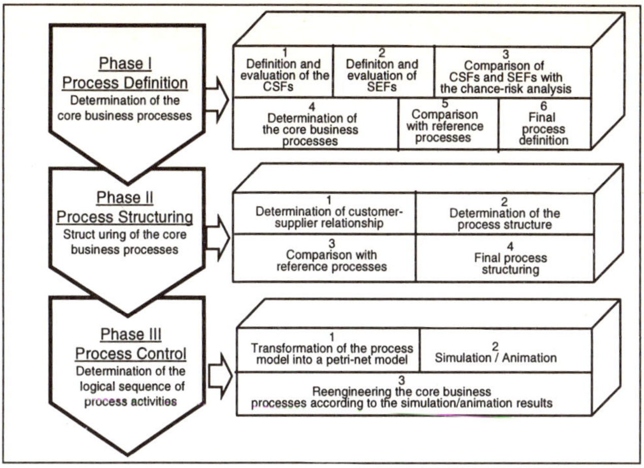

Figure 5: PROPLAN model for business process planning

The process definition will be achieved through the following steps:

1. Critical success factors (CSF) analysis: The critical success factors will be determined in brainstorming meetings with a group of competent employees. The critical success factors will then be evaluated using various methods.

2. Strategic environmental factors (SEF) analysis: In addition to CSFs, strategic environmental factors must be determined, analysed and evaluated. This can be done in the same way as the CSF analysis.

3. Comparison of CSF and SEF results: By comparing the CSF and SEF results with a chance-risk analysis, the process planners can determine, how the development of the business environment compares to that of the company itself. The different combinations identify which actions should be taken for the present and the future.

4. Determination of the core business processes: As there are no analytical methods for determining business processes, the best way is group-based brainstorming. The results from the three previous steps are essential as a basis for this activity. The brainstorming leads to the proposition of core processes.

5. Comparison with reference processes: The proposed processes will be compared with existing reference processes using criteria, such as company-specific factors, business goals, business strategies. This can be useful, for example, to uncover missing activities.

6. Final determination of the strategic business processes: In the final step, the results will be consolidated and a group consensus regarding the strategic business process will be defined.

Phase II: Process Structuring

The phase "process structuring" consists of several subphases.

1. In a team process, the planners structure the processes defined in the first phase of the planning process. In order to emphasize the interfaces between the different activities of a process, the method of the so-called "customer-supplier relationship" originating in the speech act theory is used[155]. In PROPLAN, the graphical notation of this method was, on one hand, enlarged in order to place a more powerful method at the planners' disposal enabling them to develop a formal process model and, on the other hand, changed in virtue of visualization[156]. At the end of subphase 1 the process is structured as a chain of customer-supplier relationships.

2. The planners must agree on one unique process structure. The unification process is maintained for example by CONSUL.

3. In this subphase the defined process structure can be equalised by reference processes.

4. Finally, the planners have to define the final process structure.

Phase III: Process Control

In this phase, the semi-formal process model will be transformed into a formal model. The underlying formal method is the petri-net model as the basic structure for simulation and animation processes. As a result of process animation/simulation, reengineering of the defined processes might be necessary.

The process logic phase implements the processes from phase II in a simulation/animation environment where it is possible to schedule and structure single activities of processes.

1. Process Modelling with Petri-Nets: The process structures from phase II are modelled as a petri-net for a forthcoming analysis. Petri-nets have an exact mathematical definition and theory and provide high flexibility for implementing complex structures such as business

---

155 See Medina-Mora/Winograd/Flores/Flores, 1992; Dunham, 1991; Scherr, 1993; and the tool of Action Technologies for conversation structuring.

156 See Elgass, 1994.

processes. It may be useful for the animation/simulation to have detailed data about each process such as cost and time consumption of activities even though it is not a requirement.

2. Simulation/Animation: Dependent on the availability of process data, the business processes can be animated or simulated to test their behavior. Animation and simulation can be performed on different process levels.

3. Reengineering: The simulation/animation might uncover potential problems in process structure and behavior. These problems can be eliminated through a final reengineering step thus leading to streamlined and efficient processes.

After the third phase, processes have to be implemented in the company; this is beyond the scope of the PROPLAN concept.

4.3.2. PROPLAN Prototype

In comparison to common process planning tools (e.g. ARIS Toolset[157], BDF[158], Workflo[159]), the special features of the PROPLAN Prototype are team orientation, an interface- and communication-driven approach to process structuring, and an integrated planning method. As of autumn 1994, the PROPLAN prototype consists of a single tool supporting the steps of the three planning phases. These are a process definition tool for phase I, a process structuring tool for phase II and a petri-net editor for phase III. The group processes such as discussion, unification, and problem solving can be supported either by CONSUL or other software such as GroupSystems[160].

Process Definition Tool: For the process definition phase, a utility was designed supporting the evaluation and comparison of the critical success factors identified by each planner. First, each planner has to define and evaluate the critical success factors for the organization or business and then evaluate them. A graphical part of the utility permits the demonstration of the evaluated CSFs within a polarity profile. The planners will then be able to compare all evaluations and start the discussion in regard to a common accepted profile.

Process Structuring Tool: The process structuring tool consists of two subtools "visualizer (PROPLAN/G)" and "definer". The visualizer (see figure 6) allows the visualization of the

---

157 ARIS Toolset is a software product from IDS Scheer GmbH, Saarbrücken, Germany.
158 BDF (Business Design Facility) is a software product from Texas Instruments Information Engineering (Deutschland) GmbH.
159 Workfo is a software product from FileNet GmbH, Bad Homburg, Germany.
160 GroupSystems is a software product from Ventana Corporation, Tuscon, Arizona, USA.

customer-supplier relationships and the definer allows a description of the underlying communication protocols defining exactly the course of the conversation by means of the so-called "speech acts".

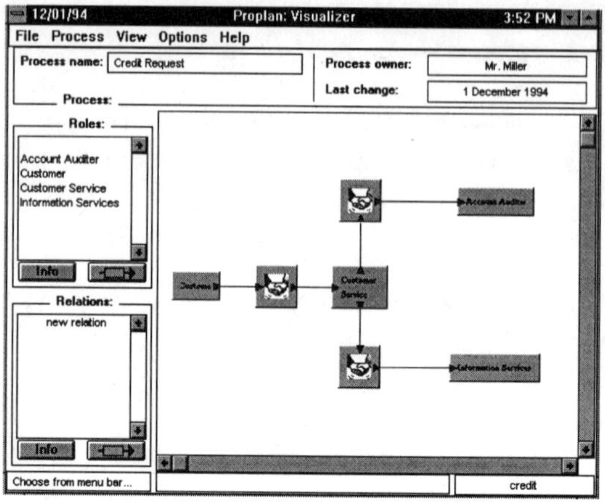

Figure 6: Process-Structuring Tool - Example of a business process of a bank, loan department

Petri-Net Editor: For phase III (process logic), a simple petri-net editor allows generating state/transition petri-nets of processes. The editor allows insertion, modification and deletion of states, transitions and markings. The user can assign names to the net objects and will also be able to view predecessors and successors. The editor can also be used for random animation of processes.

Open questions on the PROPLAN concept and prototype

The in-depth reflection on business process planning leads to a multitude of open questions in the concept domain as well as in the prototype domain. One leading theme is the search for a definite method (formal or semi-formal) in phase I. It is interesting to note to what extent analytical methods can be used. We are currently developing a model which transforms the semi-formal process model (model of customer-supplier relationships) into a formal model based on petri-nets[161]. Another question is the acceptance on the side of the companies. Therefore, we will conduct several workshops with experts from different companies evaluating the concept and the prototype. Likewise, it is necessary to study the effects of the team orientation in the planning process.

---

[161] See Elgass/Krcmar/Oberweis, 1994.

4.4. ISPLAN

ISPLAN (**I**nformation **S**ystems **Plan**ning Tool) is a concept and tool that is used for strategic information systems planning. Information systems planning is a relatively well researched area. Thus far the research approaches are rather theoretical and abstract and do not provide sufficient information for translating it into actions or computer support. Another point often missing is that information system planning is a strategic task that should be carried out by a couple of managers as a group decision process. We designed a flexible model for the information system planning process allowing implementation and empirical evaluation.

4.4.1. ISPLAN Concept

Based on existing literature[162] and interview results[163], we designed ISPLAN using a phase concept. Strategic information systems planning is seen as the decision process about projects ideas that do fit in the IS environment of a company and therefore will be realized. ISPLAN itself covers only project planning. ISPLAN does not support any further steps such as project controlling or implementation, even though these tasks could be based on data derived from the information system planning task. ISPLAN is structured in four main phases "project collection", "evaluation definition", "project evaluation", and "evaluation discussion".

Phase I (Project Collection): In the project collection phase, new IS projects are proposed and entered into the project database. The project database maintains project information relevant to planning, i.e. data entries which are useful for planners who must decide whether the proposed system fits into the information system infrastructure of a department or company and the proposed system or not.

Phase II (Evaluation Definition): In the evaluation definition phase, the planners define how the project ideas will be evaluated. A structure - called a system - must be defined by the planners so that all projects can be evaluated. For ISPLAN, we chose a portfolio structure which has four dimensions: benefit, risk, strategy fit and environmental fit[164]. Each of these four dimensions consists of one or more criteria. In accordance with cost benefit analysis, there is a single value per dimension that is derived from a number of weighted criteria and items.

---

162 See Österle/Brenner/Hilbers; 1991. Ward/Griffiths/Whitmore, 1990.

163 See Reitermann, 1992.

164 "Benefit" and "risk" are theoretically accepted standard dimensions while "strategy fit" and "environment fit" were developed as a result of industrial co-operation.

Phase III (Project Evaluation): In the project evaluation phase, the planning group evaluates all the projects. Every member enters a value and a comment to each criterion per dimension and per project. While entering values and comments, everyone has access to the project database to browse through project information. As soon as the project evaluation phase is finished, the discussion phase begins. A graphical portfolio and reports comparing all evaluated projects is produced. There are different possible representations, such as the portfolio of all projects from one planner or the portfolio of all planners for one project.

Phase IV (Evaluation Discussion): A discussion on the differences of the project evaluations can be initiated by the planners or about the general project portfolio. After the discussion, a new round of evaluation can take place. The final group goal is to get a common, acceptable portfolio through the revolving process of evaluation and discussion. The final group portfolio each planner accepts is the basis for the realization of IS projects in a common sense. Based on the group portfolio, the group decides which project plans will be realized and which will not.

The main difference between the ISPLAN planning method and existing methods[165] is the underlying group concept. The ISPLAN method is based on a planning team where all activities and decisions are made by common group consensus.

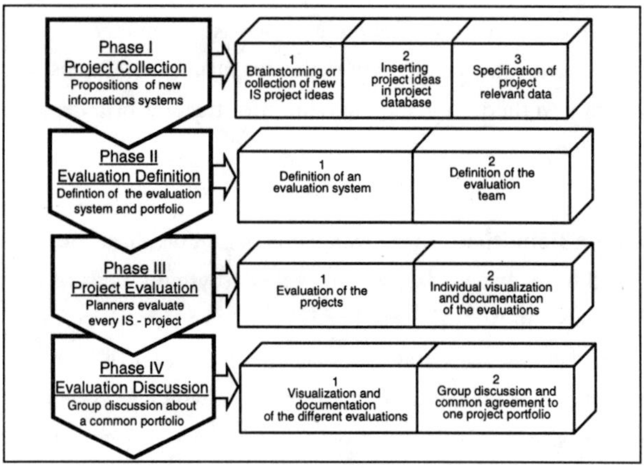

Figure 7: ISPLAN - phase model

---

165 See Österle/Brenner/Hilbers; 1991. Ward/Griffiths/Whitmore, 1990.

4.4.2. ISPLAN Prototype

The ISPLAN prototype is a one tool-environment where almost all steps of the ISPLAN concept described above are implemented. To allow the evaluation by project planning teams, we strove to make the prototype as easy as possible. It consists of administrative and end-user components. The ISPLAN administration component allows the creation and deletion of user accounts. This permits log in/out, project evaluation, and graphical composition of the evaluation results. The administrator maintains the general data for new project ideas and then specifies the systems with the dimension criteria. After creating the system, the administrator assigns a group of persons the task to evaluate one or more projects. The end-user part of ISPLAN assists the IS planner to evaluate projects he was assigned and then to view the results of the evaluation in comparison with other planners. A planning group can do their evaluation synchronously or asynchronously. The method chosen by the planning group depends on infrastructure, habits of the group, and very likely on the importance and size of the projects. A resulting portfolio can be seen in figure 8.

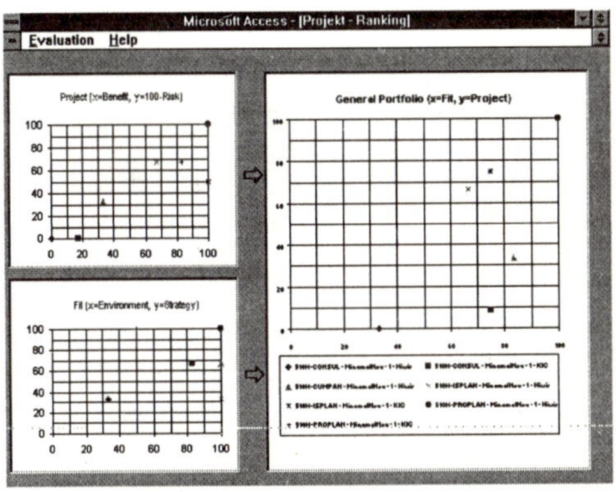

Figure 8: ISPLAN - an example of a project portfolio

Open questions on the ISPLAN concept and tool

It needs to be further investigated whether a common set of data elements for each project can be defined for supporting the planner to obtain objective decisions. Another issue is how much discussion on the overall portfolio will be needed to reach the final result. The planned evaluation will help to find answers to these issues and additional proposals for improvement.

5. Conclusion

The successful prototype implementations show that our goals were not too ambitious. We developed for each research question a general concept for the structuring and refinement of Information Management tasks. A common usable groupware-architecuture was also defined. This allows us to give software development recommendations for each of the subject areas as well as enhance the understanding of groupware implementation issues.

References

Austin, J.L.: How To Do Things With Words, Cambridge (Ma.), Harvard University Press, 1962.

Blair, G.; Gallagher, J.(ed): Object-Oriented Languages, Systems and Application. Pitman, London 1991.

Coad, P.; Yourdan, E.: Object-Oriented Analysis. Second edition, Prentice Hall, Englewood Cliffs, 1991.

Davenport, T.H.; Short, J.E: The new industrial engineering: Information technology and business redesign. In: Sloan Management Review, Summer 1990, page 11 - 27.

Elgass, P.: Untersuchung zur Geschäftsprozeßplanung in deutschen Unternehmen, Internal Working Paper, IS-Department, Universität Hohenheim, 1994a.

Elgass, P.: Computergestützte Geschäftsprozeßplanung, Internal Working Paper, IS-Department, Universität Hohenheim, 1994b.

Elgass, P.; Krcmar, H: Computerunterstützung für die Planung von Geschäftsprozessen. In: Hasenkamp U.; Kirn S.; Syring M. (Ed.): CSCW - Computer Supported Cooperative Work - Informationssysteme für dezentralisierte Unternehmensstrukturen. Addison-Wesley, 1994, page 67 - 83.

Elgass, P.; Krcmar, H.; Oberweis, A.: Prozeßmodellierung - Vom informalen zum formalen Prozeßmodell. In: Conference proceedings EMISA / MOBIS-Workshop 13.10. and 14.10.1994, Münster.

Gaitanidis, M.: Prozeßorganisation: Entwicklung, Ansätze und Programme prozeßorientierter Organisationsgestaltung. Farlan, München 1983.

Habermas, J.: Wahrheitstheorien. In: Habermas, J.: Vorstudien und Ergänzungen zur Theorie des kommunikativen Handelns. Frankfurt am Main, Suhrkamp Verlag, 3. Auflage, 1989, page 127 - 183.

Hammer, M.: Reengineering don't automate, obliterate. In: Harvard Business Review. July-August 1990, page 104 - 112.

Hammer, M.; Champy, J.: Reengineering the Cooperation - A Manifesto for Business Revoloution. London, 1993.

Kaplan, S.M.; et al: Flexible, Active Support for Collaborative Work with Conversation-Builder. In: CSCW'92 - Proceedings of the Conference on Computer-Supported Cooperative Work vom 31. Okt. - 4. Nov. 1992 in Toronto. Edt.: Turner, J.; Krauts, R. ACM Press, New York 1992, page 378 - 385.

Kilbert, Gryczan, Züllighoven: Objektorientierte Anwendungsentwicklung. Braunschweig 1993.

Krcmar, H.: CATeam-Werkzeuge: Beispiele und praktische Erfahrungen. Working Paper, No. 32, 1992a, IS Department, University of Hohenheim.

Krcmar, H.: Computerunterstützung für die Gruppenarbeit - Zum Stand der Computer Supported Cooperative Work Forschung. In: Wirtschaftsinformatik, 34. Jg., No. 4, August 1992b, S. 425-437.

Krcmar, H.; Schwarzer B.: Prozeßorientierte Organisationsmodellierung - Gründe, Anforderungen an Werkzeuge und Folgen für die Organisation, In: Schriften zur Unternehmensführung, Edt. W.-A. Scheer, Gabler Verlag Wiesbaden, 1994.

Kunz, W., Rittel, H.: Issues as Elements of Information Systems. Working Paper S-78-2, Institut für Grundlagen und der Planung, University Stuttgart. Berkeley, 1970, page 1 -7.

Ludwig, B.: Argumentation in Gruppen - oder auch: Einige Grundlagen der zwischenmenschlichen Koordination. Internal Report, IS Department, University of Hohenheim, Version 5, October 1994a.

Ludwig, B.: Evaluierung des Konversationsstrukturierungswerkzeuges Consul. Internal Working Paper, IS Department, Universität Hohenheim, 1994b.

Medina-Mora, R.; Winograd, T.; Flores, R.; Flores, F.: The action workflow approach to workflow management technology. In: CSCW Proceedings November 1992.

Österle, H.; Brenner, W.; Hilbers, K.: Unternehmensführung und Informationssystem: Der Ansatz des St. Galler Informationssystem-Managements. Teubner, Stuttgart 1991.

Reitermann, V.: Konzepte und Vorgehensweisen der Informationssystemplanung in der Praxis. Master's Thesis, IS Department, University Hohenheim, 1992.

Reuter, W.; Werner, H.: Thesen und Empfehlungen zur Anwendung von Argumentativen Informations-ystemen. Institut für Grundlagen der Planung, University of Stuttgart, Working Paper A-83-1, 1983.

Scherr, A.L.: A new approach to business processes. In: IBM Systemss Journal, Vol. 32., No 1, 1993.

Schönwälder, S: Objektorientierte Prototypenentwicklung mit der Programmiersprache Smalltalk 4.1 und dem Datenbankverwaltungssystem GemStone 3.2 - Erfahrungsbericht über Installation und Evaluation der Systemumgebung; Internal Working Paper, IS-Department, Universität Hohenheim 1994.

Searle, J.R.: Speech Acts. Cambridge University Press, Cambridge 1969.

Taylor, D.: Object-Oriented Technology. Servio, Alameda 1990.

Toulmin, S.: The Uses of Argument. Cambridge, Cambridge University Press, 1958.

Ward J.; Griffiths, P.; Whitmore P.: Strategic Planning for Information Systems, John Wiley & Sons, 1990, John Wiley Information Systems Series.

The *GroupFlow* Framework: Enterprise Model and Architecture of the Workflow System

Ludwig Nastansky, Wolfgang Hilpert

Abstract

The *GroupFlow* environment integrates concepts that are typically referred to as *workgoup computing* or *Groupware* on the one hand, and *workflow management* or *business process design* on the other hand. *GroupFlow* offers business process and technology frameworks to set up versatilc and flexible workflow systems for distributed information management within organizations and their outside communication partners.

This article describes the Enterprise Information Management Model and the distributed data and object architecture layout of the *GroupFlow* framework. The procedures for the specification of workflows based on this framework are outlined.

Keywords: Workflow management, workgroup computing, business process design, groupware, distributed organizations, wide area information exchange, Lotus Notes

1. The GroupFlow Project Environment

GroupFlow is to be considered as a comprehensive system approach supporting business process engineering, deployment, monitoring, and the operational infrastructure of distributed workflow management frameworks within an organization. The GroupFlow system comprises the tools necessary for business process design and monitoring as well as a complete set of operative modules for the various tasks and processes within a flexible LAN- and/or WAN-based workflow supporting runtime environment.

The conceptual approach of the *GroupFlow* system with respect to business process modeling, distributed data and object architecture design, user and process/agent interaction is in concordance with research and discussions that are drawn along the lines of studies such as published in Harrington (1991), Keen (1991), Davenport (1993), Hammer & Champy (1993), Ishii & Ohkubo (1991), Marshak (1992), or Medina-Mora, Winograd, Flores & Flores (1992). The importance of business process and workflow oriented system approaches to corporate information management has lead to the development of the *GroupFlow* framework. In another paper (Nastansky & Hilpert 1994), we have been focusing on complementary aspects of the entire *GroupFlow* framework, like e.g.:

- The business process paradigm underlying the design of workflow systems: a continuous scale between cooperation and automation.

- The architecture of GroupFlow enabling various classes of workflows on a continuous scale between flexibility and predefined structures.

- Further aspects of the GroupFlow Modeler like integration in a distributed operative environment or the clustering approach.

GroupFlow has been implemented using Lotus Notes as the basic development platform and underlying distributed architecture. The user interfaces on the client sides are either based on Notes-native FORM and VIEW concepts, or developed using graphical front end tools. On the back end server side of *GroupFlow*, Notes technology has been exclusively used for data repositories of the actual business information content, for the workflow structuring parts, and the set of workflow runtime modules supporting processes like messaging, replication, event management, gateway connections, or cross-platform data exchange and process coordination.

2. The *GroupFlow* Enterprise Information Management Model

According to Bracchi & Pernici (1984) the major target of conceptual office modeling is to make office information system design easier and more reliable. Thus, goals for a conceptual design of office models are:

(a) Obtain a description of the enterprise. The large number of exceptions and special cases makes it impossible to reach a complete formal description of the office. However, the model should describe as many aspects of the enterprise as possible in a definitive way. It is important that this description is comprehensive not only to an analyst or systems designer but also to the staff members, managers and planners in the office. They should be able to validate the system, suggest modifications, identify inconsistencies, and maintain and further develop the system themselves.

(b) Identify processes that are no longer useful in achieving the current enterprise goals but are still performed, perhaps only because of habit. These processes are to be modified or completely replaced. In literature we find many different approaches for office or enterprise models. Some of them are discussed more deeply in Desai (1991), Dutton (1993), Lochovsky, Hogg, Weiser & Mendelzon (1988), Kubota & Ishii (1989), or Tueni, Jianzhong & Fares (1988). An enterprise model that is applicable to workflow design and processing obviously has to subsume at least the following layers of information management within the organization: The information flow of an organization, the sequence of activities, the agents and resources such as office workers or organizational units playing specific roles when performing activities. The enterprise model is to encompass the decomposition of the whole application environment into a workflow-based sequence of tasks, the resources required for these tasks, and the objects accessed and manipulated during task processing. Also, task and process decomposition require to refine lower-level task activities and sub-level processes. *Fig. 1.1* represents the fundamental structure of the enterprise information management model underlying *GroupFlow*.

Infrastructure model	Process model	Information processing model
unit	business process	object type
agent	task	information links
role	activity	folder
workgroup	rule	
resource	time	
relationship		

Fig. 1.1: Outline of the Enterprise Model underlying *GroupFlow*

(1) The *infrastructure model* defines the structural components of the organization which can be represented within *GroupFlow*. This infrastructure model comprises the people who work at different locations/positions in different organizational units of an organization, the resources they use to perform their tasks, the formal groups/teams they belong to and the relations and formal communication paths between these groups. It determines the interrelationship between the units such as superior units. Also, the assignment of roles to agents describes what the actor of a role is expected to do within his working environment or within a special process.

An agent can be both a human/person (actor) or an automated software agent. A human agent holds a position related to an organizational unit within the infrastructure model and in addition can play different roles to perform office tasks. Automated software agents perform a variety of information processing and communication procedures automatically using specific software modules. Examples could be archiving, relational database queries, complex price or status calculations and so on.

A formal unit matches the human agent with the organizational structure. A unit describes the elementary components of the organizational structure. The enterprise model underlying *GroupFlow* allows a unit to either be elementary or to be aggregated, like divisions or departments. Workgroups, on the other hand, offer flexible concepts for perpetual organizational (re-) modeling. Particularly informal, short-lived task forces can easily be built/grouped together.

(2) The *workflow routing specifications* are based on the process model of the enterprise. It holds information about the business process layout and definition, the involved agents, resources, etc. This module focuses on the process dynamics/specifications, their interdependencies, the steps to be taken within a process, their serial or parallel sequences, etc.

As opposed to workflow systems supporting automation of bulk data processing tasks within rigid sequencing-patterns the *GroupFlow* approach primarily is user and team focused in supporting the actual processing of business data. In this user-interaction focus *GroupFlow* is taking a similar starting point as that used in Medina-Mora, Winograd, Flores & Flores (1992). The core of the *GroupFlow* application architecture is modeled around the groupware paradigm underlying its host environment Lotus Notes, and extending its functionality to a scale ranging from single user interaction to automatic software agent processed operations. The defined office procedure classes and their respective workflow routing specifications are distributed via the built-in replication mechanism of the underlying development and application platform. The actual routing and status management is handled in a local manner: the "intelligent" document compares its actual status with the also decentralized available routing information in order to find the next agent for further task performance.

(3) The *information processing model* traces the outline of the object types or information items such as messages, documents or forms that are manipulated and exchanged within the organizational infrastructure. It also describes the information links that can exist between the several objects. Information items or document objects can be included into folders. The functionality that actually drives the workflow routing is captured in *program objects sets* that are linked dynamically into the information object. The system architecture is designed in a modular and layered manner.

3. The GroupFlow Distributed Data and Object Architecture Layout

The architecture of the *GroupFlow* system framework (*Fig. 3.1*) consists of three major components that are outlined in a layered architecture model:

(1) The *GroupFlow* back end components encompass the distributed *workflow structure repository*, the workflow-protocol or routing-status tracking functionality, and the replication and workflow routing engine. These components manage the structural information of the workflow as well as the messaging and synchronization activities. The scaleable business process structuring model that underlies *GroupFlow* is being discussed in Nastansky & Hilpert (1994). The protocol information stored in the *GroupFlow* repositories is further used to perform analysis comparing actual with planned, allowing anomalies to be spotted and corrected.

(2) The *GroupFlow target application* side encompasses the entities defining the authentic application functions of the business processes being enabled by a workflow system. Much of the processing within the *GroupFlow* system is performed based on predefined Lotus Notes-native form, view and macro/script templates. Continuous processes with certain routine characteristics are best modeled in *shared* document databases: The involved persons know about the existence of information in the database and the respective tasks to be performed. The complementary *send* (e-mail) model is basically applied for rather simple ad hoc routing applications. The integration of both the send model and the share model as technically supported by the Lotus Notes platform can efficiently result in a variety of combinations over a wide spectrum.

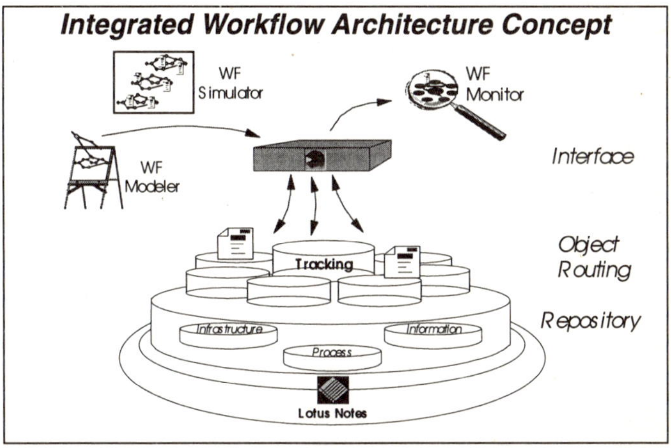

Fig. 3.1: *GroupFlow* Framework

(3) The *GroupFlow tool environment* provides an open set of independent interactive graphical tools enabling a variety of workflow related functions. Currently, the *GroupFlow* system offers as its key tool environments: *GroupFlow Modeler*, a graphical workflow modeling editor, and the graphical *GroupFlow Monitor*. The *GroupFlow Modeler* supports both workflow top-down as well as bottom-up design, dynamic clustering, update, redesign, and simulation of workflows. The organizational layout can also be graphically modeled and related to workflows using the higher clustering levels of the *GroupFlow Modeler*. Any data defining the graphically modeled specifications are stored in Lotus Notes database objects and hence can be exchanged across distributed locations using the replication mechanism. The *Group-*

Flow Monitor supports various message tracing functions between agents. Particularly planned and actual workflow routing can thus be visualized and compared. A subset of the monitoring functionalities - the *GroupFlow Analyzer* - visualizes document routing and message exchange within any Lotus Notes database application. The results of this kind of analysis allow to derive information for possible re-design options for the workflow with the *GroupFlow Modeler*.

4. Procedures for *GroupFlow* Specification

In order to actually utilize the *GroupFlow* system in a comprehensive workflow application a few major deployment phases have to be run through. It is important to recognize that these phases are highly interdependent. In an actual installation, typically it will be necessary to iterate back and forth between the outlined phases. The phases are as follows:

(1) analysis and workflow concept design,

(2) implementation of the workflow system,

(3) application of the workflow system, and

(4) monitoring and analysis of actual workflow

4.1. Workflow Concept Design

In a first phase the business process side of an application has to be analyzed and (re-)constructed before the actual implementation of the workflow system can go under way. This involves the investigation of existing or planned processes to eliminate potential bottlenecks and/or redundancies. The flow of the information, the decision points and the various forms of data and information presentation have to be investigated.

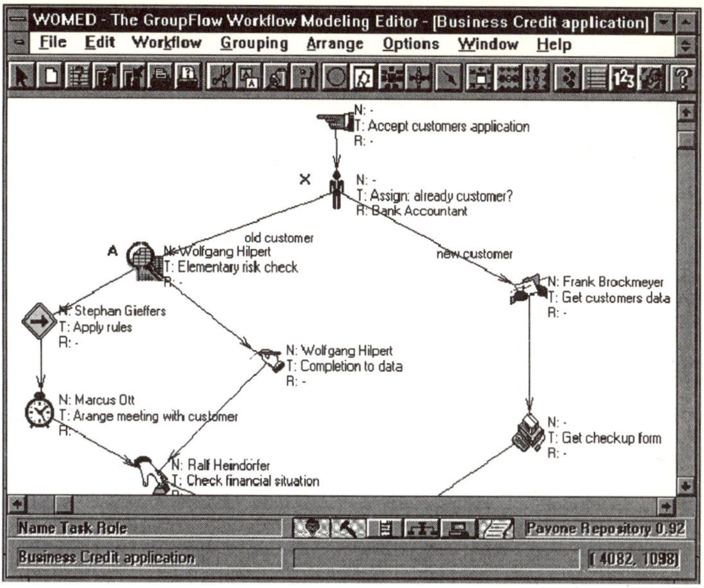

Fig. 4.1: The workflow modeling editor „*GroupFlow Modeler*"

In this first phase the concept of the process is developed. This includes the design of a graphical workflow model as well as of the related organizational structure layout. The *GroupFlow* modeling tools support the efficient presentation, discussion, and refinement of the new system design. In order to support the *ex ante* analysis of the business process model the derived workflow can be simulated. The simulation may focus on static structural aspects based on the workflow visualization, or, it may include dynamic sequencing patterns based on basic object flow simulation in the workflow graph. Thus, consistency checks and bottleneck detection are possible beforehand.

4.2. Implementation of the Workflow System

In order to implement a workflow application the graphical representation of the workflow as designed with the modeling editor is automatically transferred into operable workflow definitions. The graphical workflow model consisting of nodes and edges with its embedded specific properties and attributes is logically transformed and stored as operable routing specifications in the workflow repository. The transformation process involves both conceptual and technical interface capabilities.

The target workflow-enabled database applications interoperate with the workflow repository to use its specifications and to manage the actual workflow routing. These applications are used to activate the document object routing. They are designed to be driven by the specifications entered in the workflow repository and are used as prototype applications and thus form the basis for the design of the actual operative application databases.

4.3. Workflow Routing

For the application of the workflow system the users initiate actual workflow instances based on the specification and design performed at the former steps. Various alternatives exist of how a (human or process) agent can route a workflow object to the next appropriate agent in the chain.

(a) Standard Routing of Predefined Workflow:

The user initiates the object routing by composing new documents in the target workflow database application. All agents with access to the shared databases can locate their tasks in several different contexts or views. The current agent of a workflow finds her work to be done in her work assignment area. The scenario described here is based on the shared database approach. There are many advantages to this solution, the most important being the team responsiblity for keeping track of processes. Still, there may be situations where a quick response is necessary. This implies the need for the application of a send approach for the workflow routing. Within the *GroupFlow* system we apply a combination of both models: basically, the document objects are hosted in common, shared databases accessable by all team members and are assigned for processing to one or more agents. In addition, an E-Mail notification supplied with a hypertext-/document-link that leads the addressee directly to her new task, is sent.

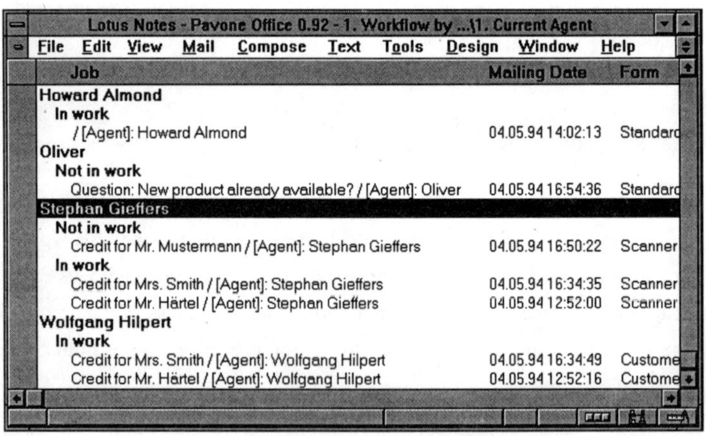

Fig. 4.2: View "Current agent"

When pushing the button for the 'next task routing' the user incorporates a key feature of the *GroupFlow* architecture. A background process determines who will be the next person in the routing chain based upon the process specifications in the workflow repository for the chosen type of workflow and the individual circumstances of the current case (see fig. 4.3).

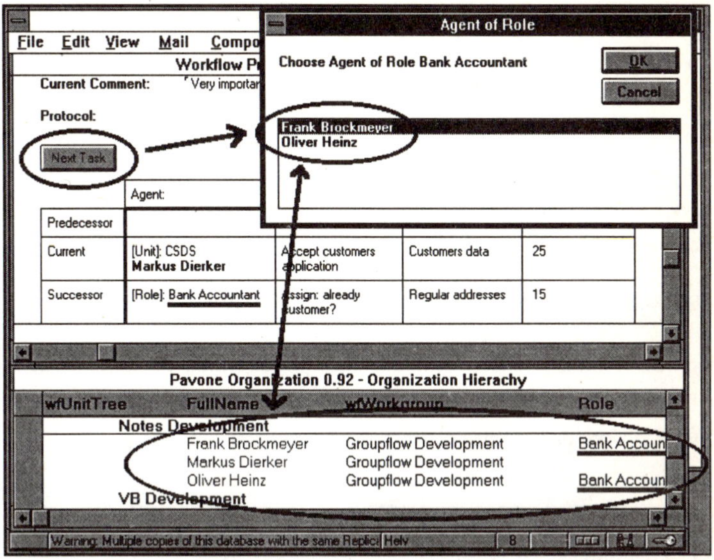

Fig. 4.3: Specify next agent more precisely at runtime

(b) Flexible ad hoc Modification and Exception Handling of Predetermined Workflows

The *GroupFlow* architecture supports modification of the standard routing sequence *within a predefined* workflow at run-time by ad hoc modifications and dynamic re-routing of tasks for special cases and exceptions. The *GroupFlow* environment integrates a set of structured mechanisms to handle exception or disruption problems of various kinds in predefined workflows as described in Nastansky & Hilpert (1994).

The possible modification rules applying to given workflows have been modeled on common exception situations in business processes, such as:

- *check-back* with previous agent,
- *inquiry* or question to anyone else,
- *task delegation* invoking a detour in routing path, or
- complete *change* of the underlying workflow.

As with all other activities of this workflow system, the exception handling to the standard workflow specifications must be thoroughly recorded.

4.4. Workflow Monitoring (*ex post* analysis)

The *GroupFlow Monitor* visualizes the *actual workflow* of the workgroup. Based upon the entries both in the target workflow application databases and the protocol in the tracking database, an *ex post* as well as a concurrent analysis of the business process can be performed. The most interesting feature of a *Monitor* is the possibility to compare the entries of the actual workflow instances with the underlying *common* or *planned* workflow type specifications in the workflow repository. In order to monitor the progress of the processes we propose three major dimensions to focus on:

(1) *Snap shot*: static workflow analysis

For this view all document objects of all business processes that are currently being worked on are included in their actual status at present. This view helps in estimating the current workload and the workload balance between team members.

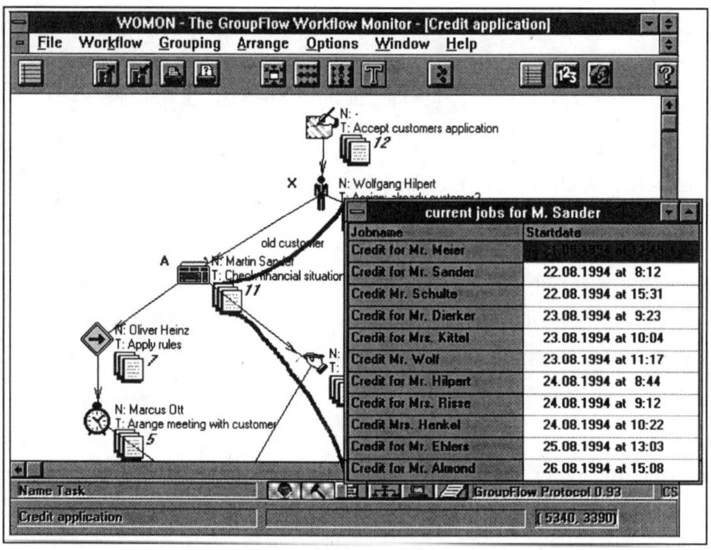

Fig. 4.4 : Monitoring of workflows

(2) Process specific: dynamic workflow analysis

By determining a particular workflow or a specific cluster of workflows all document objects that have been dealt with during a process can be followed in their development over time. This view shows the currently active workflows, preferred routing paths and also relationships between activities such as time restrictions.

(3) Actor specific: involvement in various processes

The third dimension of analysis investigates the activities of single actors or workgroups on document objects of various workflows. It can be shown how individual actors are involved in different workflows within the team over a longer period of time.

5. References and Acknowledgments

Bracchi, G.; Pernici, B.: The Design Requirements of Office Systems; ACM Transaction on Office Inform. Systems, Vol. 2, No. 2, (1984), S. 151ff.

Clark, B.; O'Donnell, S.: Computer supported co-operative work; Br. Telecom Technol J, Vol 9 No 1 January 1991, (1991), pp. 47-55.

Davenport, T.H.: Process Innovation, Reengineering Work through Information Technology; Harvard Business School Press, Boston, 1993.

Desai, S.M.: Unification of Underlying Concepts in Different Office Models; DataBase Winter/Spring, (1991), pp. 38-45.

Dutton, J.E.: Commonsense Approach to Process Modeling; IEEE Software, 4., 10, (1993), pp. 56-64.

Hammer, M.; Champy, J.: Reengineering the Corporation, A Manifesto For Business Revolution; Harper Business, New York, NY,USA, 1993.

Harrington, H.J.: Business Process Improvement: The Breaktrough Strategy for Total Quality, Productivity, and Competitiveness, McGraw-Hill, New York, 1991.

Ishii, H.; Ohkubo, M.: Message-driven groupware design based on an office procedure model, OM-1; Journal of Information Processing, Japan, Vol. 14, No. 2, (1991), S. 184-191.

Jari, A.; Nils, E.; Risto, M.; Markku, R.; Reijo, S.: Workflow in Newspaper Prepress Departments; Groupware 93 - Europe, (1993), pp. 279-295.

Keen, P.G.W.: Shaping the Future: Business Design through Information Technology, Harvard Business School Press, Boston, 1991.

Kubota, K.; Ishii, H.: Office Procedure Knowledge Base for Organizational Office Work Support; Office Information Systems: The Design Process, Pernici, Verrijn-Stuart, A.A. (Ed.), Elsevier Science Publishers B.V., North-Holland, (1989), pp. 55-72.

Lochovsky, F.H.; Hogg, J.S.; Weiser, S.P.; Mendelzon, A.O.: OTM: Specifying Office Tasks; ACM Computing Survey, (1988), S. 46-54.

Marshak, R.T.: Pavone GroupFlow - Providing a Workflow Suite for Lotus Notes Environments; Workgroup Computing Report, Seybold, Boston, USA, Vol. 18, No. 11, 1995, (1995), S. 3-23.

Marshak, R.T.: Requirements for Workflow; Office Computing Report, Seybold, Boston, USA, Vol. 15, No. 3, 1992, (1992), S. 3-16.

Medina-Mora, R.; Winograd, T.; Flores, R.; Flores, F.: The Action Workflow Approach to Workflow Management Technology; CSCW 92 Proceedings, 1992.

Nastansky, L.; Hilpert, W.: Critical Success Factors for Workflow Management as a Key Component in Banking Services; Proceedings, WKWI Conference Nürnberg, Germany, October 7./8., 1993.

Nastansky, L.; Hilpert, W.: The GroupFlow System: A Scalable Approach to Workflow Management between Cooperation and Automation; in: Wolfinger B. (Ed.): Innovation in Computer and Communication Systems, proceeedings of the 24. GI annual conference within the frame of the 13th World Computer Congress, IFIP Congess '94 in Hamburg, Germany, 28. August - 2. September 1994, Springer, Berlin (1994), pp. 473-479.

Newman, W.: Office Models and Office Systems Design; Integrated Office sytems, N. Naffah, Ed., North-Holland, Amsterdam, October, (1979), S. 3-10.

Ott, M.: Conceptional design and implementation of graphical workflow modeling editor in the context of distributed groupware databases, master thesis, University of Paderborn, May 1994.

Scherr, A.L.: A new Approach to Business Processes; IBM Systems Journal, 32, 1, (1993), pp. 80-98.

Tueni, M.; Jianzhong, L.; Fares, P.: AMS: A knowledge-based approach to tasks representation, organization and coordination; ACM, (1988), S. 78-87.

The authors express their gratitude to **Howard Almond** who has revised this article as a native English speaker.

ALLFIWIB: Customer Consulting in Financial Services with Distributed Knowledge Based Systems

Ulrike Einsfeld, Mark Roemer, Peter Roßbach, Klaus Sandbiller, Andreas Will

Abstract

This paper's objective is to show that Distributed Artificial Intelligence offers methods well suited to provide support to the process of customer consulting in financial services. Firstly, the demands made upon this type of advisory support system will be highlighted. Then, the design and realization of a distributed problem-solving system will be described. Some of the results have already been published.[166] New developments are the inclusion of distributed solving of asset allocation problems under risk (cf. section 2) and the expansion of the system to incorporate a formerly stand-alone system acting as a problem-solving agent to provide support for buy-or-lease decision-making (section 3).

Keywords: Banking IS, customer consulting, Distributed Artificial Intelligence (DAI), distributed problem-solving, distributed systems, financial sector

1. System Support for the Client Adviser in Financial Services

In recent years customers' demands towards their financial service companies have changed significantly.[167] Due to increasing income and improved information concerning financial services customers became more rational and challenging. As a consequence financial institutions are forced to implement business strategies based on the individual needs of their clients.[168] Only those strategies focusing on individual needs instead of products can meet the requirements of a customer oriented buyers' market.

The financial institutions have responded to this demand by adopting a strategy of offering the entire range of services for the customers 'under one roof'. The process of customer consulting constitutes the main part of this new strategy. Financial products are difficult to comprehend and also difficult to choose between, especially as individual solutions often require the combination of several different single products. The new strategy advocates advising the customer on a one-to-one basis, with the intention to build up the customer's loyalty to the

---

[166] for an overview cf. Buhl, Will (1993), Roemer (1994), and Roßbach (1996). „ALLFIWIB“ is the (German) acronym for „Customer Consulting in Financial Services with Distributed Knowledge Based Systems“.

[167] cf. Talmor (1994), p. 71

[168] cf. Jablonsky (1993), p. 14

adviser and so to the financial service company. This results in increasing demands upon the client adviser to build up the necessary skill for the interface between bank and client and no longer to specialize in single types of product.[169]

The adviser is faced with a continually expanding range of products and permanently ever shorter product life cycles.[170] Furthermore, as it is in many cases advantageous to combine products, the adviser must also have knowledge regarding the interdependencies and interactions of the product range at his disposal. For this reason, the required expert knowledge extends far beyond the capabilities of the client adviser, especially when considering that he also has to know much about sales psychology. If the advisers have only partial knowledge of the available range of products, they will only recommend those products they know best.[171] In this case the advice given is often not ideally tailored to the client's individual needs.

To cope with these problems supporting the consulting process with IT seems natural. The objective should be to support the adviser during the entire consulting process. This covers the precise analysis of the client's preferences which are often not sufficiently defined, the subsequent search for alternative products or product packages which meet the preferences and, finally, the selection of the most advantageous solution. A system should support the adviser actively in order to compensate for possible lack of knowledge and to guarantee a comprehensive consultation.

A look at the current situation shows that financial service companies are far from achieving the necessary level of system support.[172] With few exceptions the only systems existing are confined to particular financial products and are purely calculation programs which can be used by the client adviser only to evaluate alternatives already worked out. In such cases the client adviser is only supported passively and the process of searching for products or product packages needs to be done by himself.

Although it has been revealed that methods of Artificial Intelligence can offer some advantages for the solution of financial problems, especially for product selection or the handling of risks, only a few of the systems actually used are employing those methods.[173] This is mainly due to the fact that the use of knowledge based systems is advantageous only within relatively narrow domains, in which the knowledge can be strictly delimited.[174] The domain of financial customer consulting however is too large, too varied, and too complex to be modeled with a single knowledge based system in the traditional sense.[175] Even if such a knowledge based

---

[169] cf. Roßbach (1996)
[170] cf. Wigston (1994), p. 12
[171] cf. Roßbach (1996)
[172] for the German financial sector cf. Buhl, Hasenkamp, Müller-Wünsch, Roßbach, Sandbiller (1993)
[173] e.g. Hoppe (1992); for a comprehensive survey cf. Chorafas, Steinmann (1991)
[174] cf. Davis (1991), p. 221
[175] cf. Roßbach (1996)

system could be developed, the upkeep and maintenance of the system would be nearly impossible to manage.[176]

However, the area of financial services has an inherently distributed structure. For example, there is a functional distribution arising from the various components of financial services, requiring the application of a wide range of different methods of analysis and evaluation. Furthermore, there is an institutional aspect of distribution. Most of the financial service companies are divided into decentralized departments concentrating on specific product groups. This is particularly the case in cooperative partnerships which are becoming increasingly popular between traditionally established financial service companies, such as banks and insurance companies.

This distributed structure makes the process of customer consulting a distributed problem-solving process. Therefore, an application model of Distributed Artificial Intelligence with cooperating agents for each subdomain seems a promising basis for the development of an adequate IT support. Basically, this approach can be successful if the necessary cooperation and communication effort does not predominate the advantages of the modular structure and the task sharing among the agents.

Based on these considerations the prototypically consulting support system ALLFIWIB applying methods of Distributed Artificial Intelligence is introduced in the following. In section 2.1 we describe two typical types of financial problems, namely deterministic and asset allocation problems. Their solution is the objective of the system ALLFIWIB. Then, the design of the prototype is sketched, following the successive steps of the problem-solving process (section 2.2 - 2.5). The necessary control is described in section 2.6.

A further advantage of a DAI approach is the relatively simple expandibility of the system. Existing stand-alone systems can be integrated into the distributed system with little effort. This opens up a wide field for software reuse. Section 3 describes the reengineering and integration of FES, a formerly stand-alone system supporting the buy-or-lease decision, into ALLFIWIB.

2. Design of the ALLFIWIB System

For the design of the ALLFIWIB system the blackboard approach was chosen. Here, the conceptual model contains three modules: the agents, a blackboard, and a control module (cf. Fig. 1). For an integrated solution of customer problems the agents cooperate via the blackboard, a

[176] cf. Wiederhold, Rathmann, Barsalou, Lee, Quass (1990), p. 61

global logical memory representing the current state of the solution space; the agents do not cooperate directly with each other. The control module serves to coordinate distributed problem-solving. After a look at the types of problems which should be solved by the system we can understand this concept better and discuss it in more detail.

2.1. Problem Types in Financial Consulting

We distinguish two basic problem types, which are typical for financial consulting situations.

Deterministic problems: These problems can be characterized by the customer's objective to maximize the expected net present value of payments (NPV). They are typical for commercial customers in financial planning situations (e.g. searching a financing program for a given investment as well as investing surplus liquidity for some periods) or for private customers, e.g. financing a real estate or car purchase. The desired cash flows over time ('payment patterns') restrict the value maximization: a solution is feasible, if it matches the payment pattern. Deterministic problems are formally represented by the objective function NPV and the constraining payment pattern.

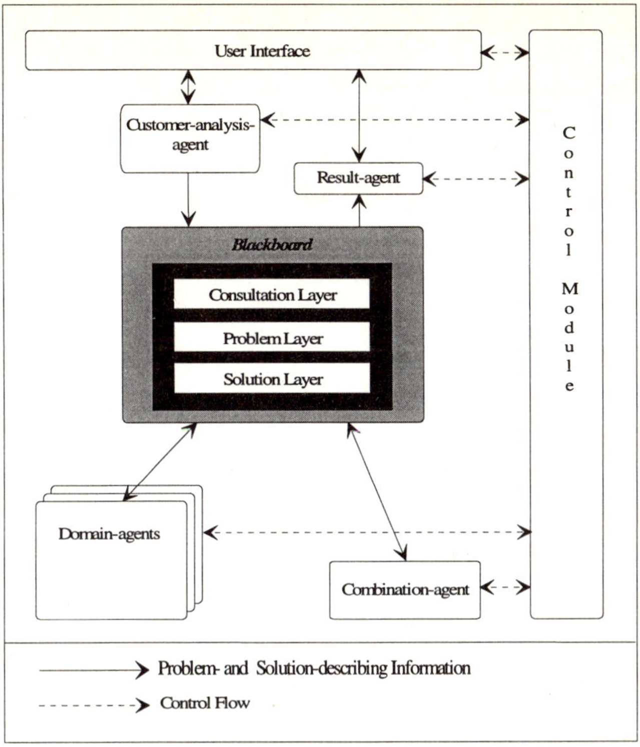

Fig. 1: System Design of ALLFIWIB - Overview; cf. Buhl, Will (1993)

Asset allocation problems: Private customers investing in risky assets often tend not to maximize the expected value of payments, but rather the expected utility of this value. Often they cannot specify exact payment patterns but only an amount to be invested today saving for a specific future date (e.g. retirement). Asset allocation problems are represented by the customer's utility function (representing his risk attitude), the amount to be invested, and the planning horizon.

The general objective of the ALLFIWIB system is the elaboration of good and feasible solutions to problems of both types. The distinction between the problem types allows to focus on two interesting research topics: in the case of deterministic problems (with the need to meet the payment pattern) the construction of feasible solutions by independently acting agents and in the case of asset allocation problems the construction of good solutions because of non-linearities in the utility functions of risk averse customers (whereas the NPV is a linear function).

2.2. Analyzing and Formalizing a Customer Problem

The analysis of a customer problem is performed by the Customer-analysis-agent. The relevant information to be gathered includes personal data, the customer's objectives, the type of customer (private or commercial), his risk attitude, desired payment modalities, and the like. The Customer-analysis-agent can access the financial services provider's local or remote databases via a specific domain scheme[177] so that previously recorded data need not to be requested again. A graphical user interface supports the acquisition of new data.

The formal representation of problems is written on the blackboard. To provide an easy operability for efficient distributed problem-solving, the blackboard is partitioned 'horizontally' into a consultation layer, a problem layer, and a solution layer. The consultation layer contains all information remaining unchanged during distributed problem-solving; examples are the customer's tax rate and the utility function for asset allocation problems. The problem layer contains payment patterns or the amount to be invested, depending on the type of problem. The solutions finally will be stored in the solution layer.

In addition, the blackboard is partitioned 'vertically'. This means that, (i) several consultations can be performed concurrently, (ii) several competing solutions to each problem can be pursued, and (iii) subproblems (as the result of a decomposition of a problem) can be solved concurrently.

2.3. Decomposing a Problem

For many financial problems, good solutions, consisting of several products from different application domains, are known. This explicit 'combination-knowledge' is represented in a specialized agent: the Combination-agent. When treating ***deterministic problems*** its analysis starts by 'splitting-up' complex payment patterns into simpler ones, e.g., it may make two or more pure investment or pure finance problems out of a complex mixed problem. For example, a real estate problem can be split into some saving periods, the investment, and subsequent financing periods. If the result of this decomposition allows the application of combination-knowledge, the corresponding Domain-agents are triggered to solve the subproblems by writing the decomposed payment patterns onto the blackboard's problem layer. Thus, the Combination-agent initiates an explicit collaboration of Domain-agents.[178] This explicit knowledge may lead to a better solution than the search process described in section 2.4.

---

[177] cf. König (1993)
[178] cf. Sandbiller, Weinhardt, Will (1992)

The Combination-agent as the expert on combination-knowledge decides on its own whether to decompose a problem or not. For this reason, it is partitioned into a condition part and an action part. The condition part specifies conditions to be met for a successful decomposition of the problem. The Combination-agent compares each problem found on the blackboard with these conditions and decides autonomously and self-selecting if the problem can be decomposed. If so, the action part performs the decomposition as well as writing back the resulting subproblems on the blackboard. This principal concept of agent-architecture is the same for the Domain-agents, too.

For ***asset allocation problems*** decomposing the problem makes no sense at this point of the problem solving process: we need to know a number of single products (bonds, shares, etc) in order to decide which combination is best for the customer. Thus, solving asset allocation problems we always start with working out single products (cf. next section).

2.4. Solving a Problem

The functionally and institutionally distributed domain knowledge is represented in several Domain-agents. Like the Combination-agent, the Domain-agents are quite autonomous units, each specializing in one branch of the area of financial services (life insurance, credit, bonds, etc). Their task is to solve problems written on the blackboard's problem layer. The independent design of each Domain-agent allows the implementation of the best problem-solving strategy (e.g. selection of securities or configuration of credit-contracts), respectively.

Looking at the solving of ***deterministic problems*** first, an easy bottom-up heuristic proves to be profitable (cf. section 2.5) for the customer when compared to usual standardized products - even if there is no a-priori knowledge of good combinations. Each Domain-agent tries to accomplish two solutions: one feasible solution (meeting the customer's desired payment pattern) and one 'locally' optimized single product. For instance, the following results of 'locally' optimized single products have been derived for net present value maximizers:[179]

- Due to the German corporate taxes, commercial loans without any interest and discharge payments up to contract end prove optimal compared to all other loan types.[180]
- For both, the investor and the issuing bank or firm, zerobonds are better than all straight bonds, whenever bonds are profitable for them in the after-tax world at all.[181]

[179] cf. Buhl, Sandbiller, Will (1994)
[180] cf. Buhl (1994)
[181] cf. Buhl, Sandbiller, Will (1993)

Such locally optimized solutions are accomplished by the action parts of the Domain-agents. The resulting payment streams are written on the blackboard's solution layer. It is obvious that optimized payment streams often do not meet the requirements of a customer's desired payment pattern. In this sense, the solution is not feasible and a residual problem remains to be solved. These residual problems can be calculated by algebraic operations on the required payment pattern and the payment stream of the non-feasible solution.[182] The Domain-agents write residual problems on the blackboard's problem layer, where it can be read by other agents. If one or more Domain-agents solve this residual problem or if the Combination-agent decomposes the problem, these agents are said to collaborate implicitly with the first Domain-agent.[183] Solutions of the residual problem will either be 'locally' optimized products (with further residual problems) or they will make the (combined) solution feasible.

An example illustrates that this heuristical way of constructing combined solutions by integrating locally optimized solutions may prove very profitable for a customer:[184] For a DM 1 Million office building financed with private funds, a customer obtains a negative present value of DM 555,000 as a reference solution. In contrast, a lease with upfront one-time payment, a loan financing the one-time payment, and a zerobond for the private funds provide a net present value advantage of about 280,000 DM or 51 % compared with the reference solution.

Given an ***asset allocation problem***, it can be assumed that an involved Domain-agent will always offer a feasible solution, i.e. a solution investing the total amount up to the planning horizon. This is because in all domains like shares, bonds, or investment funds various terms can be offered covering (nearly) any amount for any (realistic) planning horizon. Thus, a residual problem like in the case of deterministic problems will never arise.

Often a Domain-agent can offer a number of feasible solutions to a problem. The best solution is the one maximizing the customer's utility. This is illustrated by Fig. 2: Solutions are represented by a (m,s^2)-tupel for the expected final value of the investment and its variance. The utility function of a risk-averse customer is represented by its indifference curves with increasing utility to the upper left. An agent may be able to offer solution 1 and solution 2, with solution 1 maximizing the customer's utility.

[182] cf. Will (1995)

[183] cf. Sandbiller, Weinhardt, Will (1992)

[184] cf. Buhl, Sandbiller, Will (1993). This example is calculated with realistic German tax and interest rates. The providers of the optimized solution obtain a positive net present value of DM 66,000, while with the reference solution they do no business at all.

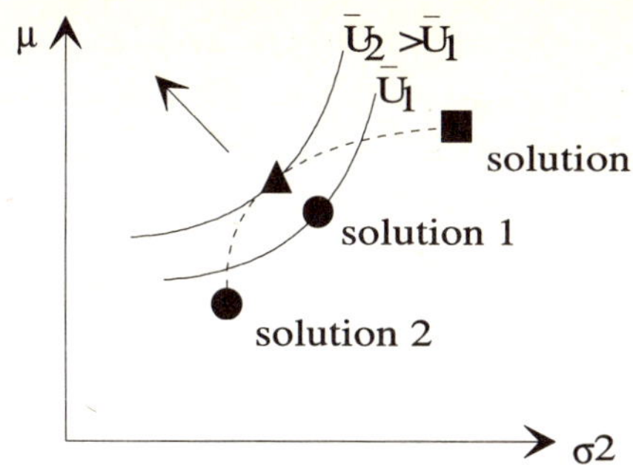

Fig. 2: Maximizing utility of risk-averse customers

Thus, an agent, which is 'egoistic' in the sense that it is aiming at investing the total amount and not willing to cooperatively participate in a combined solution, would offer only solution 1. But for a risk-averse customer the combination (here: the portfolio) made up of two or more solutions can be worth more than the sum of its parts (non-linear utility function). It is possible to raise the utility by diversification. In Fig. 2 this is illustrated by solution 3, which might be offered by another agent: The portfolio 2+3 built of solution 2 and solution 3 provides a higher utility than its parts. Moreover, this combination provides a higher utility than the 'egoistic' solution 1.

Keeping in mind that there might be an 'altruistic' agent willing to cooperate and offering a solution similar to solution 2 the first agent will offer not only the maximizing solution 1, but solution 2, also; otherwise it would probably do no business. This implies that each Domain-agent offers more than one solution to an asset allocation problem: one utility-maximizing solution, and one or more solutions that the agent expects to be 'good' parts of a portfolio built from solutions offered by other agents. In practice, offering a low risk solution and a high return solution additional to the utility-maximizing one leads to good results. So, a number of competing solutions represented by (m,s^2)-tupels is written on the blackboard's solution layer.

2.5. Aggregating and Presenting Solutions

We will consider ***asset allocation problems*** first. Constructing portfolios from a number of solutions raises two major problems: (i) As mentioned above, the search for the utility-maximizing portfolio is a non-linear problem. (ii) Let solution 2 and 3 contribute to an optimal portfolio (cf. Fig. 2); then both solutions have to be revised because now only a share of the primarily invested total amount remains.

At this point the Combination-agent comes into play again. Its task is now to calculate the optimal portfolio respecting the given solutions by employing a non-linear optimization program. The results are shares of the total amount which the corresponding Domain-agents should contribute to this optimal portfolio. These shares are written back on the blackboard's problem layer as subproblems, so that the agents can revise their formerly found solutions.

In the case of ***deterministic problems*** it is very easy to build a combined solution from the partial solutions. Because of the linearity of the net present value function, value additivity holds: Given two partial solutions 1 and 2, the NPV of the combined solution is:

$$NPV(1+2) = NPV(1) + NPV(2)$$

Thus, combined solutions can simply be constructed by adding the partial payment streams as well as the NPVs of the partial solutions. A high value of locally optimized solutions adds to the value of the combination. If the customer calculates with realistic interest rates, it will (nearly always) be possible to make a solution feasible by one or more product with a non-negative net present value. This means that the heuristic of locally optimizing products, adding them, and making the combination feasible by a last „brick" of non-negative value proves to be profitable for the customer. Obviously this way does not guarantee an optimal solution, but in many cases it produces a solution better than usual standardized products.

Since further involvement of the Domain-agents is not necessary, the task of aggregating is performed by the Result-agent which is activated after the problem-solving process has finished. The primary task of the Result-agent is to offer the best (combined) solutions to the customer. For both problem types, the Result-agent presents a ranking of the best (combined) solutions via a graphical user interface. This involves the presentation of the specific terms of the offered products or contracts as they can be found (using the references on the blackboard) in the databases of the providers.

2.6. Design of the Control Module

To coordinate the distributed problem-solving process efficiently, the control module is divided into three distinct units:[185]

The task of the Event-manager is to inform the condition parts of the agents when new problems are put on the blackboard's problem layer. After writing a problem on the blackboard, the Customer-analysis-agent, the Combination-agent, or a Domain-agent send a message to the Event-manager. The Event-manager informs the condition parts of all active agents of this

---

185 cf. Roemer (1994)

event. This way, the agents are relieved of continuously looking for new problems on the problem layer. Moreover, the sending agent needs no knowledge of the currently active agents which have to be informed of a problem entry.

The processing sequence is controlled by the Agenda-manager. It collects the condition parts' applications for problem-solving and determines priorities of execution for all incoming applications. If the resulting sorted list (the agenda) is empty, the process of problem-solving is terminated by activating the Result-agent. The task of the Agenda-manager will be illustrated with the example of determining the execution priority of the Combination-agent: For a deterministic problem, applications of the Combination-agent get highest priority to perform the decomposition of the problem. In contrast, with asset allocation problems the Combination-agent has to combine already supplied solutions. Hence, in this case the Agenda-manager will schedule the Combination-agent at last.

The execution of the action parts is performed by the Load-manager. It reads the Agenda-manager's agenda, starts execution of the action parts of the top record on the agenda, and deletes this record from the agenda. The instruction to start execution is accompanied by information identifying the problem to be solved. If there are several applications from one agent (for solving different problems) the Load-manager can start execution of this agent several times. Moreover, when starting execution in a network the Load-manager pays attention to a balanced netload in order to achieve higher performance.

3. Expandibility of the ALLFIWIB System

As mentioned in section 1, in most financial service companies there are already existing advisory support systems for particular products. Often large sets of data are stored in these systems and knowledge of (generations of) experts is coded. Therefore, in developing a new advisory support system existing applications must be reused. The problem-solving competence of the previous stand-alone application should be preserved and reengineered so that it can be integrated into the new system. The agent concept of ALLFIWIB supports this way of integration by using only a few and clearly defined interfaces. In the following section we describe the concept of FES, a stand-alone system supporting the buy-or-lease decision. As an example for the expandibility of the ALLFIWIB system we show the reengineering steps necessary to integrate FES into the distributed problem-solving environment.

3.1. Financial Engineering System FES

The Financial Engineering System FES[186] designed as a stand-alone system is a buy-or-lease decision support system. The concept of the system is illustrated by Fig. 3.

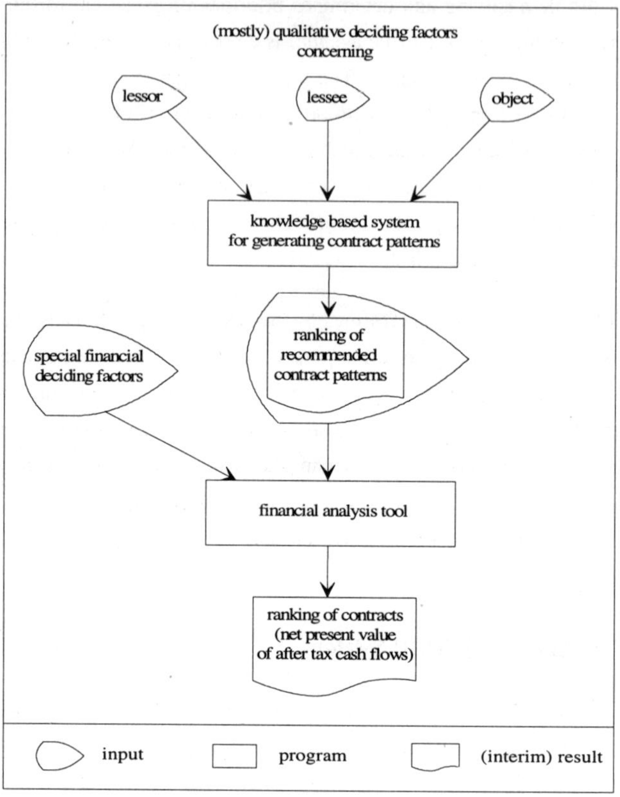

Fig. 3: System Design of FES; cf. Weinhardt (1993)

At the beginning of the advisory process the deciding factors of the buy-or-lease decision problem concerning the lessor/seller, the lessee/buyer, and the accompanying object will be ascertained. From this, a knowledge based system generates recommendations of useful kinds of contracts, called contract patterns, and puts them in order according to the suitability of these patterns judged by the given criteria. In the next step contract patterns out of this set of recommendations can be completed by further user input to contracts ready to sign. These

[186] FES, a cooperation project of the university of Gießen and IBM Germany, was finished in spring 1993. For a more detailed description cf. Weinhardt, Detloff, Gomber, Krause, Schneider (1994).

contracts will be evaluated by a financial analysis tool. The result is a ranking of the contracts based on the net present value of the contracts' cash flows after taxes. All inputs and results of the customer consulting process are stored in a database.

3.2. Concept of Integration

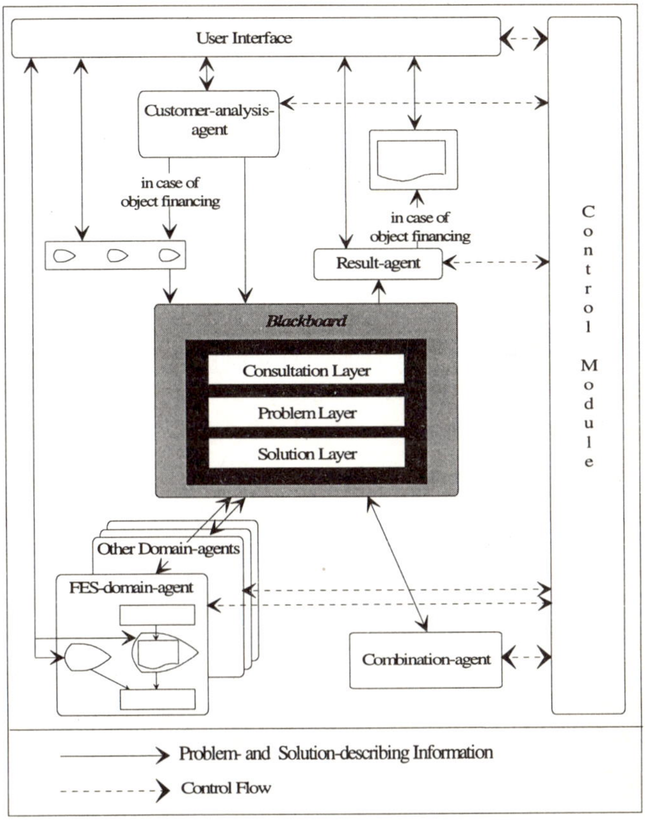

Fig. 4: Integration of FES in ALLFIWIB

In the ALLFIWIB system FES should support the case of object financing as one agent in the distributed process. Integration into the distributed environment of ALLFIWIB requires detailed coordination. Therefore, we have to divide FES into three parts: (i) the data collection referring to the problem, (ii) the problem-solving part, i.e. selection and evaluation of alternatives, and (iii) the presentation and explanation of the results (cf. fig. 4).

i. The data collection becomes part of the ***Customer-analysis-agent***, running only in the case of object financing.

ii. The second part constitutes the ***FES-domain-agent***. Contrary to the other agents the FES-domain-agent needs to have its own user interface for completing the contract patterns. Except for the interface the FES-domain-agent acts like each Domain-agent in ALLFIWIB. If it can offer a solution (proved by the condition part) the action part of the FES-agent reads the problem from the blackboard and, after problem-solving, writes the solution as well as the residual problem (if necessary) on the blackboard. To enable the FES-agent to communicate (cf. section 2.6) is one of the main reengineering tasks.

iii. Finally, the presentation of the contracts evaluated by FES has to be ensured. Therefore, the result presentation of FES with its abilities to analyze the payments of each contract and to present them for example in bar charts can be activated by the ALLFIWIB ***Result-agent***.

In conclusion, the integration has to be a compromise between the possibilities of adaptation and the reengineering effort for the integrated system on the one hand and the invariability of the concept of the integrating system on the other hand.

4. Evaluation and Outlook

The first prototype developed was designed to solve deterministic problems. Four Domain-agents for loans, real estate leasing, bonds, and life insurance as well as a Combination-agent and the control module were implemented.[187] Testing activities proved the general practicability of the ideas sketched. Even 'mixed' problems starting with periods of saving, followed by a real estate investment and subsequent periods of financing could be solved by the system of cooperating agents.

In a second step, the prototype was improved by applying the concepts of distributed problem-solving to asset allocation problems and the integration of FES. The following results of this work can be summarized:

- The strict distinction between problem- and solution-describing information from control information makes it easy to expand distributed problem-solving into new problem types like asset allocation problems. While the message-based control flow can be left un-

[187] The environment is a LAN of IBM PS/2 under OS/2 Warp and IBM LAN Server. The blackboard was implemented with the relational DBMS IBM DB2/2. The agents were developed with Trinzic ADS 6.2, the managers with C.

changed, all information concerning the problem type is written on the blackboard. Thus, the decision on if or how to solve a problem is left to the autonomous agents.

- The flexibility of a distributed system with separate agents communicating only indirectly to exchange information on problems and solutions, allows the reuse of previously existing systems with a minimum of adaptation effort.

The results show that ALLFIWIB is able to meet the requirements and produces solutions of high quality. This should, therefore, prove the readiness of the concept for practical implementation.

Acknowledgement

We owe a substantial debt to anonymous referees and many colleagues who have contributed to this paper by helpful comments. Special thanks are due to Piers Davison for his thoughtful review of the paper.

Bibliography

Buhl, H.U.: Optimale Kreditfinanzierung; Zeitschrift für Betriebswirtschaft 4 (1994), pp. 515-529.

Buhl, H.U., Hasenkamp, U., Müller-Wünsch, M., Roßbach, P., Sandbiller, K.: Wettbewerbsorientierte Systemunterstützung in der Finanzberatung; Wirtschaftsinformatik 3 (1993), pp. 262-279.

Buhl, H.U., Sandbiller, K., Will, A.: Vorteilhaftigkeit und Systemunterstützung kombinierter Allfinanzprodukte; Discussion Paper No. 48, Professur für BWL-Wirtschaftsinformatik, Universität Gießen 1993.

Buhl, H.U., Sandbiller, K., Will, A.: The Advantage of System Support for Combined Bank Assurance Products; Bachem, A. et al. (eds.): Operations Research '93; Heidelberg 1994, pp. 76-79.

Buhl, H.U., Will, A.: Unterstützung von Allfinanz-Angebotsprozessen mit verteilten wissensbasierten Systemen (ALLFIWIB); Information Management IM 2 (1993), pp. 42-50.

Chorafas, D.N., Steinmann, H.: Expert Systems in Banking; Worcester 1991.

Davis, S.R.: From Technology Push to Market Pull: Expert Systems in the Front Office; IEEE (ed.): Artificial Intelligence Applications on Wall Street; Washington 1991, pp. 220-225.

Hoppe, U.: Methoden des Knowledge Engineering. Ein Expertensystem für das Wertpapiergeschäft in Banken; Wiesbaden 1992.

Jablonsky, A.: Systems for Survival; The Banker 7 (1993), pp. 14-15.

König, H.-J.: Dezentrale Datenhaltung in der Allfinanzkundenberatung; Informationstechnik it-ti 1 (1993), pp. 45-54.

Roemer, M.: IV-Unterstützung zur Erstellung wettbewerbsorientierter Allfinanzangebote - Konzeption und prototypische Realisierung; Wirtschaftsinformatik 1 (1994), pp. 15-24.

Roßbach, P.: Supporting the Process of Customer Consulting in the Field of Financial Services; Intelligent Systems in Accounting, Finance and Management 1 (1996).

Sandbiller, K., Weinhardt, Ch., Will, A.: Cooperating Agents Solving Financial Problems: A Scenario; Tagungsband des Arbeitskreises "Verteilte Künstliche Intelligenz" in der GI; Erlangen 17. - 18.12.1992.

Talmor, S.: Step by Step; The Banker 1 (1994), pp. 71-75.

Weinhardt, Ch.: Financial Engineering - A Knowledge Based Buy/Lease Decision Support System; Karmann, A., Mosler, K., Schader, M., Uebe, G. (eds.): Operations Research '92; Heidelberg 1993, pp. 572-575.

Weinhardt, Ch., Detloff, U., Gomber, P., Krause, R., Schneider, J.: IV-Unterstützung in der Finanzierungsberatung - Integration von Methoden und Paradigmen; Wirtschaftsinformatik 1 (1994), pp. 5-14.

Wiederhold, G., Rathmann, P., Barsalou, T., Lee, B. S., Quass, D.: Partitioning and Composing Knowledge; Information Systems 1 (1990), pp. 61-72.

Wigston, I.: Encouraging Innovation; The Banker 1 (1994), pp. 12-13.

Will, A.: Die Erstellung von Allfinanzprodukten - Produktgestaltung und verteiltes Problemlösen; Wiesbaden 1995.

A Generic Approach for Computer-Assistance of Complex Decision Processes

T. Heissel, H. Krallmann, U. Meyer, M. Müller-Wünsch, C. Schopf, A. Woltering

Abstract

The increasing globalization of markets has increased the competitive pressure. The urge to adapt to rapidly changing conditions has forced many companies to introduce more flexible organizational forms. There is common agreement about the importance of supporting these changes through an information management that is aware of the strategic role information plays as a factor for success. One of the key success factors of a corporation will be the capability to perform high quality decision processes in various fields of the company.

The workbench TUB-MAGIC[188] has been designed and implemented to support the development of distributed, intelligent decision support systems which use intelligent agents to assist the decision-making process in complex situations. The concepts and the realization of TUB-MAGIC were tested by the development of two applications. The application MAGNIFICO[189] has been implemented to support a cooperative general financial consulting process of a financial institution, e.g. banking corporations. The second application, MAGNUM[190], is designed for an environmentally oriented analysis and reengineering of business processes, for example, the development of new products.

Keywords: decision support systems, distributed artificial intelligence, multi agent systems, cooperative general financial consulting, environmental management, computer supported cooperative work

6. Introduction

Recent changes in competitive business practices in Western societies reflect a shift in ethical values. Rather than the simple consumption of goods and services today's consumers are looking for self-fulfillment, satisfaction, and individuality. These same societal value changes have led to a shift in corporate emphasis from product-orientation to customer-orientation.

---

[188] TUB-MAGIC: Technical University of Berlin - Multi Agent Architecture for Intelligent Consulting. The project is funded by the DFG (*German Research Association*) within the research area "Distributed DP Systems in Business and Management"

[189] MAGNIFICO: Multi Agent System for Intelligent Financial Consulting

[190] MAGNUM: Multi Agenten System für Umweltmanagement (Multi Agent System for Environmental Management)

Employee's needs and working conditions are being supported instead of traditional corporate hierarchies and information barriers. Team-work has replaced the axioms espoused by Taylor. All of this has resulted in the introduction of new management concepts, such as KAIZEN, team organization, TQM (Total Quality Management), and simultaneous engineering.

Integrated information management and information processing concepts are critical components if a company needs to react immediately to customers needs and market requirements (e.g. Amadio, Fassina (1993), pp. 36). If the decision making process is to be optimized, the quality and timeliness of information processing must be improved to achieve the new corporate goals of

- customer orientation,
- employee orientation, and
- business process orientation[191].

For the most part decision support systems have focused on a single problem (i.e. market planning) or a single setting (i.e. the production)[192]. But, today, an isolated examination of these problems will not result in significant success. Meanwhile, a new understanding of organizing and controlling corporations with modern technical means is being established. Concerning the organizational aspects, an integrated view of business activities is common. Business process management means that corporate tasks are no longer finely segmented and the individual resulting actions of the segmentation process are no longer optimized at a single spot[193]. Today, business processes are inspected more generaly and subsequently delegated into working groups that have the skills and competence to perform ongoing tasks without regard for organizational hierarchies and communication barriers. Not only are simple tasks processed this way, but also complex and *new* situations.

These complex, and often semi-structured decision problems, have often been supported by group decision support systems (GDSS) as a subset of DSS[194]. Moreover, experience with knowledge-based DSS has helped to develop powerful DSS with great functionality. Still, there are application gaps for users and development gaps for developers that have limited the broad use of computer-assisted decision aids.

Based upon our own experiences[195] in the area of corporate stratcgy planning, it is useful to apply a semi-formal problem solving process model in most complex decision situations. By

---

191 Binner (1993)
192 Rockart, DeLong (1988)
193 Cuena, Garela-Serrano (1993)
194 Hatcher (1992); Watabe, Holsapple, Whinston (1992)
195 Krallmann, Müller-Wünsch, Woltering (1992); Müller-Wünsch, Schopf, Woltering (1991)

identifying single phases and impacts of decision processes, it is easier to find computerized solutions. Scientifically it can be demonstrated that the participation of several experts improves the outcome in complex decision situations. Of course, it must always be kept in mind that different experts may have different opinions on how best to achieve the results and their opinion may differ on what goals should be pursued, as shown by the following example (cf. Radford (1988)).

Suppose four specialists are involved in a complex decision issue. Over the course of time each of the participants is engaged in possible future outcomes of the decision situation (see fig. 1).

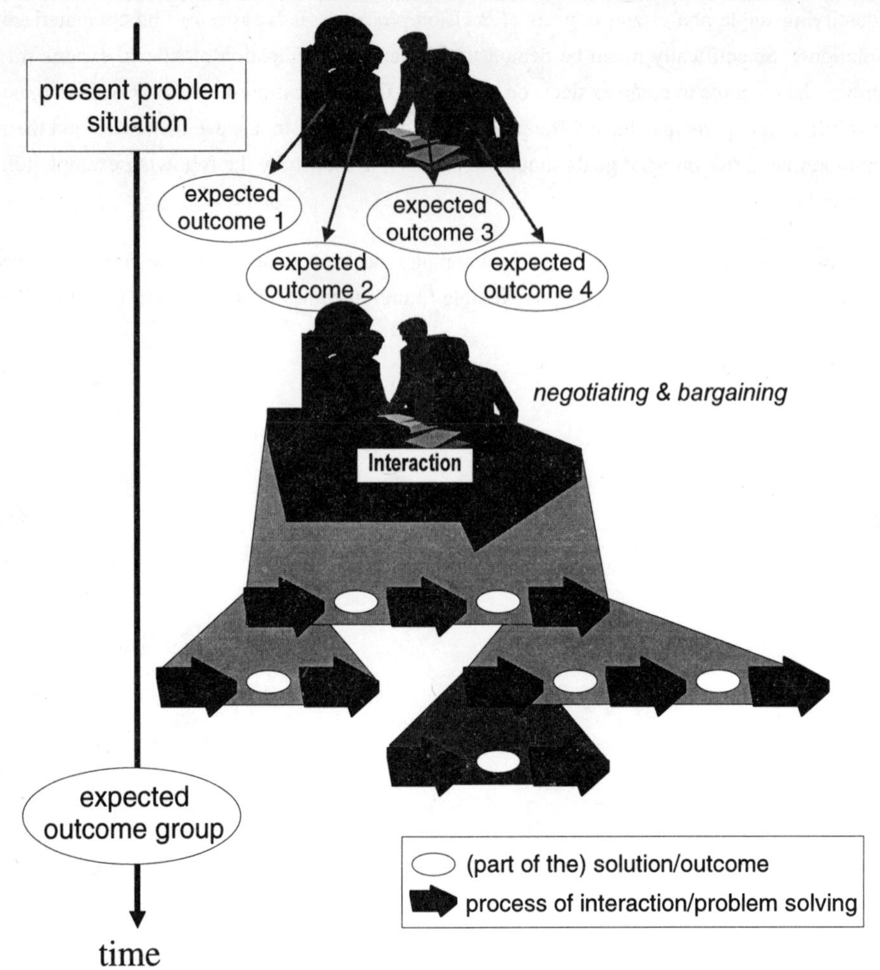

Fig. 1. Model of a complex decision process.

There are often many different possible solutions for a given decision problem. Four of these outcomes (possibly derived from different preferences of the specialists) are shown here.

Finally, if business process theory is used, experts have to agree to a certain outcome. The manner by which the specialists assess possible outcomes of a problem situation are often different. To achieve an agreement upon a final goal or goal system, they go through several decision solving phases (see fig. 1).

To achieve desired goals, specialists participate in an iterative feed-back loop, comprised of *information gathering, information analysis* and repeating *interaction.* The resolution of a situation is more complicated if the specialists have different perceptions of the possible outcomes and of the preferences of other specialists. In such circumstances, interaction between specialists may be necessary before the problem can be solved. End goals may also depend on the power of specialists within a group. Specialists in complex decision situations often enter into coalition with other specialists in order to achieve a particular goal. Over the course of time a coalition can break down due to changing conditions in the environment or changes within group dynamics.

Not only are the interaction processes diverse, but also the information analysis is an interesting process. Different specialists may use different methods to solve the problem: for instance, numerical computations, case-based reasoning, or heuristic reasoning.

Several of the above-mentioned problems have been studied by researchers in decision support systems (DSS), distributed artificial intelligence (DAI), and computer supported cooperative work (CSCW). Our approach is deeply influenced by this work[196]. Our aim is to develop a generic development environment for complex decision situations, such as consulting processes in highly complex environments. Such a development environment should contain the following concepts for modeling:

(a) preferences and intentions of problem solving specialists,

(b) available problem solving methods with their potential interaction, and

(c) methods for conflict resolution such as bargaining and negotiating between specialists.

Our workbench, TUB-MAGIC, has been implemented since the beginning of 1992. After generic concepts of TUB-MAGIC are introduced (see section two), MAGNIFICO, a financial application, is presented. It uses the concepts of TUB-MAGIC and assists in the process of general financial consulting. In section four, a second application, MAGNUM, is presented to validate the concepts of TUB-MAGIC. MAGNUM is designed to analyze business processes. Here, an example is given for the product development processes within a specific corporation. Not only are the usual analyzing dimensions for business processes examined, such as costs and duration, an computer analysis of the ecological impacts on the business processes is also created.

---

[196] Bond, Gasser (1988); Müller (1993); von Bechtoltsheim (1993)

Finally, basic ideas for the future development of TUB-MAGIC will be discussed. These ideas result from field tests of the workbench with students from the department of computer science.

7. TUB-MAGIC

7.1. Concepts and Terminology for TUB-MAGIC

TUB-MAGIC is a tool that has been designed and implemented to develop systems that support companies in certain decision situations. The characteristics of such situations have been described above. We want to reformulate the situation from the viewpoint of the tool designer:

The focus is on the decision-making process of a team. The members of the team represent different task areas, fields of knowledge, or skill levels. Although the decision-making process is characterized by environmental conditions and specific goals, the team members have their own ideas and goal conceptions. Cooperation between the team members (as well as competition among them) is part of the decision-making process. The process itself and the decision framework are normally restricted. For example, the process has to be finished within a limited period of time or certain requirements (costs, quality, composition, etc.) have to be met.

TUB-MAGIC calls such a situation "scenario" and attempts to include all critical components within its model. A representative called an "agent" is assigned to each team member. The term is derived from DAI. Agents must be able to follow "intentions", pursue "goals", and fulfill "tasks". They can use "resources" to which they have priviledges. The quality of the problem solution depends on the explicit modeling of general concepts such as competition, cooperation, communication, and interests. Additionally, specific terms may need to be modeled. For example, in MAGNIFICO the term "risk" was modeled.

2.2. Description of the Architecture

The multi-agent architecture TUB-MAGIC was originally designed according to the COSY-architecture of the Daimler-Benz research institute in Berlin (cf. Burmcister, Sundermeyer (1991)). During our project, a complete redesign of the modules within the agents was made in order to meet the requirements of our applications.

TUB-MAGIC defines the structure of all objects from the consulting scenario and the relations between the single objects. Four different types of objects are contained in the scenario

(In the following, the names of objects in the architecture will be written in *italics* and according to the spelling of the programming language).

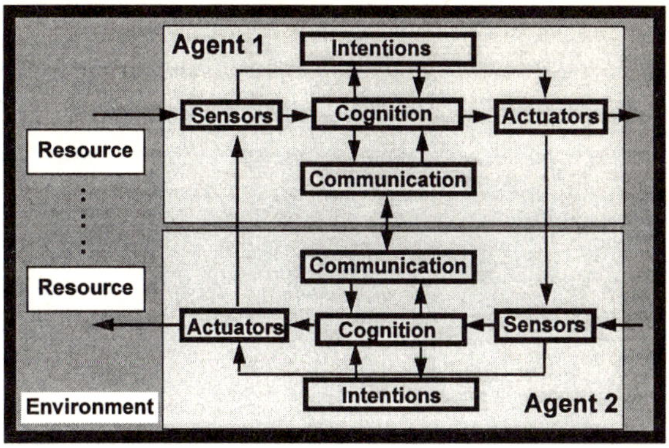

Fig. 2. Multi agent architecture.

First of all, there are the agents, units that are embedded in the environment together with other agents (see fig. 2). An agent contains five modules:

- The intention module contains the goal-oriented intentions and the action-oriented intentions.
- The cognition module contains four components: a *ProblemSolvingComponent*, a *CooperationComponent*, a *KnowledgeBase,* and a *TaskScheduler*. The *ProblemSolvingComponent* is responsible for updating the knowledge and the intentional structure as well as generating tasks. The *TaskScheduler* handles the selection, allocation, and execution of tasks. The *CooperationComponent* is responsible for the integration of the communication acts into the problem-solving process and the control of possible forms of cooperation. The *KnowledgeBase* contains all the data needed by the agent.
- The communication module handles the sending and receiving of communication acts between agents.
- The sensors module permanently updates the environmental data. It perceives changes of the environment and other agent's actions.
- The actuators module executes actions chosen by the agent and changes the state of the environment.

The second type of object in the scenario are resources. These are established in the environment of the agents, e.g. data bases to which the agents have access. Furthermore, data structures are included to which common access is possible. These exist only temporarily during the run-time of the system (e.g. the investment proposal of MAGNIFICO, which is contained as an object in the environment). These resources are generated by an action of an agent. Other agents can have access to the object.

Application terms are the third type of object embedded in the scenario. They represent formalized terms or taxonomies of the application. For example, MAGNIFICO models the term "risk" which provides risk grades such as "low" or "speculative". In a more formal language, the application terms are types which contain values and define methods. There is a possibility of defining variables of the given types. This form of modeling enables the agents to exchange information about communication terms, to give statements and to draw conclusions from other statements.

The fourth type of object models the behavior of the agents:

- Cognitive actions can be executed by the agent. They change the inner state of the agent, especially its knowledge and beliefes. The execution of cognitive actions cannot be perceived by other agents.

- Effectoric actions can be executed by the agent. They change the state of the environment. The execution of effectoric actions can be perceived by other agents.

- Sensings represent the perception ability of the agent. They are activated and processed if a change in the perceived environment occurs.

- Tasks represent what the agent has to do. A task can be created according to the pursual of a goal or as a sub-task to other tasks. Agents can also receive tasks from other agents by communication. Tasks only express *what* has to be done not *how* to do it. They can be fulfilled by executing actions, communication acts, and forms of cooperation. Multiple tasks can be active at the same time.

- Goals represent the desires of the agent. They can be activated and deactivated during runtime.

- Communication can be done in four ways. *Inform* tells another agent the actual value of a variable. With *Request,* the value of a variable can be queried by another agent. *Order* tells another agent to work on a specified task. An *Order* cannot be rejected. *Petition* asks to work on a task. A *Petition* can be rejected.

- Cooperation — is a context of interaction. A cooperation has members and a goal that is pursued. It is divided into phases and their progress is controlled by a subset of the members. So far, different forms of cooperation have been designed but not yet implemented.

The behavior of an agent is organized according to the following cycle:

The agent processes new information supplied by the input from its sensors and communication module. The cognition module processes the gathered information and represents it in the form of knowledge. This can change the state of the goal-directed intentions and the goals of the agent (cf. Meyer (1993)). As a result, the start or end of pursuing a goal leads to the creation of tasks that are handled by a *TaskScheduler*. This scheduler is responsible for assigning priorities to the tasks, allocating the tasks for execution to the action-directed intentions, and controlling the execution itself. The execution produces changes in the environment which, in turn, can be perceived by other agents or the agent itself.

2.3. Description of the Modules

2.3.1. The Intention Module

The processing of an agent corresponds to its modeled intentions. The intentions are represented in the intention module and control the behavior of the agent. TUB-MAGIC differentiates between *goal*- and *action*-oriented intentions. The goal-oriented intentions control the pursual of goals; that is, how a goal can be achieved or a certain state can be preserved. In this sense, goals represent the desires of the agent. Goals are modeled as states and are evaluated to be *true, false* or *unknown*. The action-oriented intentions control the processing *and* the omission of actions. They respond to active tasks.

As shown in fig. 3, both sorts of intentions have conditions to be fulfilled and references. A condition is modeled by a formula and expresses the situation under which the intention is true ("activated"). The possible values of the formula can be "true", "false" or "unknown". The references of an intention are a subset of the four kinds of object in the scenario. They represent objects needed or changed during the realization of the intention. The structural difference between the two kinds of intention is found in their meaning:

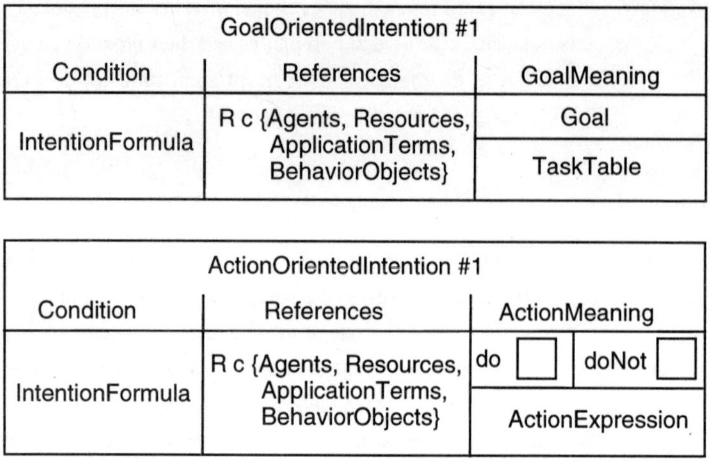

Fig. 3. Structure of goal-oriented and action-oriented intentions.

- Goal-oriented intentions are associated with a goal that is to be achieved or kept. For this, purpose tasks are supplied. These are held in a table. The rows refer to the possible changes of the intention's condition (the change of activation). The columns refer to the possible state of the goal's achievement (also "true", "false" or "unknown"). Tasks can be entered in the fields of the table. These tasks are activated as specified by the field's row and column header.

- Action-oriented intentions contain an *ActionExpression,* consisting of certain kinds of behavior objects (cognitive actions, effectoric actions, tasks, communication acts, and forms of cooperation). These objects can be combined by the four operators *seq* (sequence), *par* (parallel expression), *cond* (conditional, if-then-else), and *condLoop* (while-loop). The complex *ActionExpressions* can be either executed (*do*) or can be forbidden (*doNot*) by the intention. The latter is useful if a goal is already achieved and is to be preserved.

An example for an intentional structure is given in 2.4.

2.3.2. The Cognition Module

The cognition module is responsible for the knowledge processing of an agent. It includes the *ProblemSolvingComponent* (PSC), the *CooperationComponent* (CC), the *TaskScheduler* (TS), and the *KnowledgeBase* (KB) (see fig. 4). Additional objects are the PSC→CC-agenda and the CC→PSC-agenda. These both control the data exchange between the aforementioned components.

The *ProblemSolvingComponent* contains an interpreter which is responsible for the management of the goal-directed intentions. The first step of the control loop updates the world model of the agent. All new information gathered by sensing (1) and receiving communication (2) is evaluated and stored in the KB (3), if necessary. The second step updates the *IntentionFormulas* in the conditions of the goal-directed intentions (3, 4). Afterwards, the evaluation of the goal-directed intention's formulas may give new logical values. The third step initializes new tasks out of the goal-directed intention's task table. The new tasks are transferred to the *InputAgenda* of the TS (5).

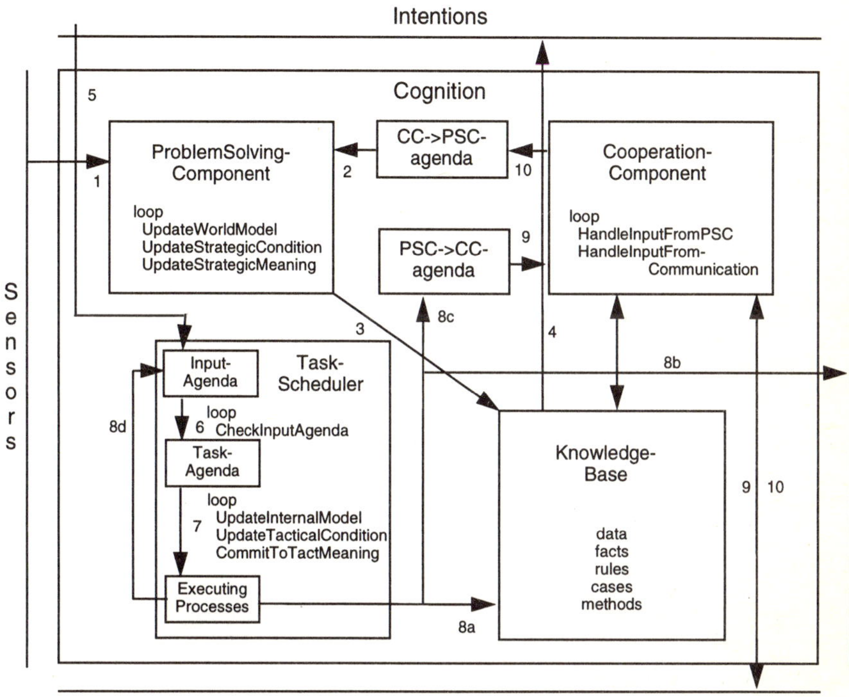

Fig. 4. Structure of the cognition module.

The TS has its two own processes to manage tasks. The first process continualy checks the *InputAgenda* and selects the tasks that are transferred to the *TaskAgenda* (6). The second process is divided into three steps (7). The first step updates the internal model of the agent. This is necessary due to the activation of the tasks by the *ProblemSolvingComponent*. The second step updates the conditions of the action-oriented intentions (4). These compete for the execution of the tasks in the *TaskAgenda*. Within the third step the competition is resolved and tasks are allocated to the intentions. The meaning of the intentions is evaluated and the execution of the *ActionExpressions* is started if the meaning is *do*. The expression is forbidden if it is *doNot*. The execution of *do*-meanings leads to the execution of the cognitive actions (8a), effectoric actions (8b), communication acts and forms of cooperation (8c), and sub-tasks (8d) specified in the *ActionExpression*.

The *CooperationComponent* (CC) has its own interpreter. Currently, this only handles single communication acts. In the future, we plan to control more complex forms of cooperation. In the first step (9), all the agent's communication acts are read from the PSC→CC-agenda, initialized, and sent to the communication module. In the second step, all received communication acts are collected from the agenda in the communication module and transferred to the CC→PSC-agenda (10).

The KB contains all objects that are necessary for the problem solving of the agent. Currently, these are basic data structures, facts, rules, and methods. Extensions to the problem solving capabilities are under development. Our goal is an approach based on mixed-paradigm-reasoning.

2.3.3. The Other Modules

- The communication module processes the direct communication between agents. Two data structures manage the entering and the sending of communication acts. An agenda collects the incoming communication acts until they are processed by the *Cooperation-Component*. Outgoing communications acts pass through a list and are sent immediately. Their registration in the list is only for the purpose of visualization and testing.

- All changes in the environment (i.e. updates in the data base) are perceived by the sensors module and collected in an agenda. The processing of the changes is initiated by the *ProblemSolvingComponent* in the cognition module, which updates its world model cyclically. By doing so, the sensors module is asked whether there are changes in the environment or not. For performance reasons, the changes are not transferred directly. Rather they become available if the sensors module evaluates wether the changes effect an particular agent. With this mechanism the sensing of an agent is restricted and, therefore, more efficient.

- If the agent wants to make changes in the environment, this is done via the actuators module. This module holds the effectoric actions of the agent. They are initiated during the evaluation of the *ActionExpressions* in the action-oriented intentions. Alternately they can be directly activated by sensorial input. The latter case models the reactive behavior of the agent. All effectoric actions can be perceived by the sensors module of other agents.

2.4. An Example

Here is an example of the use of an intentional structure. This example also demonstrates the interaction between the intention module and the cognition module. A simple strategy for the management of a portfolio in the stock market is presented. The example is based on the following ideas:

An agent can buy and sell national and foreign stocks in the stock market for a customer. Its strategy is to have a certain amount of foreign stocks in the portfolio if the risk for the foreign currency is low. Otherwise it wants to concentrate on national stocks.

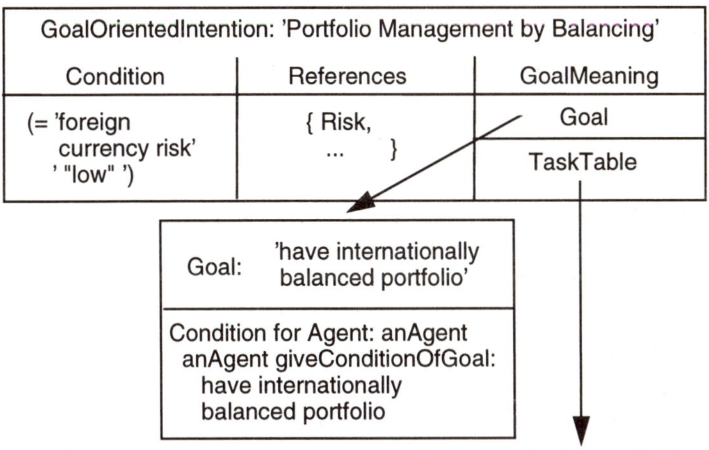

TaskTable:	Goal is fulfilled	Goal is not fulf.	Cond. unknown
Int. Cond. T->T	KeepPFTask	ChangePFTask	
Int. Cond. T->F			
Int. Cond. T->U			
Int. Cond. F->T	KeepPFTask	ChangePFTask	
Int. Cond. F->F			
Int. Cond. F->U			
Int. Cond. U->T	KeepPFTask	ChangePFTask	
Int. Cond. U->F			
Int. Cond. U->U			

Fig. 5. The goal-oriented intention 'Portfolio Management by Balancing'.

To model the example we need a goal-oriented intention, a goal, a *TaskTable*, two tasks, a risk-type (application term) that supplies constants like 'low' and 'high' as well as variables, a percentage-type, and three action-oriented intentions. We assume the necessary actions such as 'BuyStocks' as given. Figure 5 shows the structure of the goal-oriented intention.

The goal-oriented intention 'Portfolio Management by Balancing' has a condition that formalizes the situation under which the strategy is to be applied with the help of an *IntentionFormula*. The predicate '=' is defined for all the types in TUB-MAGIC. 'foreign currency risk' is a variable of the risk-type 'Risk'. 'low' is one of the constants of this type. In the references we can see the usage of the type by the intention.

The goal 'have internationally balanced portfolio' has, like every goal in TUB-MAGIC, a condition relative to every agent. Let us assume that for this agent the goal is fulfilled, if the amount of foreign stocks is 50%.

The *TaskTable* distinguishes six different cases:

- condition of the intention has been true and still is true, goal is fulfilled, KeepPFTask

  During the last two cycles of the interpreter in the *ProblemSolvingComponent* the risk has been estimated low. The agent has a balanced portfolio and wants to preserve this state. The task for keeping the stocks is activated. If this is not the first cycle where the agent has fulfilled the goal (the agent has just reached a balanced portfolio) this task was already activated in the last cycle. Whether two activations of the same task are useful or not depends on the task itself and the structure of the meaning of the action-oriented intention allocated to the task. In every case the *TaskScheduler* can handle this problem.

- condition of the intention has been true and still is true, goal is not fulfilled, ChangePFTask

  During the last two cycles of the interpreter in the *ProblemSolvingComponent* the risk has been estimated low. The agent has no balanced portfolio. The task for changing the portfolio is activated. We can assume that this task was already activated in the last cycle. The usefulness is checked by the *TaskScheduler*.

- condition of the intention has been false and now is true, goal is fulfilled, KeepPFTask

  The risk hasn't been low up to now and is estimated low in this cycle for the first time. For some reason the goal is already fulfilled. Perhaps other strategies were activated that have the side effect of producing balanced portfolios under certain circumstances. The new interest in the goal is made explicit by activating the task for keeping the stocks. This may influence other strategies.

- condition of the intention has been false and now is true, goal is not fulfilled, ChangePFTask

  This is the classical case. The risk hasn't been low up to now and is estimated low in this cycle for the first time. The portfolio is not balanced. So the task for changing the portfolio is activated.

- condition of the intention has been unknown and now is true, goal is fulfilled, KeepPFTask

  For some reason the risk could not be estimated in the past, but now is estimated to be low. The agent has a balanced portfolio and wants to preserve this state. The task for keeping the stocks is activated.

- condition of the intention has been unknown and now is true, goal is not fulfilled, ChangePFTask

  For some reason the risk could not be estimated in the past, but now is estimated to be low. The agent has no balanced portfolio. The task for changing the portfolio is activated.

Now we want to look at three different action-oriented intentions that can be used within the example. As shown in fig. 6, the task for changing the portfolio can have two different realizations, depending on the amount of foreign stocks in the portfolio in the moment.

- If the foreign contingent is less than 50%, more foreign stocks have to be bought (see first intention; for simplicity's sake we don't consider the possibility of selling national stocks). The *condition* is a formula that combines the activation of the task with the foreign contingent. The *action-meaning* is a sequence of choosing appropriate stocks for buying (a cognitive action), the buying itself (an effectoric action), and informing the customer about the change (a communication).

- If the foreign contingent is higher than 50%, foreign stocks have to be sold (see second intention; for simplicity's sake we don't consider the possibility of buying national stocks). The foreign contingent can't equal 50%, since otherwise the task wouldn't have been activated - the goal was not fulfilled.

The task for keeping the stocks is realized by an intention that responds to its activation. The *doNot*-meaning is a parallel expression containing the actions for selling and buying stocks.

The semantic of a parallel expression in a *doNot*-meaning is to forbid all sub-expressions. So here the agent can neither buy nor sell stocks as long as the intention is fulfilled.

ActionOrientedIntention: 'Buy Foreign Stocks'		
Condition	References	ActionMeaning
(and (isActive 'ChangePFTask') (< 'foreign contingent' 50))	{ChangePFTask, Percentage, ...}	do [X] doNot [ ] (seq ('ChooseF.Stocks') ('BuyStocks') ('Inform Customer'))

ActionOrientedIntention: 'Sell Foreign Shares'		
Condition	References	ActionMeaning
(and (isActive 'ChangePFTask') (> 'foreign contingent' 50))	{ChangePFTask, Percentage, ...}	do [X] doNot [ ] (seq ('ChooseStocksFor Selling') ('SellStocks') ('Inform Customer'))

ActionOrientedIntention: 'Keep Shares'		
Condition	References	ActionMeaning
(isActive 'KeepPFTask')	{KeepPFTask, ...}	do [ ] doNot [X] (par ('BuyStocks') ('SellStocks'))

Fig. 6. Three action-oriented intentions.

8. MAGNIFICO

A typical example for complex decision-making can be found in the field of general financial consulting. General financial consulting means offering a private customer all financial services through one consultant. Of course, the consultant has to contact experts in the various investment areas to cope with the complex and wide area of financial consulting. In some banks such teams of financial experts really do come together from time to time. But, in most cases, the consulting quality suffers from an insufficient cooperation between the investment experts.

In the project MAGNIFICO a prototype is being developed to support financial consultants and the cooperation between team members. The basis for this prototype is the previously described workbench TUB-MAGIC. The team members are modeled as agents that interact to configure for example the customer's portfolio.

8.1. Modeling an General Financial Consulting System

The knowledge of a financial consultant in MAGNIFICO is modeled in the client advisory agent. Together with the client agent, who represents the real customer, this pair can be found in the system repeatedly. Investment experts of different investment fields are responsible for the maintenance of their special agents. These experts can be actual human teams as well. Every consultant has access to the knowledge of all the investment experts at any time and from any place where networks are available. The resulting structure of the organization is shown in fig. 7.

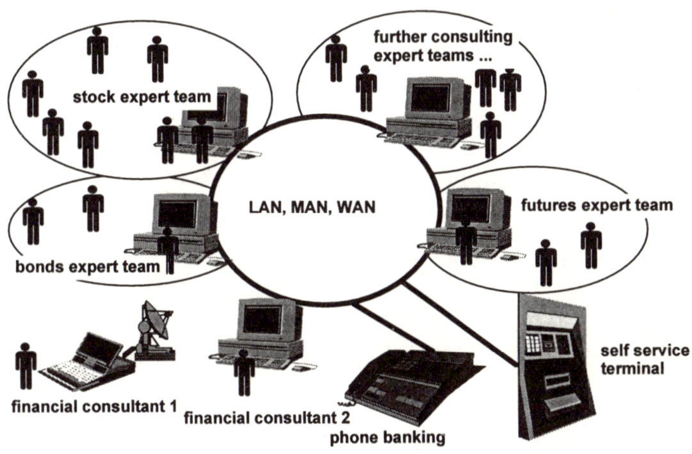

Fig. 7. Organization of a Computer Assisted General Financial Consulting.

For the first prototype, the extensive service offered by a general financial consulting system is limited to the section of a freely disposable investment amount. The client advisory agent contains consultant knowledge, including all investment sections. The client advisory agent distributes the investment amount to partial investment sections assigning the appropriate exemplary distribution to the client. This assignment is guided by heuristic classification[197]. The integration of the financial portfolio selection theory, according to Markowitz[198], is being developed. This will lead to optimal distribution of the investment amount, taking the parameters "yields" and "risks" and a preference function of the client into account. Upon completion of the assignment, the client advisory agent engages the investment expert to work out investment proposals for each partial investment amount.

A bond agent, a stock agent, a real estate agent, a life insurance agent, and a future agent are partial experts in certain investment sections. A tax advisory agent and a national economy expert are available as advisory experts. They put their knowledge at disposal, upon request or unasked, in order to compile an offer.

Customizing the consulting process is made possible by representing the human client in a formal model. This model includes five components: The component *characterization* contains data relevant in an administrative sense, the component *SocioDemo* contains socio-demographic data of the client relevant for investment, the component *investment data* contains all decisive data relevant to the investment, and the component *capital* models the client's current capital structure. A capital value and a value which indicates the corresponding expenditures is assigned to each attribute. The component *income/expenses* gathers the client's main income sources and expenses according to the client's current value and target value. The modeling of the client's cash flow restictions are planned in the form of two further components. The client model is implemented in the client agent.

In a more advanced project phase, the agents will be in a position to collaborate independently according to specified goals or to compete with other agents. In the next section first experiments made with a stock agent and a future agent are described.

8.2. Generation of Investment Proposals Based on a Cooperation between Stock and Future Agent

The future agent is an expert for options on the German futures exchange (DTB). Dealings in standardized options on the DTB are completely computer-supported. Because of the standardization the market is very fluid. Hence, there are fair negotiable prices for private investors at almost any time. Additionally, low charges and well-conducted judicial regulations lead to an increasing interest of private investors in dealing on the DTB.

---

[197] Clancey (1985)
[198] Markowitz (1952)

However, the DTB is very complicated. In spite of the standardization there are about two thousand calls and puts available on the DTB. These options are more complex when combined with one another or when combined with stocks. As a result, it is possible to profit from almost any anticipated market tendency. The private investor needs extensive consultation for dealing at the DTB.

The reasons for a private investor to deal at the DTB can be trading or hedging. "Hedging" means to offer security for losses because of declining stock prices. "Trading" means making profits from anticipated market tendencies. A stock expert will be needed for judging combinations of stocks and options as well as for helping to anticipate the prices of options.

Trading is a component of the cooperation between the stock agent and the future agent. The goal of this cooperation is to generate "customer-optimal" trade. Therefore, the two agents have to agree on the stock on which the option is based and on the period for the anticipation. An easy way to achieve this agreement is for the stock agent to propose until the DTB-agent accepts the proposal. Otherwise, the stock agent has no more proposals and quits the cooperation.

After agreement upon a stock and an anticipation period, the additional parameters of the trade have to be settled. This part of the cooperation is based on fixed rules with an agreement at the end. The stock agent estimates an interval for the expected price at the end of the consideration period. The width of the interval is based on the customer's risk aversion. According to these parameters, the DTB-agent configures up to four trades which have their profit-interval corresponding to the anticipated interval and proposes them to the stock agent. It judges the proposals, picks one of them as the best result or rejects all and tries to find another stock (see fig. 8).

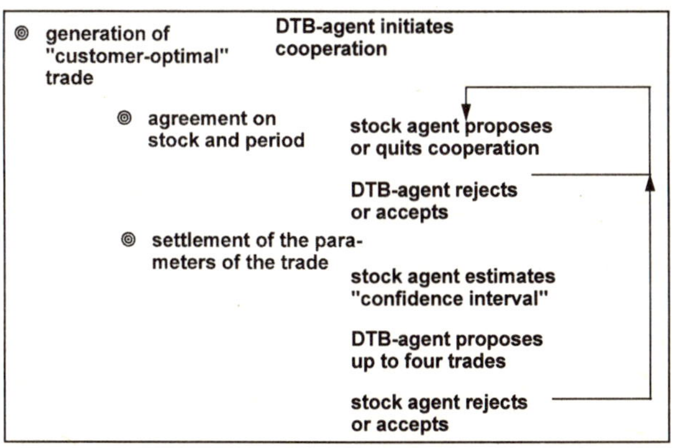

Fig. 8. Cooperative Trading with DTB-options.

This simple cooperation may help us to find generic cooperation forms. As a first result, the example above describes a simple form of agreement which works well when the agents know each other well. Otherwise, backtracking around the reasons for rejection is unavoidable.

4. MAGNUM

Our second area of interest copes with the problem of optimizing business processes. In the past, economic decisions have been deeply influenced by the requirements made by market conditions and production constraints. In particular, information about costs and time have been considered in typical management decision-processes.

Today, a new ecological attitude in management has been established. This leads to a more detailed consideration of ecological features and values during managerial decision-making. But this integration of ecological aspects also increases the complexity of the problem. The basic idea is the addition of an ecological view to the common views of business processes. Three different aspects of processes have to be considered:

- costs of a single process
- time consumption realated to a single process
- information about relevant environmental influences

As a consequence, the usual model of business processes has to be extended. Research has already been done in the field of extending the model of business processes with costs[199]. The resulting concepts are being analyzed for their capability of representing ecological data.

First results show that in most cases a model containing all three dimensions is too complex to be analyzed by a single decision-maker. As a consequence, different experts have to support the primary decision maker. As far as ecological information is concerned, we distinguish three factors:

- analysis of ingredients and components,
- recycling and disposal of waste, and
- environmental laws and standards.

---

[199] Langhoff, Müller-Wünsch (1993)

The goal of MAGNUM is to support the decision making process in an organization. A system is being developed using the TUB-MAGIC architecture. A possible modeling of the scenario is shown in the following figure:

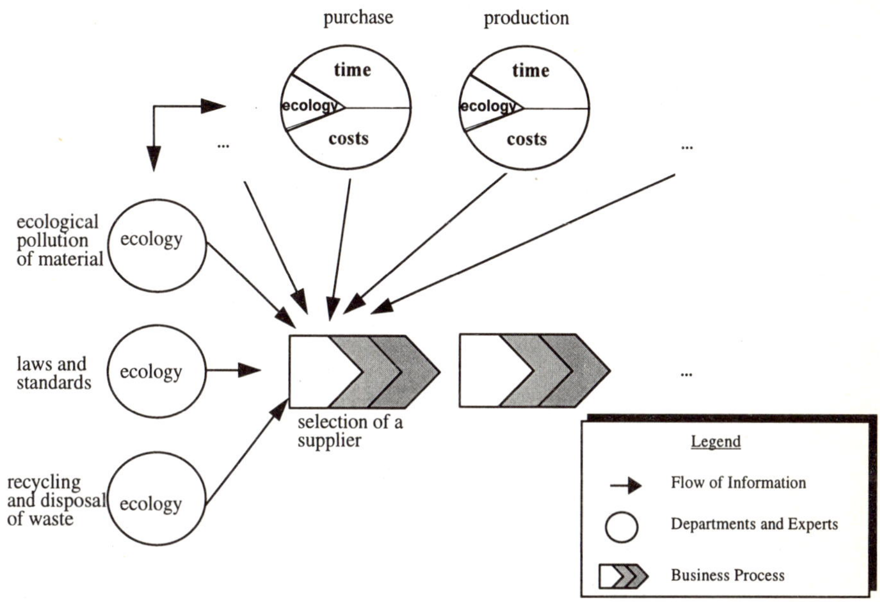

Fig. 9. The scenario of MAGNUM.

In a first approach, each department and each ecologist is modeled as an agent. The goal of an agent is to minimize costs, time consumption, and ecological pollution. In most cases, more than one goal is active. Furthermore, priority rules have to be established to handle different goals in situations where goals compete. Currently, the agents modeling the ecologists only have the intention to respond to *requests* from the other agents.

At this time it is not possible to describe the dimension ecology by a single value. This is because there are no satisfactory rating methods to aggregate all environmental influences. In respect to the information needed in ecological balances, a data model has to be built. All agents will have access to this data model troughout the process and they will be able to enter information they consider to be relevant[200].

[200] Hallay, Pfriem (1993); Braunschweig, Müller-Wenk (1993)

5. Future Research

As far as the technical aspects are concerned, the emphasis of our project was on the integration and use of DAI-based methods, DSS concepts, and ideas from CSCW. We expect to achieve numerous benefits from opening the architecture towards an interactive approach. So far, agents are able to independently interpret information. If the system does not have sufficient knowledge to solve a problem, it is currently not possible to integrate knowledge of human experts during runtime. CSCW and HCCW (Human Computer Cooperative Work) offer methods that we consider to be promising candidates to overcome this restriction.

Beyond the extension of TUB-MAGIC to CSCW and HCCW facilities another area of interest lies in the cognitive processes involved in expert reasoning. This is a much neglected area in episodic problem solving. In response to this, hybrid problem solving architectures which combine cases, rules, and models have been developed. These architectures allow the strengths of each form of reasoning to complement those of the others[201].

For this reason, we are working on integrating case-based reasoning techniques (CBR)[202], neural computing mechanisms, and "conventional" DSS technology. The TUB-JANUS shell is a development environment to generate *case-based decision support systems* in the area of typical business classification tasks[203]. Further work will attempt to integrate other problem-solving methods -here model-based and rule-based methods- into the TUB-JANUS shell. The goal is to build a hybrid DSS generator for semi- and ill-structured tasks in complex decision situations. The primary aim of this work is to extend this stand-alone approach to meet new requirements by supporting distributed decision processes or group decisions (e.g. the general financial consulting process).

In the short run, we are considering the integration of TUB-JANUS and other problem solving methods into the *CognitiveActions* of the TUB-MAGIC environment. In the terminology of TUB-MAGIC, hybrid problem solving will change the way an agent executes its cognitive actions. Currently, these actions are pure methods or rule-based reasoning processes.

Concerning the representation of knowledge, an integration of CBR-techniques will lead to a redesign of the knowledge base in the agents. Currently, the structure of the knowledge base is designed according to the epistemological approach of the multi-agent architecture. The structure will have to be changed according to the needs of a knowledge representation language that is able to capture the diversity of the different knowledge types as well as the epistemological knowledge about agents in a scenario.

---

201 Rissland, Skalak (1989); Golding, Rosenbloom (1991); Skinner, Luger (1992)

202 Kolodner, Simpson, Sycara-Cyranski (1985); [Kolodner (1993)

203 Jeske, Müller-Wünsch, Woltering (1992); Schiemann, Woltering (1994)

6. Acknowledgments

The TUB-MAGIC development has been highly motivated by fruitful discussions with our colleagues and students, especially Helmut Frank, Susanne König, Niels Jäger and Jörg Lindemann. Moreover, we would like to thank our partners from other participating universities, especially the University of Marburg, the University of Giessen, the University of the Saarland, and the University of Hohenheim for their interesting and influencing contributions. Also, we appreciate discussions with the DFKI, especially Donald Steiner and his team, and the Daimler Benz Research Group in Berlin with Kurt Sundermeyer and his team. We also appreciate the great support of Peter Castine and Gay Wood in creating an english version of our work.

7. References

Amadio, P.; Fassina, I.: The case studies. In: Power, R.J.D. (ed.): Cooperation among organizations. Berlin: Springer, 1993, pp. 26 - 40.

Binner, H. F.: Strategie des Generalmanagement. Berlin: Springer, 1993.

Bond, A. H.; Gasser, L. (eds): Readings in Distributed Artificial Intelligence. San Mateo: Morgan Kaufmann, 1988.

Braunschweig, A.; Müller-Wenk, R.: Ökobilanzen für Unternehmungen. Bern: Paul Haupt, 1993.

Burmeister, B.; Sundermeyer, K.: Cooperative Problem-Solving Guided by Intentions and Perception. In: Pre-Proceedings of the 3rd Workshop on MAAMAW. D. Steiner, J. Müller (eds.), Kaiserslautern: DFKI GmbH D-91-10, 1991

Clancey, W. J.: Heuristic Classification. In: Artificial Intelligence, 27, 1985, pp. 289 - 350.

Cuena, J.; García-Serrano, A.: Intelligent computer support. In: Power, R.J.D. (ed.): Cooperation among organizations. Berlin: Springer, 1993, pp. 72 - 102.

Golding, A.; Rosenbloom, P.: Improving Rule-Based Systems through Case-based Reasoning. In: Proceeding of the 9th AAAI, 1991, pp. 22 - 27.

Hallay, H.; Pfriem, R.: Öko-Controlling. Heidelberg: Campus, 1993.

Hatcher, M. E.: Group decision support systems: decision process, time and space. In: Decision Support Systems, 1992, no. 2, pp. 83 - 84.

Jeske, M.; Müller-Wünsch, M.; Woltering, A.: Extension of Standard Software Systems by the Case-Based Reasoning Approach to a Hybrid Architecture for Intelligent DSS. In: J. Biethahn et al. (eds.): Wissensbasierte Systeme in der Betriebswirtschaft - Anwendungen und Integration mit Hypermedia. Wiesbaden: Gabler Verlag, 1992, pp. 201-223.

Kolodner, J. L.: Case-Based Reasoning. San Mateo: Morgan Kaufmann, 1993.

Kolodner, J. L.; Simpson, R. L.; Sycara-Cyranski, K.: A Process Model of Case-Based Reasoning in Problem Solving. In: Proceeding of the 9th International Joint Conference on Artificial Intelligence (IJCAI), Vol. 1, 1985, pp. 284 - 290.

Krallmann, H.; Müller-Wünsch, M.; Woltering, A.: CASA: A knowledge-based tool for management consultants. In: Expert Systems with Applications, 1992, Vol. 5, pp. 257 - 265.

Langhoff, M.; Müller-Wünsch, M.: Rechnergestützte Prozeßkostenanalyse. In: CIM Management, 4, 1993, pp. 38-42.

Markowitz, H. M.: Portfolio Selection. *In*: The Journal of Finance, 1952, pp. 77-91.

Meyer, U.: Intentionalität in der Modellierung von Agenten. In: Proceedings des Gründungsworkshop der Fachgruppe Verteilte Künstliche Intelligenz der Gesellschaft für Informatik, Saarbrücken: DFKI GmbH D-93-06, 1993, pp 22-33

Müller, J. (Hrsg): Verteilte Künstliche Intelligenz. Mannheim: BI-Wiss. Verlag, 1993.

Müller-Wünsch, M.; Schopf, C.; Woltering, A.: Using standard software systems in a hybrid and distributed architecture for an intelligent decision support system for corporate strategy development. In: Proceedings Int. Soc. of Decision Support Systems, 1991, FAW Ulm, Germany.

Radford, K. J.: Strategic and tactical decisions, 2nd Edition. New York: Springer, 1988.

Rissland, E. L.; Skalak, D. B. (1989): Combing case-based and rule-based reasoning: A heuristic approach. In: Proceeding of the 8th International Joint Conference on Artificial Intelligence (IJCAI), Vol. 1, pp. 524 - 530.

Rockart, J. F.; DeLong, D. W.: Executive Support Systems. Illinois: Homewood, 1988.

Schiemann, I.; Woltering, A.: Integrating the Kohonen Feature-Map Model into the CBR Cycle - The TUB-JANUS Shell. H. Krallmann (ed.): Working Paper, Technical University of Berlin - Department of Systems Analysis, RAP/3/1994, 1994.

Skinner, J. M.; Luger, G. F.: An Architecture for Integrating Resoning Paradigms. In: R. J. Brachman, H. J. Levesque, R. Reiter (eds.): Procs. of the International Conference on Principles of Knowledge Representation and Resoning. San Mateo: Morgan Kaufmann, 1992, pp. 753 - 761.

von Bechtolsheim, M.: Agentensysteme. Braunschweig: Vieweg, 1993.

Watabe, K.; Holsapple, C. W.; Whinston, A. B.: Coordinator support in a nemawashi decision process. In: Decision Support Systems, 1992, nor. 2, p. 85 - 98.

Group Scheduling - Methods and Tools for Distributed Scheduling Processes in a Corporate Environment

Leena Suhl, Erwin Reinecke, Uwe Pape

Abstract

We discuss the problem of generating a schedule by a team in a corporate environment. It is assumed that each team member is responsible for a partial schedule but has to share common resources. We propose the concept of a group scheduling support system consisting of an individual workbench for the interactive work, a communication component and a negotiation subsystem. A prototype implementation called GS^3 under Windows for Workgroups for a PC-LAN is discussed. The communication and coordination kernel of GS^3 can be integrated into existing corporate planning environments.

Keywords: group scheduling, communication, coordination, negotiation, workbench

1. Introduction

The process of allocating *tasks* or *activities* to corporate resources can be very complex and is often carried out by a group of schedulers in team work. The resources can be production machines, transportation vehicles, service facilities, or employees, for example. A schedule determines the allocation of activities to resources over time together with the sequences of tasks on each resource. The resource allocation process is subject to numerous more or less exactly defined constraints.

A corporate resource allocation process is typically a *semistructured* decision problem. Given the objectives, resources, constraints, and activities with their resource requirements, the problem can be defined as an exact optimization problem. However, normally not all practical restrictions and tasks can be formalized and expressed in the optimization model. Furthermore, there may be special cases and exceptions requiring human intervention. Thus a combination of algorithmic and interactive scheduling techniques seems to provide an ideal solution. A single-user scheduling support system has to be integrated with coordination and communication techniques, many of which can be found in contributions to Computer Supported Cooperative Work and Coordination Theory.

The project Group Scheduling began at the Technical University of Berlin in February 1993. It focuses on complex schedule generation processes carried out by groups of professional schedulers in organizations. A basic process to be modelled was the airline scheduling process which we had studied in an earlier project[204]. However, the results were to be generalized for other corporate resource allocation processes as well.

Recent developments of information technology give us new powerful possibilities of supporting the group scheduling process by computers. Recent experience shows that we should not just implement manual processes on computers but rethink how to organize complete business processes in an optimal way[205].

Many practical distributed resource allocation processes are not optimally supported by computers yet[206]. One problem is that due to lack of communication one organizational unit is not aware of resources available in other units. This may happen, as an example, when a site of a car rental agency is lacking the information of reservations of other, nearby sites. In the construction process of an airline schedule several expert schedulers are allocating same resources (aircraft, crews and so on) for various connections all around the world. The process is not optimally coordinated, if one scheduler may reserve a resource for a longer period than needed - like for the whole scheduling period. On the other hand, without the use of computer-based consistency checks this was the only possible way of avoiding chaotic planning situations where noone has a total overview.

2. Goals of the Project Group Scheduling

The project Group Scheduling focuses on schedule construction problems where several expert schedulers use same resources for the schedules they generate. We assume that each scheduler is responsible for a partial schedule but has to coordinate the use of common resources with his/her colleagues. There are three basic forms of coordination: hierarchy, market

---

[204] cf. Franken & Suhl (1992), Suhl (1993)
[205] cf. Hammer & Champy (1993), Scheer (1994)
[206] cf. Herzhoff (1994), Suhl (1993)

and network[207]. There is no research known to us comparing these organization forms for scheduling construction processes. Thus onc goal of our project was to design a testbed for the comparison of organization forms for scheduling applications.

The main goal of the project Group Scheduling can be stated:

Search for optimal organizations of corporate schedule generation processes

In more detail, the project includes the following parts:

- Understanding and modeling the basic components of a generic schedule generation process in corporations from the viewpoint of a single scheduling expert.
- Modeling the most important organizations of the scheduling process carried out by a team.
- Building a prototype for the purpose of testing various applications and organizations.
- Carrying out laboratory experiments with several types of distributed scheduling problems.
- Extending the experiments to cover also field tests.

Currently (spring 1994) most of the modeling work has been completed. The concept of the prototype system is finished and to a great extent implemented. Results of the laboratory and field experiments will be reported in a subsequent paper.

The goal of the project Group Scheduling is to introduce new conceptual models for the distributed resource allocation process that allow optimal coordination and communication between distributed planners thus contributing to the competitiveness of a corporation. The concepts are illustrated by the prototype system GS^3.

We hope to contribute methodologically to the state-of-the-art of group support systems, by introducing support techniques for the case that a distributed group of planners is solving a complex schedule generation problem where they schedule shared resources.

---

[207] cf. Veryard (1994), Malone & Crowston (1991)

3. Related Research

Systems discussed in this paper involve complex planning and scheduling problems to be solved by a team possibly distributed in space and time. To our knowledge the system GS^3 presented in this paper is the only one explicitly supporting both schedule construction and team-oriented decisionmaking. The methods and tools used in GS^3 exploit results from areas like scheduling algorithms, Constraint-Based Scheduling, Coordination Theory, Distributed Data Bases, Group Decision Support Systems, Computer-Supported Cooperative Work, and Human-Computer Cooperative Work.

Scheduling Algorithms

Scheduling algorithms have been studied in Operations Research since several decades. A mathematical scheduling problem can be stated by defining the resources, activities with their resource requirements, constraints and objective(s). Three types of scheduling problems are important in practice: 1) Deadline-oriented scheduling (like in manufacturing and project scheduling), 2) Interval scheduling (like school timetabling where resources are allocated in given intervals of time), 3) Routing and scheduling (like the airline scheduling problem where routes of aircraft are determined simultaneously with flights schedules). An overview of scheduling in computer and manufacturing systems is given in Blazewicz et al. (1993). Interval scheduling for the school timetable construction is discussed in Maier (1994), and airline scheduling problems in Suhl (1993).

Most practical scheduling problems are NP-hard, so that there is not much hope in the worst case to solve them optimally. However, hardware improvements and specially tuned algorithms today make it possible to find good solutions for problems which were intractable a decade ago. For example, in Suhl (1993) the solution of airline scheduling problems by the mathematical programming code MOPS (Mathematical Optimization System) is described.

Knowledge-Based Scheduling

Recently Artificial Intelligence techniques, especially knowledge-based systems, have been proposed for scheduling in manufacturing systems[208]. An AI system in this area should not replace the human scheduler or supervisor, but extend his/her capabilities by doing more problem solving than was possible manually. Some algorithmic techniques have proven successful for portions of the scheduling problem and can be combined with AI methods.

Two basic components of a knowledge-based system are a knowledge base and an inference engine. What-if rules are a widely used representation form of knowledge. Rule-based systems constitute a means of modeling the problem solving know-how of human experts. They are able to explain their reasoning, since they can make their logic transparent. An incremental scheduling procedure is a good candidate for a rule-based system.

Rule-based systems were developed by Lufthansa for flight scheduling and physical aircraft management[209]. Combined routing and scheduling problems are the subject of the ESPRIT-project PONTIFEX (Planning On Non-specific Transportations by an Intelligent Fleet EXpert)[210]. An overview of constraint-based scheduling systems for manufacturing is given in Atabakhsh (1991). Few of the knowledge-based scheduling systems have been successfully used in practice until now. They suffer from the common problem of all formalized schedule generation systems: It is not known how to combine the non-formal portion of expert knowledge and intuition optimally with a formalized rule-based system.

Computer-Supported Cooperative Work

Coordination and communication within joint work carried out by group members in an organization is the subject of the discipline called Computer-Supported Cooperative Work (CSCW). The concept of CSCW is still relatively young and not yet established. It was introduced by Cashman and Greif in 1984, and the first CSCW-conference was held in Austin, Texas in 1986[211].

---

208 cf. Atabakhsh (1991), Blazewicz et al. (1993), Müller (1993)
209 cf. Lufthansa (1990), Franken & Suhl (1992)
210 cf. Ruijtenbeek & Scharenborg (1991)
211 cf. Grudin (1991)

Software tools, developed for a network of cooperating humans, are generally called groupware. The development of electronic mail and distributed data bases provide the basis for groupware. However, the use of these tools alone is not enough for a system to be called groupware. Essential is the shared intention of the participants to follow a common goal.

Three important areas of CSCW are[212]: 1) Synchronous meeting facilitation, like electronic meeting rooms, computer conferencing and videoconferencing; 2) Workflow management, with other words systems that support process-oriented workflows within organizations where several people in different organizational units are working on the same process; 3) Message-oriented systems, which support asynchronous communication of team members through e-mail, speech acts[213] or semistructured messages[214]. Note that message-oriented systems can also support group decisionmaking, for example in form of negotiations. Our system GS^3 represents message-based groupware able to support synchronous and asynchronous schedule generation processes with negotiation on resource allocation.

Group Decision Support Systems

The concept of Group Decision Support Systems (GDSS) emerged in mid-1980s, and is usually associated with synchronous decisionmaking (all decisionmakers being simultaneously in contact negotiating about a joint decision). Technical developments in electronic communication, computing, and decision support, coupled with interest of organizations to improve meeting effectiveness, provided the basis of GDSS. One of the first definitions of GDSS was given by DeSanctis and Gallupe, stating that GDSS are used to support synchronous decision making, where decision makers work together to find a complex decision[215]. A typical example of a GDSS is the software system GroupSystems developed at the University of Arizona[216]. Since the definition of DeSanctis and Gallupe, GDSS have been extended to include also asychronous systems, where a negotiation process is based either on message-passing or on a shared data base[217].

---

212 cf. Lewe & Krcmar (1993), for example
213 cf. Winograd (1987)
214 cf. Malone & Crowston (1987)
215 cf. DeSanctis & Gallupe (1987)
216 cf. Lewe & Krcmar (1993)
217 cf. Jarke, Jelassi & Shakun (1987)

Another classification of GDSS is given in Eden (1992): those involving direct keyboard entry from members of the group (like GroupSystems); those that are facilitator driven but involve real-time computing that is integral to the activity of the group; and those that are facilitator driven with no computer support.

According to Eden (1992), the design for something that claims to be a GDSS must, at the very least, reflect on the following: the nature of group decision making as a process; the nature of decision making in organizations; and the nature of support and intervention by a „system", be it facilitator/chauffeur/consultant/software tool in relation to a group.

Negotiation Support Systems

Negotiation Support Systems (NSS) can be understood as a special case of GDSS focusing on components to facilitate negotiations. Negotiation support systems can be classified according to the degree of third-party control[218] (i.e., most control with autocratic styles and arbitration, and least control in mediation and bargaining styles). Agents in market settings, such as real-estate-purchase transactions, are examples of self-interested third parties.

Another dimension of NSS is the structure of the solution domain as an outcome of the negotiation. A simple domain would be a given number of alternatives. For example, Jarke, Jelassi and Shakun (1987) discuss the decision where two negotiators (husband and wife) want to select a car among 10 alternatives. On the other hand, the solution space can be a continuous interval of one variable, like in the simplified case of labor-management negotiations, where only one number (percental increase of salary) is determined.

Characteristic to the schedule generation problem, which is the subject of this paper, is that it is extremely difficult to determine its solution space. Being an NP-hard problem, it has an astronomical number of potential solutions. Moreover, the partial solution of each individual scheduler depends on other partial solutions, since the allocation of a resource to a task implies that this resource is not available for other tasks during the reserved time.

During the schedule generation process, there is not one big question to negotiate about, but many small ones - like which scheduler may use a certain resource at a certain time for an ac-

[218] cf. Valley, White & Iacobucci (1992)

tivity in his/her responsibility. The willingness to make concessions depends to a great extent on the incentive determined by the organizational structure.

Coordination Theory

Many disciplines, like computer science, economics, management science, linguistics, and biology, are studying questions about coordination of systems. In recent years the question has arised, what general types of coordination there are and which type is suitable for a given system. The term coordination theory was introduced by Malone & Crowston (1990) to refer to theories about how coordination can occur in diverse kinds of systems.

Malone and Crowston define coordination in a broad sense as „the act of working together harmoniously“[219]. In Malone & Crowston (1991) a narrow definition is given for the cases where they want to focus specifically on the aspects that are unique to coordination: „Coordination is the act of managing interdependencies between activities“. They offer a conceptual framework for coordination as requiring four basic components: *actors* performing *activities* directed towards *goals*, with goal-relevant *interdependencies* between the activities.

Three main theories of coordination are used in literature both as descriptive and as prescriptive theories: hierarchies, markets and networks[220]. A *hierarchy* is held together by administration, command and control. Each part is precisely defined to perform a specific function. Efficiency in a hierarchy is thought of in terms of the division of labor. Ideally, each function is carried out by a single part, with no overlaps. Additional parts are responsible for control functions.

A *market* is a system of agents, providing products and services to one another. A market is held together by exchange, based on formal contracts. In economics, a market is defined as efficient if no agent has the power to distort the market. Various forms of monopoly are regarded as inefficient, since the monopolist may ask higher prices or degrade the quality of service without redress.

A *network* is a 'flat' organizational form, in contrast to the 'vertical' organizational form of the hierarchical organization. A network allows direct connections between two members, so

---

[219] cf. Malone & Crowston (1990)
[220] cf. Veryard (1994)

that it is not always necessary to connect along the hierarchical structure. Sociologists use the term 'network' to denote a system held together by informal communication, based on trust. In today's Management Science networks are often favored over hierarchical forms, since they make the system more flexible, which is emphasized in rapidly changing market situations.

The research on coordination theory is still at the beginning, and there is not yet a coherent body of theory in this domain. Especially, it is not clear, which coordination form is best suited for a given team-oriented scheduling process. One goal of our project is to build a test-bed, where various coordination forms can easily be tested.

4. Requirements for a Scheduling Support System

The special character of corporate scheduling support requirements is best demonstrated by a practical example[221]. Some airlines construct aircraft rotations on the basis of a tentative schedule, where the flight legs, requested aircraft types, and days of the week for each flight are given. Each flight has to start within a given time window, which may be a fixed time, an interval of a few hours, or the whole day. The block time for each flight and the minimum ground time for each aircraft type and airport are given. The main objective is to minimize the number of aircraft needed to carry out all given flights, taking various physical, organizational, and political restrictions into account.

The process of designing an aircraft schedule appears to be well structured at a first glance, and there have been several attempts to automate it. However, no automatic scheduling system so far could model all poorly structured (soft) constraints. For example, sometimes an aircraft can fly faster than standard flight time by using more fuel than normally. Sometimes the ground time can be reduced by a special agreement with the ground personnel. It is impossible to model all variants of constraints in a computer-based system - many questions can only be solved by human judgment and intuition. On the other hand, in case of a well defined complex planning problem the computer often outperforms the human scheduler.

Since the problem of generating aircraft rotations can be partially automated, and partially not, it is a semistructured planning problem. Such problems can best be supported by delegating to a computer routine computations and resolution of interactions too complex for the human expert to perform. Such judgments that the computer could neither make, nor recognize they are needed, are left to the human. This is a typical example where the computer and the expert *together* make better decisions than either of them alone.

The requirements for a computer-based scheduling support system can now be summarized:

Incremental Scheduling

Often a new schedule is based on an older version, in such a way that not many changes are required. In such a case a scheduler can use his/her experience and knowledge to construct the new schedule by a sequence of incremental, elementary changes. Basic elementary operations include Insert, Delete, Change, and Interchange of activities. All decisions are made by a human scheduler, but the system is able to check consistency after each change. However, it should be possible to store also inconsistent system states, since a scheduling process may be interrupted in order to be continued at a later time.

An incremental scheduling process can be supported by proposals generated by the system. For example, a proposal may suggest to undercut a block time of a flight by a few minutes, if this would save an aircraft. The actual decision is based on the judgment of a human scheduler, who may accept or reject the proposal of the system.

Algorithmic Scheduling

If a completely new schedule is to be generated, or many changes in an existing schedule have to be done, the human scheduler may prefer invoking an algorithm to compute a completely new schedule. An exact optimization algorithm provides the advantage that a guarantee of the solution quality is given. In cases, where the problem is too large for an optimizer or its solution would take too long, a heuristic algorithm can be used to compute an approximate solution. Fast algorithms are useful for what-if-analyses, where the scheduler wants to find out the consequences of given changes in the scheduling problem itself.

In most practical processes the schedule produced by an algorithm has to be modified by a human scheduler, in order to take such components into account, which cannot be expressed in

---

[221] cf. Suhl (1993)

an analytic model. For this reason the global and incremental scheduling components have to be integrated, so that a scheduler can switch between both modes in a flexible way.

Simulation

Deviation from standard data often occur during the execution of a plan in practice. All frequent flyers know how often flights are late, or arrive too early, because of various disruptions. Thus a schedule should contain enough buffer to recover from such situations. The behavior of a schedule in case of disruptions can be tested in advance by simulating the schedule under real conditions. In an integrated system the simulation component uses data and methods integrated with other planning components.

Individual Work Organization

Discussions with professional schedulers have shown that the individual arts to construct a schedule manually are very different. If the scheduling process is supported by computers, the schedulers would like to keep their individual preferences. Some of them construct a schedule in elementary steps according to a mental idea. Others run several what-if-analyses to find out the optimal problem definition. A scheduling support system should allow the user to change problem definitions and solution strategies in a flexible way.

Support of Cooperative Work

A distributed schedule generation process normally involves several organizational units, like long, medium, and short haul planning, or long and short term planning. However, all units use the same resources, like aircraft and crews in airlines. Thus the work has to be coordinated so that finally one consistent schedule is produced. There is no coherent theory how to model such processes yet. The communication and coordination model in GS^3 is an attempt to model this process in such a way that it can be effectively supported within a computer network.

Graphical User Interface

A computer-aided scheduling system is at most as good as its user interface. A user-friendly (graphical) interface is of special importance in the interactive mode, since each change in the schedule has to be individually carried out by the scheduler. An interface based on an industrial standard, like MS-Windows, X-Windows or Presentation Manager, brings the advantage of similarity with other applications to the end user, and standard development tools to the developer.

The Workbench Concept

The requirements for a computer-supported scheduling system can be realized in a software system concept called workbench. A scheduling workbench provides several tools to be chosen and used in the construction work. As an example, a graphical schedule editor, exact and heuristic optimization methods, a rule base for the interactive work and a simulation environment can be integrated under a graphical user interface. Only one data base and user interface have to be realized. Software developers can easily integrate, test, and exchange various components of the system.

5. Concept of a Group Scheduling Support System

Our project Group Scheduling aims to combine a single-user scheduling support system with coordination and communication facilities needed to support planning teams. We propose a conceptual system with two main parts: Scheduling Workbench and Group Scheduling Assistant.

The *Scheduling Workbench* (SWB) provides planning tools like optimization algorithms, heuristic methods, a proposal generator, and a schedule simulator under a graphical user interface[222]. A human planner can flexibly choose and combine the given techniques. The consistency of a schedule is automatically checked. Usually a planner starts with a given initial plan, which may be computed by an algorithm under the SWB. He/she may also simply take the plan of a previos planning period to start with. This schedule is gradually modified in an interactive process under SWB.

The second part of the proposed system, *Group Scheduling Assistant* (GSA) takes care of coordination and communication needs in team-oriented planning. If a planner wants to make

[222] cf. Suhl (1993)

his/her partial plan public to other team members, he/she invokes the GSA-component. GSA may also be used by a planner to show the partial plans of other planners on the screen. Since the individual partial plans may use same resources, they can be distinguished by different colors, for example.

The concept GSA is configurable for various problem solving organizations: the planning team may operate with or without a coordinator; the coordinator may or may not be allowed to force a planner to accept a given decision; bilateral or multilateral conflicts may or may not be allowed at intermediate planning stages and so on. GSA can be understood as a toolbox providing basic components for the system configuration for each application.

Furthermore, GSA includes a component called *Negotiation Object System* (NOS) for resolving conflicts between individual planners[223]. A resource conflict arises, if the same resource is requested by more than one planner for the same time period. A negotiation process is based on sending semistructured messages, like OFFER, REFUSE, ACCEPT, PROPOSE, FORCE, and so on. Possible responses to a given message are defined by a configurable protocol. Computer-assisted negotiations are useful in many complex planning processes, since the computer may check possible consequences of a given decision in a complex, distributed environment. This would be extremely tedious, if not impossible, for a human.

The system GSA can be understood as a *user agent* in the sense of Haugedener & Steiner (1991), since it can be configured to give automatic responses to given types of messages. For example, some allocated tasks may be so important for a planner that all requests requiring a change in them will be automatically rejected.

6. A Prototype System

A prototype called GS³ (Group Scheduling Support System) is currently being developed at the Technical University of Berlin (Fig. 1). It includes the components SWB for local schedule generation, GSA for communication and coordination between team members and NOS for solving resource conflicts. The prototype is based on an object-oriented design and has been implemented in C++ using the Borland C++ compiler. The communication components use functions provided by Windows for Workgroups (WfW) which could easily be integrated in our LAN. The planning team can communicate with other teams over an interface to Lotus Notes™.

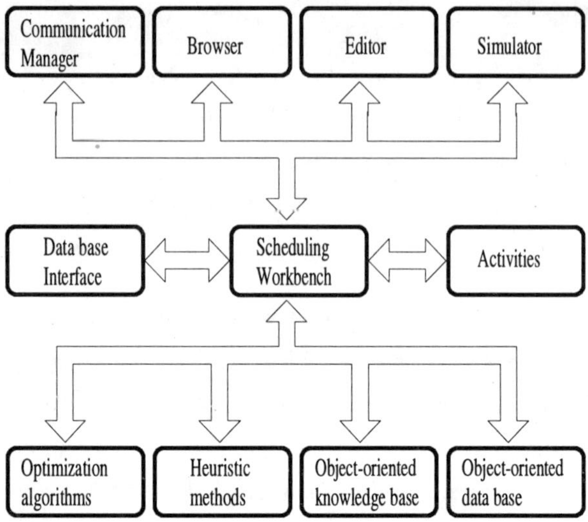

Figure 1: Architecture of the system GS^3

The prototype has been especially designed for the generation of flight schedules in an airline, but the basic ideas and methods can be modified for other planning and scheduling processes as well. Besides planning and scheduling algorithms, SWB includes a graphical editor, a browser, a proposal generator and a simulator for the modification and analysis of airline schedules (Fig. 2). The communication manager in GSA allows both synchronous and asynchronous communication between individual planners. The NOS component is realized with semistructured messages (speech acts), each message corresponding to one given type, like OFFER or ACCEPT. The nonstructured part of a message may contain comments or explanations. A negotiation consists of a sequence of messages according to the given protocol. For a complete description of NOS, see Ohly, Suhl & Reinecke (1994).

[223] cf. Ohly, Suhl & Reinecke (1994), Ohly (1993)

7. Integration into the Corporate Environment

There are several arts of integrating the system GS^3 into an existing organizational and computational environment. First of all, since our prototype has been implemented under Windows for Workgroups (WfW), it can use communication facilities like Dynamic Data Exchange (DDE) and Dynamic Link Libraries (DLL) in a LAN. Furthermore, WfW functions like mail and resource-sharing, are provided for each user.

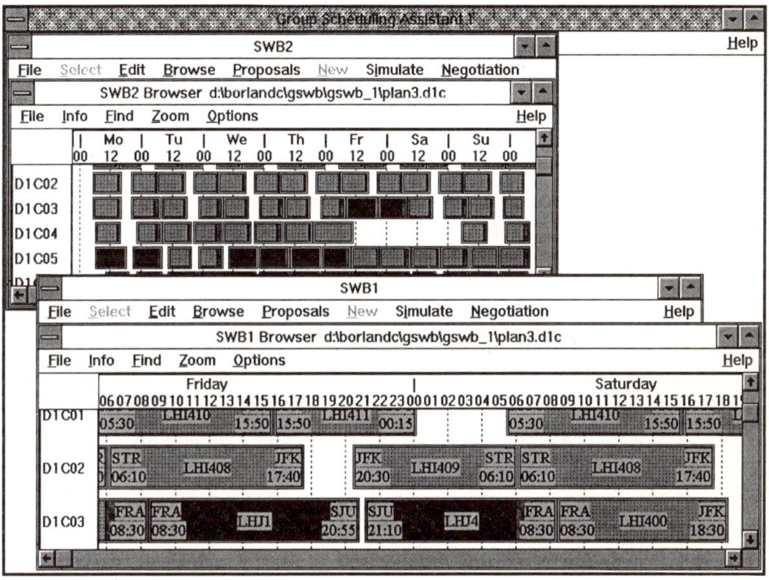

Figure 2: User interface of the system GS^3

Integration into the Macroscopic Workflow

Often the corporate resource allocation process involves several organizational planning units as well as several employees within a planning unit. The gradually refined plans which are transferred by an organizational unit to the next one form the *macroscopic* work flow within the organization. The team work carried out in each planning unit can be characterized as the *microscopic* workflow supported by workgroup computing. As an example, in the course of its creation process an airline flight schedule passes organizational units such as product planning, fleet assignment, flight scheduling, crew scheduling, airport operations scheduling and maintenance scheduling. Each unit consists of a planning team which has to cooperate in order to create a consistent, high-quality global schedule.

The system GS^3 can be used as an „island" within the macroscopic work flow in an organization. It contains components for the transformation of incoming documents into its own objects, for instance in case of newly defined tasks to be scheduled. Schedules that have been completed are transformed into outgoing documents in order to send them to the next organizational unit. Over its data base interface GS^3 can be connected with a corporate relational data base. Currently, an interface to Lotus Notes™ has been implemented so that a user has direct access to document data bases of Notes.

Integration into Existing Applications

If we remove the algorithmic and knowledge-based components from the system GS^3, what is left is a generic coordination system. We call this system the GS^3 Kernel (Fig. 4). Its communication manager provides facilities like sending unstructured or semistructured messages, viewing a global plan which consists of distributed partial plans, performing global consistency checks, making proposals according to global goals, and negotiating either bilaterally or multilaterally about resource allocation. The GSA user agents can be configurated to take over part of routine activities thus letting the human scheduler time to concentrate on really difficult problems.

The GS^3 Kernel can be integrated with existing MS-Windows applications to make them able to support teams. Thus the user can continue working in the environment he/she is used to. The organizational structure of the planning team is stored in the knowledge-base of GS^3. As an example, we plan to integrate the single-user bus line planning system ACTNET[224] with the GS^3 Kernel.

[224] cf. Reinecke & Reinecke (1992)

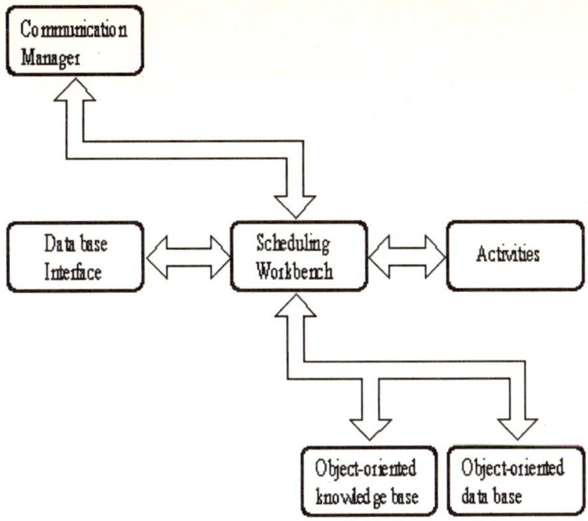

Figure 3: Architecture of the GS^3 Kernel

The fact that GS^3 is based on an object-oriented architecture, facilitates its integration into existing Windows-environments. Data exchange between applications can be supported by the DDE facility, and functions can be integrated as DDLs. Furthermore, peer-to-peer connections between individual planners are possible: It is not necessary to communicate via a central data base like in client-server applications (Fig. 5). Specific problems can be solved bilaterally by using flexible communication routes, and what-if-analyses can be carried out for partial plans without the whole team being involved.

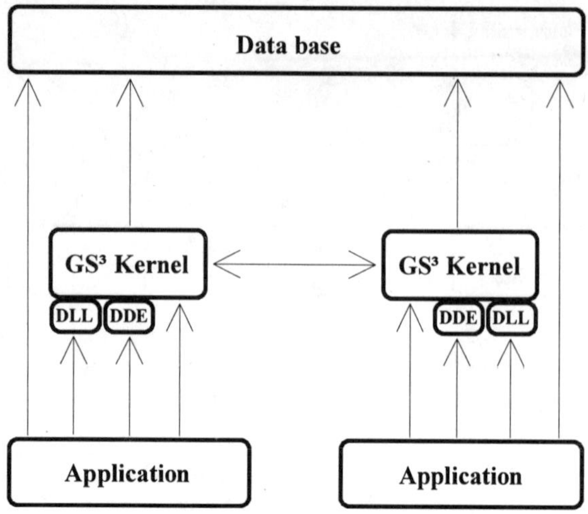

Figure 4: Network structure provided by GS^3

8. Conclusions

This paper discusses concepts and system architectures for supporting team-oriented schedule construction processes in corporations. The Group Scheduling Support System GS^3 consisting of Scheduling Workbench, Group Scheduling Assistant and Negotiation Object System can be characterized as distributed groupware able to support synchronous and asynchronous communication. It supports a planning team, allocating tasks over time which use common resources. The system can be used as a testbed for various organizational forms. It gives the user the freedom of choosing the suitable automation level by the configuration of his/her user agent. Until now a prototype for Windows for Workgroups has been implemented. Laboratory and field tests will be reported in subsequent papers.

9. References

Atabakhsh, H.: A survey for constraint based scheduling systems using an artificial intelligence approach. Artif. Intell. Eng., Vol. 6, pp. 58-73, 1991.

Blazewicz, J.; Ecker, K.; Schmidt, G.; Weglarz, J.: Scheduling in Computer and Manufakturing Systems. Springer, Berlin et al., 1993.

DeSanctis, G.; Gallupe, R.B.: A Foundation for Group Decision Support Systems Design. Management Science **33**, pp. 587-609, 1987.

Eden, Colin: A Framework for Thinking About Group Decision Support Systems (GDSS). Group Decision and Negotiation **1**(3), pp. 199-218, November 1992.

Franken, R.; Suhl, L.: Methoden der Planungsunterstützung in der Produktionsplanung dargestellt am Beispiel der Deutschen Lufthansa. In: Operations Research 1991, Springer Verlag 1992.

Grudin, J.: CSCW: An Introduction. Communications of the ACM 34(12), pp. 30-34, 1991.

Hammer, Michael; Champy, James: Reengineering the Corporation. Harper Collins Publisher, New York 1993.

Haugedener, H.; Steiner, D.: Cooperation structures in multi-agent systems. In: Brauer W., Hernandez D. (Ed.), Verteilte Künstliche Intelligenz und kooperatives Arbeiten, Informatik Fachberichte No. 291, Springer-Verlag, Berlin 1991.

Herzhoff, Astrid: Konzept eines verteilten Anwendungssystems für Autovermietungen. Diplomarbeit, TU Berlin, Fachgebiet Wirtschaftsinformatik/Angewandte EDV, 1994.

Jarke, Matthias; Jelassi, M. Tawfik; Shakun, Melvin F.: MEDIATOR: Towards a negotiation support system. European Journal of Operational Research **31**, pp. 314-334, 1987.

Lewe, H.; Krcmar, H.: Computer Aided Team mit GroupSystems: Erfahrungen aus dem praktischen Einsatz. Wirtschaftsinformatik, Vol. 35, No. 2, 1993.

Projekt EXPERT: Decision support system for aircraft rotation planning. Lufthansa internal report, 1990.

Maier, Harald: Methoden und Systeme zur Stundenplanung in Schulen. Studienarbeit, Technische Universität Berlin, Fachgebiet Wirtschaftsinformatik/Angewandte EDV, 1994.

Malone, T.W.; Grant, K.R.; Lai, K.-Y.; Rao, R.; Rosenblitt, D.: Semistructured messages are surprisingly useful for computer-supported coordination. ACM Trans. Office System, Vol. 5, No.2, pp. 115-131, April 1987.

Malone, Thomas W.; Crowston, Kevin: What is Coordination Theory and How can it Help Design Cooperative Work Systems? Conference on Computer-Supported Cooperative Work, October 1990.

Malone, Thomas W.; Crowston, Kevin: Toward an Interdisciplinary Theory of Coordination. Working Paper CCS TR #120, Center of Coordination Science, Massachusetts Institute of Technology, 1991.

Müller, Jürgen: Verteilte Künstliche Intelligenz - Methoden und Anwendungen. BI Wissenschaftsverlag, Mannheim et al., 1993.

Ohly, Florian: Ein Verhandlungsmechanismus für die computergestützte Gruppenarbeit. Diplomarbeit, TU Berlin, Fachgebiet Wirtschaftsinformatik/Angewandte EDV, 1993.

Ohly, Florian; Suhl, Leena; Reinecke, Erwin: Negotiation Support for Distributed Resource Allocation in a Corporate Environment. Paper to be presented at the IFIP Congress '94, August 28 - September 2, 1994, Hamburg Germany.

Reinecke, Y.; Reinecke, E.: Entwurf und Implementierung eines Planungssystems für den Busverkehr im ÖPNV unter einer objektorientierten Entwicklungsumgebung, Diplomarbeit, Technische Universität Berlin, Fachgebiet Wirtschaftsinformatik/Angewandte EDV, 1992.

Ruijtenbeek, R. van de; Scharenborg, N.: A knowledge based decision support system for aircraft rotation scheduling. Proceedings of ASTAIR-91 (Advanced Software Technology inAir Transport), Royal Aeronautical Society, London, Oktober 1991.

Suhl, Leena: Systems for Computer-Aided Production Planning in Airlines. Habilitation Thesis, Technical University Berlin, Dept. Computer Science, 1993.

Valley, K.; White, S. B.; Iacobucci, D.: Group Decision and Negotiation, Kluver Academic Publishers Vol. 1, No. 2, pp. 117 - 135, 1992

Veryard, R.: Information coordination: the management of information models, systems and organizations, Prentice Hall International Hemel Hempstead 1994.

Winograd, T.: A Language/Action Perspective on the Design of Cooperative Work. Human-Computer Interaction **3**, pp. 3-30, 1987.

Modeling Knowledge about Long-term IS Integration and Integration-oriented Reengineering with KADS

Karl Kurbel, Reinhard Jung, Wolfram Pietsch

Abstract

In today's enterprises, many old information systems (IS) are in use. Maintenance costs can easily account for the major portions of IS budgets. Further problems arise from lack of data integration and lack of functional integration, leading to redundancies and inconsistencies. This state of affairs can be improved by reengineering old IS and gradually integrating them into modern distributed environments. During this long-term process, many risks have to be dealt with. To treat risk explicitly, Boehm's spiral model can be employed but generally it requires experienced professionals. In this paper, we propose a knowledge-based approach to risk management. Knowledge models based on KADS methodology are presented in order to facilitate application of the spiral model.

Keywords: Software reengineering, integration, integration process, spiral model, knowledge modeling, KADS

1. IS Integration through Integration-oriented Reengineering

The 'maintenance crisis' can result in applications being backlogged for several years, preventing the development of new IS. Software reengineering, or reengineering in the context of this paper, is currently discussed as a pragmatic solution to the maintenance crisis. Reengineering, including the evolution and stepwise refinement of software, can offer significant change at far less corporate risk. Reengineering '... can help safeguard an organization's software investment better than building software from scratch or simply evolving it through traditional maintenance'[225].

A more fundamental problem than that posed by maintenance arises from the fact that the majority of old IS were developed as stand-alone systems. Lack of data integration is a very severe shortcoming because it results in additional costs while the lack of functional integration in these systems can result in serious errors and a lot of wasted labor.

---

[225] Cf. Arnold (1993).

An approach called *integration-oriented reengineering* has been developed[226] to overcome these problems. Whereas 'traditional' reengineering is primarily concerned with improving software quality, the focus of integration-oriented reengineering is on old systems' interfaces with their external or virtual software world. A prerequisite for integration in this paradigm is a conceptual understanding of the old system that extends to at least the depth of its data structures and functions. The term integration-oriented reengineering demands this level of understanding. It describes the process of reengineering old software to meet the objective of incorporating it into modern integrated application environments.

Of course old IS have to be integrated not only among themselves, but also with the company's current and future systems. Integration-oriented reengineering is thus part of the long-term process of enterprise-wide IS integration. Information systems that need to be considered in this process include:

1. Old IS that have been reengineered.

2. New IS replacing obsolete IS.

3. Standardized software modules that functionally substitute older IS.

4. New IS including standardized software modules that fill 'application gaps'.

The software and/or hardware platforms of both old and new IS are often heterogeneous. Since porting is neither appropriate nor feasible in most cases, systems are likely to stay on the platforms they were developed for. Integrating them on a conceptual level thus implies that a *distributed system* will be created[227]. We call such a system an integrated information systems environment, or *integrated environment (IE)* for short.

The efficiency and effectiveness of integration-oriented reengineering and for that matter long-term IS integration require substantial experience and knowledge about both technological and organizational factors. For instance, a decision has to be made as to whether it is better to: reengineer a particular IS, develop a new one, or buy and adapt standard software. Another example of skilled decision making is trying to choose the best sequence for integrating candidate IS into the IE.

The consequences of decisions made at one point in this process are often difficult to predict; a state of affairs which is made worse by the fact that such decisions are often wrong. Therefore, a process model for long-term IS integration should allow for explicit consideration of

---

[226] Cf. Eicker et al. (1992), Kurbel (1994).

[227] Cf. Kurbel (1994).

risk. We adapted Boehm's *spiral model*[228] to the task of planning and structuring long-term integration in a manner that allows one to incorporate explicit risk analysis in the process[229].

The IE has also to provide an infrastructure for integrating existing IS which may reside on heterogeneous nodes of a computer network. The first cycle of the spiral, which is called the *initial cycle*, therefore deals with the task of establishing that infrastructure. In particular it is necessary to decide how

(a) access to IE data is given (data access management),

(b) IE-wide integrity is ensured (integrity management),

(c) multiple updates are performed (update management).

Such questions effectively establish parameters in the design process. The resulting IE architecture is called the system's *distribution architecture (DA).* In the first cycle of the spiral the requirements for the overall IE are analyzed and then different approaches to developing it are evaluated in order to decide upon the best alternative. The process of determining parameter values and designing the DA with regard to its technical and economic implications has been described elsewhere[230].

Each subsequent cycle of the spiral encompasses a single integration project, numbered i = 1 ... n. We adopt Boehm's view that a cycle can be terminated at any time if necessary. The incremental approach, which treats one system at a time, was previously outlined[231]. The system to be integrated may be either an old one, which has undergone reengineering, or a new one. In all cases a cycle consists of four steps, covering the whole project from initiation to review:

Step 1_i 'Project selection, alternatives, constraints': First, the IS to be integrated next is selected, and an integration project is defined. Second, alternatives for integrating it into the IE are examined, with respect to their feasibility. In case of old systems, these alternatives are: reengineering, redevelopment, purchasing and adapting. The alternatives for new systems are new development vs. purchasing and adapting. Third, various constraints associated with the process and the product have to be considered (e.g. deadline, budget, user interface).

Step 2_i 'Risk analysis, risk resolution, and choosing an alternative': The risk factors for the feasible alternatives have to be identified. Besides the risks that lie within the project (e.g. deadline violation, user interface unsatisfactory), possible consequences of decisions for later cycles have to be examined. For example, the decision to stay within budget now can lead to

---

228 Cf. Boehm (1986).
229 Cf. Kurbel, Jung (1994).
230 Cf. Kurbel (1994), Jung (1993).
231 Cf. Kurbel (1994).

an increase in maintenance cost later[232]. For each alternative, suitable actions for minimizing the remaining risk are formulated, and the risk is computed. Finally one alternative is selected.

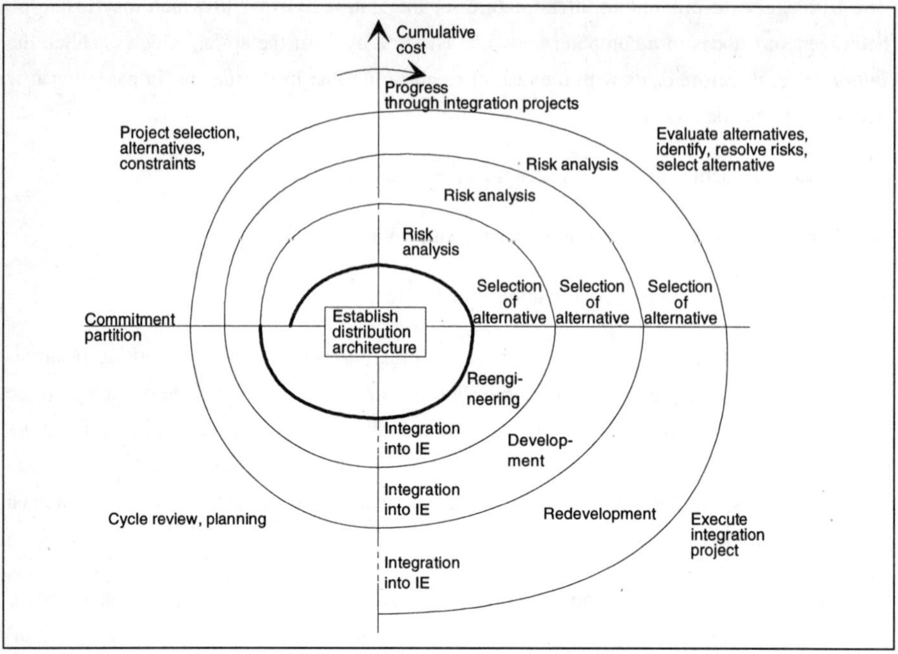

Fig. 1: An example of Boehm's spiral model applied to long-term IS integration[233]

Step 3_i 'Project execution': The integration project chosen in the previous step is executed according to the subprocess model associated with it. As a result of this step, the IS is integrated into the IE.

Step 4_i 'Review and planning': Each cycle ends with a review by all participants (project manager, IS staff, end users). Particular attention is paid to the critical evaluation of the risk-management process of step 2_i. Improvements for later cycles are also discussed.

2. Knowledge Models Facilitate Applications of Boehm's Spiral Model

Conventional software process models such as life-cycle models provide a normative framework to carry out projects of a specific class. Methodological knowledge is typically compiled

---

232 Cf. Boehm, Papaccio (1988).
233 Cf. Kurbel, Jung (1994).

into definitions, deliverables, and sequence of steps needed to implement the models. These models define standardized procedures which usually allow only minor modifications to their basic structure.

The spiral model also provides a framework for the software development process, but its focus is on planning, risk analysis and control. If applied properly this model is applicable across a wide range of project settings. As Boehm points out, however, the spiral model is not easy to understand; it is also difficult to handle and therefore requires experienced and knowledgeable teams of professionals[234]. Risk management is an integral part and not a schematic procedure. Technical knowledge and project experience are crucial to the successful use of such models.

In that integration-oriented reengineering is a new approach, which is partly based on new methodological knowledge[235], little project experience is available up until now. Experience, however, is essential for the definition of risk resolution strategies. As such it would appear that the prerequisites for successful use of the spiral model cannot be fulfilled.

Knowledge about how to conduct integration-oriented reengineering must be provided to potential users in order to make proper use of the spiral model under such circumstances. This knowledge has to be acquired and incorporated into an augmented process model. However, if the knowledge relies on the particular project settings it was derived from, it will be bound to that specific application context. Such knowledge is more useful if it is detached from contextual factors and implementation details. In data and knowledge engineering, models representing topics of the real world in an abstract, unified form are usually referred to as *conceptual models*.

In order to make results of our research applicable as widely as possible, we chose to employ the KADS methodology as our general basis. KADS[236] was developed within ESPRIT-funded projects[237]. It is on the way to becoming a standard framework for knowledge engineering in Europe and has been adopted by many knowledge-processing companies.

KADS provides among other things a comprehensive modeling technique designed to enforce reusability of knowledge models[238]. It distinguishes four levels of expertise: the domain, task, inference, and strategic level. When a conceptual knowledge model for a specific application problem has to be developed, the problem domain is matched to a library of interpretation

---

[234] Cf. Boehm (1986).

[235] Cf. Eicker, Schnieder (1993).

[236] While KADS was originally an acronym for 'knowledge acquisition and documentation structuring', it is now used as a *name* in a more general sense, neither referring to the former abbreviation nor to its meaning any more.

[237] Cf. Breuker et al. (1987), Hickman et al. (1992).

[238] Cf. Hickman et al. (1992).

models[239]. That library contains generic models for simple tasks as well as so-called real-life models for composite tasks. In his recent work, Breuker refers to the library as the 'CommonKADS library'[240]. If an adequate interpretation model (or a combination of models) is found, it then has to be adapted to the problem domain. If there is no adequate model, a real-life model has to be constructed from scratch. Normally, models will be adapted but not newly developed. If new models are constructed, they will be integrated into the library of interpretation models for reuse.

Possible inferences in KADS are depicted as 'inference structures'. Figure 2 shows a simple example of a generalized inference structure. It starts with a set of *observables* describing a certain situation and arrives at a *solution* to be applied to the given situation after a specific sequence of inference steps (<u>classify</u>, <u>match</u>, <u>specialize</u>). One viable sequence of steps within an inference structure is called an 'inference line'.

Objects to be manipulated in the reasoning process are depicted by rectangular boxes. Each box denotes a class of objects, e.g. required data or resulting conclusions. Such classes are called 'meta-classes'. They are the input and output of 'knowledge sources' (in this paper, the names of <u>knowledge sources</u> are underlined and the names of *meta-classes* are printed in italics). The meanings of all knowledge sources are specified in detail for each interpretation model. For example, the knowledge source <u>classify</u> of Figure 2 has the meaning: 'Transform instances of *observables* into *variables* which denote respective classes of instances'.

Any KADS-related methodology or toolset provides a set of predefined knowledge sources to enforce uniformity of knowledge modeling and to facilitate combination of interpretation models. The model library helps to reduce or avoid the effort of developing new models from scratch. Interpretation models provide generalized problem-solving knowledge. They guide the search for domain knowledge and its structuring.

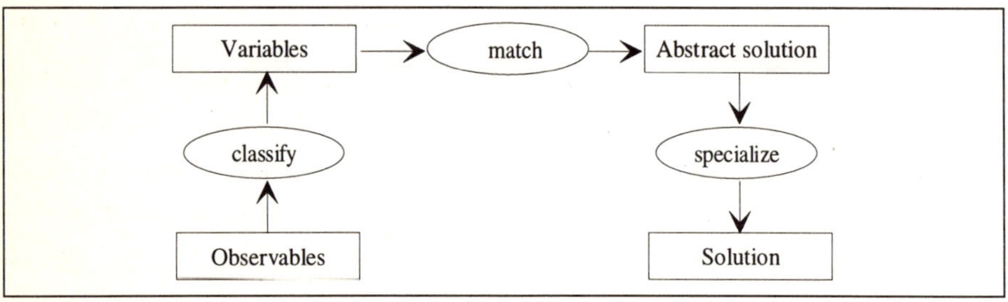

Fig. 2: Sample inference structure

[239] Cf. Breuker et al. (1987).
[240] Cf. Breuker et al. (1993).

In order to apply KADS to long-term IS integration and reengineering, it is useful to distinguish project-specific knowledge from general methodological knowledge. The work reported here focuses on more general methodological aspects. Methodologies, by definition, are meant to be applicable to many projects. Therefore, methodological knowledge should be specified in a way that it is reusable. In KADS this means refining interpretation models or designing new ones.

In our previous work, a set of interpretation models representing methodological knowledge about long-term IS integration were developed. These models will be presented below. In order to validate our approach, they will be applied to real-world projects in the future.

3. Conceptual Knowledge Modeling

In each cycle and step of the spiral model, different knowledge is required. Conceptual knowledge will therefore be grouped accordingly into five models:

1. Initial cycle: architectural knowledge.

2. Planning step: knowledge for project selection.

3. Risk management step: knowledge for assessing and managing risk.

4. Implementation step: knowledge for project control.

5. Review step: knowledge for project assessment.

Each knowledge model represents a domain of expertise. The models are of course interrelated. In particular, project selection and risk management are closely related in practice, as is the knowledge required to handle these tasks. KADS supports the design of interrelated interpretation models at the level of strategic knowledge. Our knowledge-based methodology thus provides greater flexibility than conventional task-oriented process-model specifications.

3.1. Modeling Architectural Knowledge

Architectural knowledge is the term used to refer to the knowledge about the distribution architecture and in particular to the way the parameters data-access, integrity, and update management are determined. In the following, an inference structure for establishing an adequate DA is presented.

At first glance, the inference structure for configuration tasks from the KADS library seems to be adequate for modeling architectural knowledge: Requirements are provided as input to this task, and the most suitable parameter configuration is then the output. However, a synthesis task in KADS, such as configuration, is usually characterized by a large or even infinite solution space[241]. Considering the relatively small number of 24 possible DA's (i.e. 24 different parameter constellations)[242], the reasoning process is more efficient if each possible solution is assessed. This can be done by means of the inference structure 'assessment' which belongs to the category of analysis tasks in the library of interpretation models.

The underlying strategy is then as follows: all possible parameter combinations are generated, resulting in a total of 24 DA variants. Each variant is evaluated against the requirements for the IE. The corresponding inference structure is depicted in figure 3.

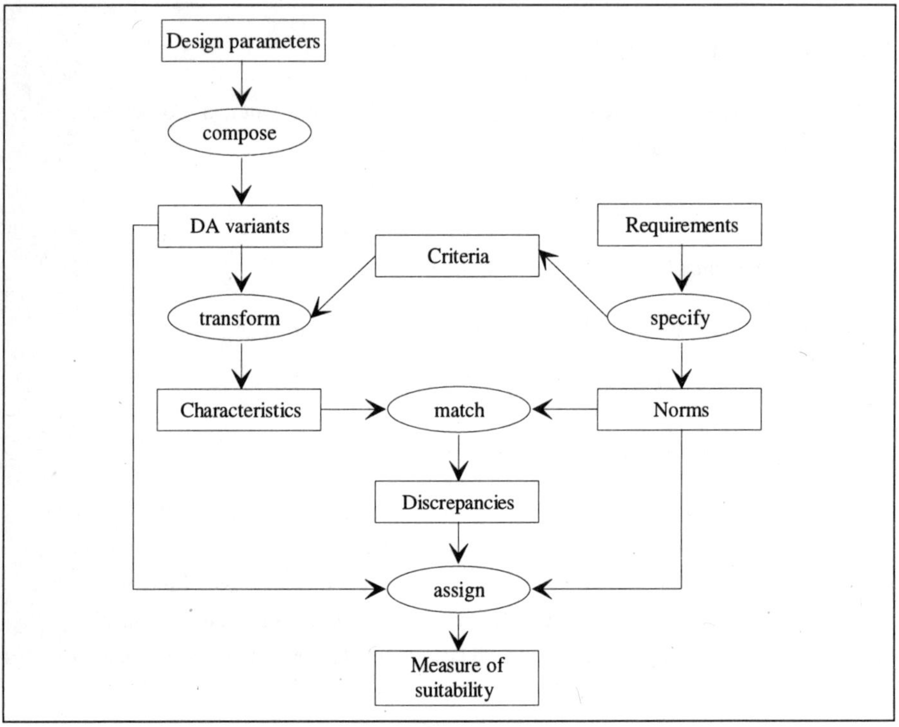

Fig. 3: Inference structure for establishing the distribution architecture

The knowledge source compose has *design parameters* as input and composes a *DA variant* as output. The knowledge source specify makes *criteria* and *norms* (criteria with desired val-

---

241 Cf. Breuker et al. (1987).
242 Cf. Kurbel (1994).

ues) out of the *requirements*. To evaluate *DA variants,* transform takes the *criteria* and transforms them into *characteristics* (criteria with expected values) of particular DA variants. *Characteristics* are then compared with *norms* by the knowledge source match. The results of the comparison are represented by means of the meta-class *discrepancies*. Finally, a *measure of suitability* is determined by assign. To do so, *norms* and corresponding *discrepancies* are assigned to *DA variants*.

On the domain level, an inference line according to this inference structure might be as follows: The user specifies, among other requirements, that good performance is a mandatory functional requirement for the IE. The knowledge source specify generates the *norm* 'performance must be good' and in addition the *criterion* 'performance'. Afterwards, the knowledge source transform evaluates a *DA variant* against this criterion. The result may be 'performance is medium'. Depending on the scale of measurement, the knowledge source match will detect a *discrepancy* between the *norm* 'performance must be good' and the *characteristic* 'performance is medium'. The discrepancy is assigned to the DA variant; this result, among others, serves as one *measure of suitability*.

3.2. Modeling Planning Knowledge

Once the DA is established, the process of integrating systems can be planned. However, modeling such planning knowledge is a challenging task. First, it strongly depends on factors external to the integration process itself, e.g. the availability of financial resources, the expertise of personnel, the expected life spans of candidate systems, the way in which quality is best measured and enforced, etc. Second, to date KADS has been rarely applied to planning problems[243]. Hence, interpretation models are rare. Third, several planning problems must be treated at the same time in order to set up an adequate integration plan. Such plans typically encompass technological integration, IS evolution, and business strategy.

We had to develop a new model because we were not able to find an existing interpretation model, or for that matter a combination of models that properly address the reasoning process for long-term planning. A model by Tansley and Hayball[244] called 'island-driving' came closest to our needs. However, our attempts to employ it for the project-selection domain led to numerous modifications which effectively amounted to a major redesign of their original model. Our resulting model was structurally different from the original model on which it was based and could not be considered to be a simple refinement of Tansley and Hayball's model.

---

243 Cf. Tansley, Hayball (1993).
244 Cf. Tansley, Hayball (1993).

In such cases KADS requires a definition of a new interpretation model for the new problem domain. However, it is difficult to design such a model beforehand exactly because the problem is not well-structured. A general approach for traditionally attacking problems of this sort is prototyping. To start with, a first tentative interpretation model was developed. In subsequent steps, the model needs to be validated and refined in practical applications. Later it might be generalized and inserted into the library.

The initial model is presented in Figure 4. Since it is supposed to capture more than one type of planning problem, it has several starting points and inference lines. One begins with a specification of the factors influencing or restricting the integration of an additional system in a specific environment. These factors are represented by the meta-class *environment-dependent factors*. Examples are: the DA chosen beforehand; the software tools available in that environment; the operating and database-management systems; the entity types that can serve as starting points for data integration (i.e. equal or similar entity types in old system and IE). The question as to exactly which factors are relevant in a specific context has to be determined when the domain-level knowledge is added to our model.

The knowledge source classify uses the *environment-dependent factors* and the specifications of *systems not yet integrated* to identify *integration candidates*. The term integration candidate is used for single IS as well as for sets of information systems with similar characteristics with respect to integration efforts. Systems that share similarities are likely to be treated at the same time during the planning process.

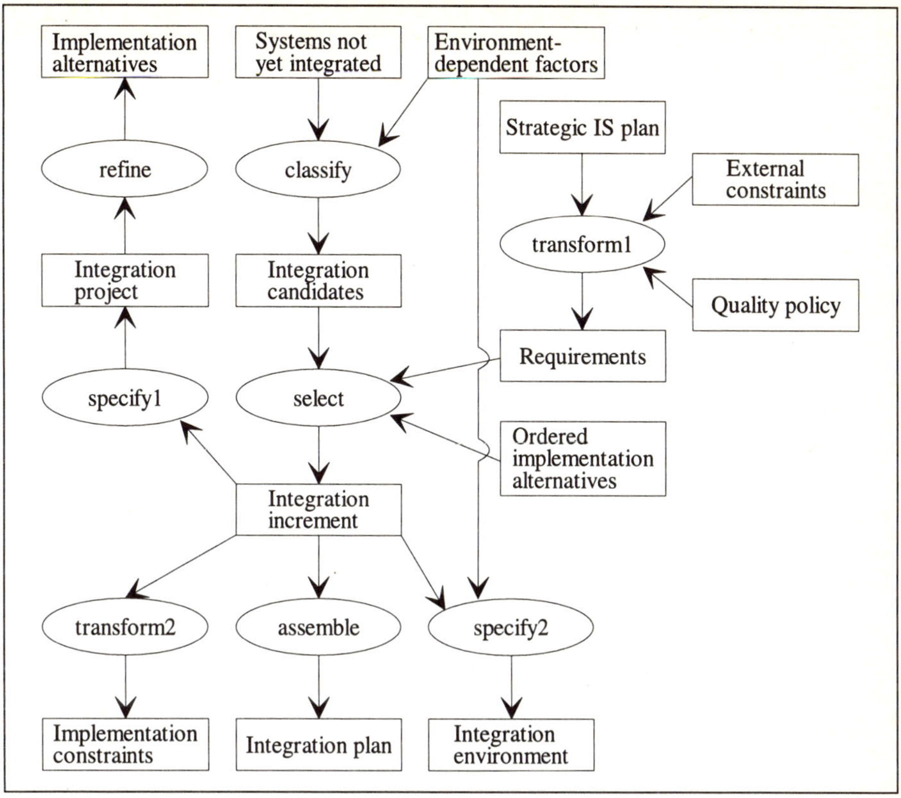

Fig. 4: Inference structure for project selection

In one cycle of the spiral, one integration candidate is under consideration. A knowledge source has to select it according to *requirements* specified in a different inference line. The selected integration candidate then becomes the next *integration increment*. In this case it is input to four inference lines, each one representing a different planning task with different outcomes:

- The knowledge source specify2 takes the *integration increment* and specifies an extended *integration environment* (old IE plus new components).
- The knowledge source assemble sets up a process model which includes temporal dependencies and restrictions *(integration plan)*.
- Transform2 analyzes properties of the *integration increment* and transforms them into *implementation constraints* (e.g. technological restrictions).

- Specify1 describes an *integration project* which subsequently is refined by *implementation alternatives* (knowledge source refine).

Functional *requirements* largely determine which *integration candidate* is selected. Requirements are derived from goals. Goals may be, for example, that the system functions efficiently, or that the data structures destined to be integrated contribute significantly to the value of the IE. Information systems will be assessed with regard to such goals, leading to the requirement that systems with certain characteristics should be treated with higher priority. Other requirements specify how standard software should be bought or how new software technologies should be introduced, etc.

In order to derive functional requirements, a separate inference structure in addition to that given in figure 4 is needed. Detaching this scheme from the project selection scheme given in figure 4 is both appropriate and necessary for several reasons: First, definition of requirements is a global problem which is intertwined with enterprise-wide strategic planning, quality management, and information strategy planning. Second, these requirements may have to be adapted whenever major external factors to integration planning change. After all in such cases the integration plan itself will probably be subject to modification. Third, functional requirements may also refer to risk management. When they are modelled in a separate inference structure, planning knowledge as well as risk management knowledge can be processed simultaneously. In KADS, the context-dependent knowledge as to which inference structure is to be employed in a certain situation is represented on the strategic level.

3.3. Modeling Risk Management Knowledge

Input to risk management in step 2_i of the spiral are the alternatives and constraints which were determined in step 1_i. The output of step 2_i then is the alternative with the lowest remaining risk. However, risk analysis with respect to implementation alternatives may also be undertaken before a decision is made as to which integration project to pursue. This may occur because a risk-analysis study can produce information that is relevant to project selection. At the strategic level, KADS supports modeling alternative ways of positioning risk analysis along the spiral.

Examining KADS interpretation models, we found that its assessment inference structure was a good match for the risk-analysis problem. An application published by Porter[245] for fraud assessment was adapted to the special case of risk management in our context. Porter added the meta-class *degree of fit* as an output meta-class for the knowledge source match; he used *de-*

[245] Cf. Porter (1992).

gree of fit as an input meta-class for the new knowledge source rank. Porter extended his model's basic structure by relating its final decision to thc ranking of possible cases. We adapted Porter's model by renaming some meta-classes and knowledge sources with respect to our type of assessment problem.

The objective of the first inference line (left hand side) is to create abstractions of the *implementation alternatives* so that risk factors can be identified. For this purpose, the meta-classes *implementation alternatives* and *risk factors* are two inputs for the knowledge source abstract1. Within the second inference line (right hand side) the knowledge source abstract2 is used to derive *risk factors* from *constraints*, as such it identifies why constraints may be violated throughout the project.

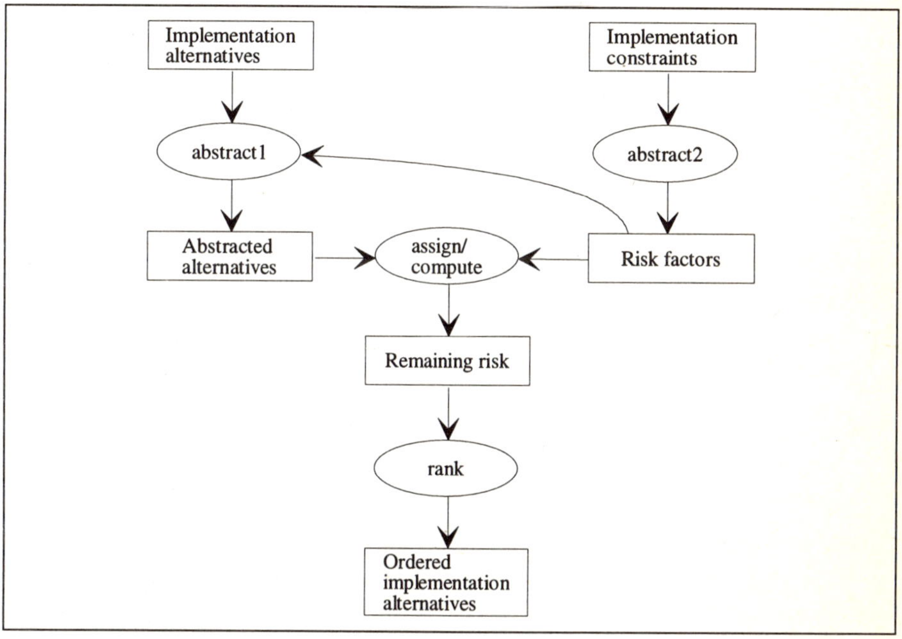

Fig. 5: Inference structure for risk assessment and selection of alternative

The crucial part of the inference structure starts with assign/compute. This knowledge source applies risk-resolving measures to the risk factors. It is a substitute for Porter's terminal knowledge source match. (A terminal knowledge source is a knowledge source which does not need further refinement.) In our case, a terminal knowledge source would not be appropriate because the risk-resolving measures are different for each risk factor. Furthermore there are a large number of possible factors. This means that assign/compute is likely to be differentiated later ('knowledge differentiation'[246]). The *remaining risk* is input to the knowledge source rank which sorts the alternatives and generates a set of *ordered implementation alternatives*.

According to this inference structure, domain-level knowledge might be used as in the following example: Consider an old IS to be integrated. *Implementation alternatives* are reengineering, redevelopment, new development, and purchasing and adapting. If a certain budget is given the corresponding *risk factor* is that costs later exceed the budget. With regard to this risk factor, the alternatives are reduced (abstracted) to their relevant characteristics. Examples of characteristics, for the 'reengineering' alternative, are quality of software, availability of documentation, etc. To assess the risk, costs for each alternative have to be estimated. Results of risk assessment (performed by assign/compute) might be probabilities that the budget is violated, for each alternative (*remaining risk*). Finally, the remaining risks of each risk factor have to be aggregated so that the alternatives can be ranked.

4. Outlook: Domain-specific Application of Knowledge Models

The three interpretation models described above comprise knowledge on a very high level of abstraction. Before they can be applied to a real-world integration process, domain-specific knowledge has to be acquired and incorporated into such models. In KADS, domain knowledge is integrated into conceptual models at another level of description; the domain level. This level is linked to the meta-classes that exist at the inference level via 'roles'.

For instance, the meta-class *alternatives* on the inference level corresponds to the choices in step 2_i among reengineering, redevelopment, new development, and purchasing and adapting. These choices may be grouped into two classes of alternatives on the domain level and are also connected to the meta-class by is-a relations. One such class comprises the choices for old systems: reengineering, redevelopment, and purchasing and adapting. The other one contains the choices for new systems, i.e. new development, and purchasing and adapting. Which class to select in a particular project depends on the type of project. The knowledge needed to select the right class is represented within the knowledge source refine; for example refine can be given by simple production rules such as:

If the project refers to an existing IS,
then alternatives are reengineering vs. redevelopment vs. purchasing and adapting.

[246] Cf. Schreiber, Wielinga (1993).

If the integration project refers to an application gap,
then alternatives are new development vs. purchasing and adapting.

Domain knowledge has to be acquired for each meta-class to be visited on an inference line. In this sense, the three interpretation models may be regarded as empty templates which guide the search for domain knowledge and give structure to it. When the conceptual models are furnished with domain knowledge, they can be used for decision support within the spiral model. Knowledge from these models may be incorporated into instruments like checklists, decision tables, or even advanced decision models.

While decision support regarding IS integration and reengineering is the primary purpose of the knowledge models, other applications can also benefit from them. As the models are employed and refined over time, they can be useful in different contexts. Evolution of model usage might pass through the following stages:

1. *Model-driven knowledge acquisition*: In a specific application, the models may be used to guide the process of knowledge acquisition. Here the knowledge engineer adds domain knowledge (e.g. the risk factors to be observed in the specific environment) to the interpretation models and thus creates a conceptual model of the domain. Inference lines are likely to be extended, refined, or adapted in this process.

2. *Decision support:* In the next stage, the models may be used as a basis for decision making when: establishing an appropriate distribution architecture; selecting the right IS to be integrated next; or choosing the best implementation alternative.

3. *Computer-supported decision making*: Suitable portions of the models will be implemented by knowledge-based systems and perhaps integrated into other systems, e.g. decision support systems, project-management systems, or strategic enterprise-modeling systems. Automatic generation from KADS models is conceivable if formal specifications are used. Up to date, research concerning knowledge specification is still on-going[247]. Commercial tools for generating real-world applications are not yet available.

4. *Model evolution and improvement of decision quality*: Model performance in various applications of the same inference lines can be compared. The results of such experiments can then be used to refine or revise the models, or even to rethink their scope, and thus hopefully improve the quality of future decision making.

---

[247] Cf. Voß, Karbach (1993), Schreiber (1993).

The models presented in this paper are tentative and require further elaboration and validation. They will be refined, applied to integration problems, and validated in future work. Furthermore we are developing a prototype decision-support system based on selected portions of the knowledge models.

Acknowledgements

The authors wish to thank DFG (Deutsche Forschungsgemeinschaft) for their support of the research underlying this paper.

Special thanks go to Linda Freeman, M.B.A., Cambridge, Massachusetts, USA and Dr. Kevin O'Mara of the University of the South Pacific, Department of Mathematics and Computing Science, Suva, Fiji Islands, for their assistance in our struggle with the English language. We are particularly grateful to Dr. O'Mara who provided us with valuable comments and constructive criticism on an earlier version of this paper.

References

Arnold, R.S.: A Road Map Guide to Software Reengineering Technology; in: Arnold, R.S. (Ed.): Software Reengineering; Los Alamitos, CA 1993, pp. 3-22.

Boehm, B.W.: A Spiral Model of Software Development and Enhancement; ACM SIGSoft Software Engineering Notes 11 (1986), pp. 22-42.

Boehm, B.W.; Papaccio, P.N.: Understanding and Controlling Software Costs; IEEE Transactions on Software Engineering 14 (1988) 10, pp. 1462-1477.

Breuker, J.; Bredeweg, B.; Valente, A.; Van de Velde, W.: Re-Usable Problem Solving Components: the CommonKADS Library; in: Löckenhoff, C.; Fensel, D.; Studer, R. (Eds.): CommonKADS, Proceedings of the 3rd KADS Meeting; Munich 1993, pp. 251-269.

Breuker, J.A.; Wielinga, B.; van Someren, M.; de Hoog, R.; Schreiber, G.; de Greef, P.; Bredeweg, B.; Wielemaker, J.; Billault, J.-P.; Davoodi, M.; Hayward, S.: Model-driven Knowledge Acquisition: Interpretation Models, Deliverable Task A1, Esprit Project 1098; Amsterdam 1987.

Eicker, S.; Kurbel, K.; Pietsch, W.; Rautenstrauch, C.: Einbindung von Software-Altlasten durch integrationsorientiertes Reegineering; Wirtschaftsinformatik 34 (1992) 2, pp. 137-145.

Eicker, S.; Schnieder, T.: Integrationsorientiertes Reengineering von Cobol-Altsystemen; Praxis der Informationsverarbeitung und Kommunikation 16 (1993) 3, pp. 162-168.

Hickman, F.R.; Killin, J.L.; Land, L.; Mulhall, T.; Porter, D.; Taylor, R.M.: Analysis for knowledge-based systems: a practical guide to the KADS methodology; Chichester 1992.

Jung, R.: Wirtschaftlichkeitsfaktoren beim integrationsorientierten Reengineering; Verteilungsarchitektur und Integrationsschritte aus ökonomischer Sicht; Working Paper No. 16 of the Institute of Business Informatics, University of Muenster, Germany 1993.

Kurbel, K.: Integration-oriented Data Reengineering Supporting Long-term Information Systems Evolution and Business Process Reengineering; in: Ng, P.A., et al. (Eds.): Proceedings of ICSI '94, Third International Conference on Systems Integration, São Paulo, Brazil; Los Alamitos, CA 1994, pp. 466-475.

Kurbel, K.; Jung, R.: An Application of the Spiral Model to Reengineering and Long-term IS Integration into a Distributed System; in: Wolfinger, B. (Ed.): Innovationen bei Rechen- und Kommunikationssystemen; Berlin et al. 1994, pp. 437-443.

Porter, D.: An inference structure for use in the fraud assessment domain; in: Bauer, C., Karbach, W. (Eds.): Interpretation Models for KADS, Proceedings of the 2nd KADS User Meeting (KUM '92); Sankt Augustin 1992, pp. 59-79.

Schreiber, G.: Operationalizing Models of Expertise; in: Schreiber, G., Wielinga, B, Breuker, J. (Eds.): KADS - A Principled Approach to Knowledge-Based System Development; San Diego 1993, pp. 119-149.

Schreiber, G; Wielinga, B.: Model Construction; in: Schreiber, G., Wielinga, B, Breuker, J. (Eds.): KADS - A Principled Approach to Knowledge-Based System Development; San Diego 1993, pp. 93-118.

Tansley, D.S.W.; Hayball, C.C.: Knowledge-Based Systems Analysis and Design - A KADS Developer's Handbook; Hertfordshire 1993.

Voß, A.; Karbach, W.: Implementing KADS Expertise Models with Model-K; IEEE Expert 8 (1993) 4, pp. 74-81.

Addresses of the Authors

Abbas, Sheena: U.M.I.S.T., Dept.of Computation, Artificial Intelligence Group, P.O. Box 88, Manchester M60 1QD, United Kingdom.

E-mail: abbas@sna.co.umist.ac.uk

Bierwirth, Christian: Bremen University, Dept. of Economics, Chair of Logistics, D-28334 Bremen.

Einsfeld, Ulrike: University of Augsburg, BWL-Wirtschaftsinformatik, D-86135 Augsburg.

E-mail: ulrike.einsfeld@wiso.uni-augsburg.de

Elgass, Petra: Hohenheim University, Department of Economics, D-70593 Stuttgart.

Falk, Juergen: University of Erlangen-Nuernberg, Department of Information Systems, Lange Gasse 20, D-90403 Nuernberg.

E-mail: wsw100@wsrz2.wiso.uni-erlangen.de

Ferstl, Otto: Business Information Systems, University of Bamberg, D-96045 Bamberg.

E-mail: otto.ferstl@sowi.uni-bamberg.de

Heissel, Thorsten: Technical University of Berlin, Department of Computer Science, FR 6-7, Franklinstr. 28/29, D-10587 Berlin.

E-mail: heissel@cs.tu-berlin.de

Hilpert, Wolfgang: Paderborn University, Faculty of Business Administration, Economics & Business Computing, Warburger Str. 100, D-33098 Paderborn.

E-mail:
Wolfgang_Hilpert%ONESTONE@notesgw.compuserve.com

Notes: Wolfgang Hilpert @ ONESTONE @ LOTUSINT

Holthaus, Oliver:	Faculty of Business Administration and Economics, Department of Production Management, University of Passau, Dr.-Hans-Kapfinger-Str. 30, D-94032 Passau. E-mail: WMHOLT01@fsuni.rz.uni-passau.de
Hunstock, Jens:	Dept. of Information Systems, Europa-Universitaet Viadrina, PO Box 776, D-15207 Frankfurt (Oder).
Jung, Reinhard:	Muenster University, Institute of Business Informatics, Grevener Str. 91, D-48159 Muenster. E-mail: WIREJU@wi.uni-muenster.de
Kirn, Stefan:	Muenster University, Dept. of Business Administration, Applied Computer Science Group, Grevener Str. 91, D-48159 Muenster. E-mail: kirns@uni-muenster.de
Koenig, Wolfgang:	Frankfurt University, Mertonstr. 17, D-60054 Frankfurt. E-mail: koenig@wiwi.uni-frankfurt.de
Kopfer, Herbert:	Bremen University, Dept. of Economics, Chair of Logistics, D-28334 Bremen. E-mail: kopfer@logistik.uni-bremen.de
Krallmann, Hermann:	Technical University of Berlin, Department of Computer Science, FR 6-7, Franklinstr. 28/29, D-10587 Berlin.
Krcmar, Helmut:	Hohenheim University, Dept. of Economics, D-70593 Stuttgart. E-mail: krcmar@rs1.rz.uni-hohenheim.de
Kurbel, Karl:	Europe University Viadrina Frankfurt (Oder), Chair of Business Informatics, Grosse Scharrnstrasse 59, D-15230 Frankfurt (Oder).
Ludwig, Boerries:	Hohenheim University, Dept. of Economics, D-70593 Stuttgart.

Mertens, Peter:	University of Erlangen-Nuernberg, Dept. of Information Systems, Lange Gasse 20, D-90403 Nuernberg. E-mail: wsw100@wsrz2.wiso.uni-erlangen.de
Meyer, Ulrich:	Technical University of Berlin, Department of Computer Science, FR 6-7, Franklinstr. 28/29, D-10587 Berlin.
Mueller-Wuensch, Michael:	Technical University of Berlin, Department of Computer Science, FR 6-7, Franklinstr. 28/29, D-10587 Berlin.
Nastansky, Ludwig:	Paderborn University, Faculty of Business Administration, Economics & Business Computing, Warburger Str. 100, D-33098 Paderborn. E-mail: NastansL@notes.uni-paderborn.de Notes: Ludwig Nastansky @ WIUNIPB @ LOTUSINT
O'Hare, Greg:	U.M.I.S.T., Dept.of Computation, Artificial Intelligence Group, P.O. Box 88, Manchester M60 1QD, United Kingdom. E-mail: greg@sna.co.umist.ac.uk
Oberweis, Andreas:	Institut für Wirtschaftsinformatik, J.W. Goethe-Universitaet, D-60054 Frankfurt/Main. E-mail: oberweis@aifb.uni-karlsruhe.de
Ortmann, Anke:	Dept. of Information Systems, Europa-Universitaet Viadrina, PO Box 776, D-15207 Frankfurt (Oder).
Ortmann, Jan:	Dept. of Information Systems, Europa-Universitaet Viadrina, PO Box 776, D-15207 Frankfurt (Oder).
Pape, Uwe:	Technical University of Berlin, Institute of Applied Computer Science, FR5-5, Franklinstr.28/29, D-10587 Berlin. E-mail: pape@cs.tu-berlin.de
Pietsch, Wolfram:	ExperTeam, Claudius-Dornier-Strasse 1, D-50829 Köln.

Pressmar, Dieter: Hamburg University, Dept. of Business Administration, Von-Melle-Park 5, D-20146 Hamburg.

E-mail: pressmar@hermes2.econ.uni-hamburg.de

Reinecke, Erwin: Technical University of Berlin, Institute of Applied Computer Science, FR5-5, Franklinstr.28/29, D-10587 Berlin.

Rittgen, Peter: Frankfurt University, Mertonstr. 17, D-60054 Frankfurt.

E-mail: rittgen@wiwi.uni-frankfurt.de

Roemer, Mark: University of Augsburg, BWL-Wirtschaftsinformatik, D-86135 Augsburg.

E-mail: mark.roemer@wiso.uni-augsburg.de

Rosenberg, Otto: Faculty of Business Administration and Economics, Department of Production Management, University of Paderborn, Warburger Str. 100, D-33098 Paderborn.

E-mail: rosenberg@prowi.wiwi.uni-paderborn.de

Roßbach, Peter: University of Marburg, FB 02, Institut für Wirtschaftsinformatik, Universitätsstr. 24, D-35032 Marburg.

E-mail: rossbach@wiwi.uni-marburg.de

Rottenbacher, Claus: Technical University of Berlin, WIL-B 4-1, Strasse des 17. Juni 135, D-10623 Berlin.

Sandbiller, Klaus: University of Augsburg, BWL-Wirtschaftsinformatik, D-86135 Augsburg.

E-mail: klaus.sandbiller@wiso.uni-augsburg.de

Scherrer, Gabriele: Technical University of Karlsruhe, Institute of Applied Informatics, D-76128 Karlsruhe.

E-mail: scherrer@aifb.uni-karlsruhe.de

Schoenwaelder, Stefan: Hohenheim University, Dept. of Economics, D-70593 Stuttgart.

Schopf, Claudia: Technical University of Berlin, Department of Computer Science, FR 6-7, Franklinstr. 28/29, D-10587 Berlin.

E-mail: schopf@CS.TU-BERLIN.DE

Sinz, Elmar: Business Information Systems, University of Bamberg, D-96045 Bamberg.

E-mail: elmar.sinz@sowi.uni-bamberg.de

Spieck, Stefan: University of Erlangen-Nuernberg, Dept. of Information Systems, Lange Gasse 20, D-90403 Nuernberg.

E-mail: wsw100@wsrz2.wiso.uni-erlangen.de

Stickel, Eberhard: Dept. of Information Systems, Europa-Universitaet Viadrina, PO Box 776, D-15207 Frankfurt (Oder).

E-mail: stickel@euv-frankfurt-o.de

Stucky, Wolffried: Institut für Angewandte Informatik und Formale Beschreibungsverfahren, Universitaet Karlsruhe (TH), D-76128 Karlsruhe.

E-mail: stucky@aifb.uni-karlsruhe.de

Suhl, Leena: Technical University of Berlin, Institute of Applied Computer Science, FR5-5, Franklinstr.28/29, D-10587 Berlin.

E-mail: suhl@tubvm.cs.tu-berlin.d400.de

Unland, Rainer: Muenster University, Dept. of Business Administration, Applied Computer Science Group, Grevener Str. 91, D-48159 Muenster.

E-mail: unlandr@uni-muenster.de

Utecht, Thomas: Bremen University, Dept. of Economics, Chair of Logistics, D-28334 Bremen.

Wanka, Ulrich: Muenster University, Dept. of Business Administration, Applied Computer Science Group, Grevener Str. 91, D-48159 Muenster.

E-mail: wanka@uni-muenster.de

Weigelt, Mark: University of Erlangen-Nuernberg, Dept. of Information Systems, Lange Gasse 20, D-90403 Nuernberg.

E-mail: wsw100@wsrz2.wiso.uni-erlangen.de

Wendt, Oliver: Frankfurt University, Mertonstr. 17, D-60054 Frankfurt.

E-mail: wendt@wiwi.uni-frankfurt.de

Will, Andreas: University of Augsburg, BWL-Wirtschaftsinformatik, D-86135 Augsburg.

E-mail: andreas.will@wiso.uni-augsburg.de

Woltering, Ansgar: Technical University of Berlin, Department of Computer Science, FR 6-7, Franklinstr. 28/29, D-10587 Berlin.

Ziegler, Hans: Faculty of Business Administration and Economics, Department of Production Management, University of Passau, Dr.-Hans-Kapfinger-Str. 30, D-94032 Passau.

E-mail: ziegler@uni-passau.de

Zimmermann, Gabriele: Institut für Wirtschaftsinformatik, J.W. Goethe-Universitaet, D-60054 Frankfurt/Main.

Zwicker, Eckart: Technical University of Berlin, WIL-B 4-1, Strasse des 17. Juni 135, D-10623 Berlin.

E-mail: zwic1431@mailszrz.zrz.tu-berlin.de

Index

R

S

T

U

V

W

Printing: Weihert-Druck GmbH, Darmstadt
Binding: Buchbinderei Schäffer, Grünstadt